REVISED AND UPDATED SECOND EDITION

ANECDOTES
of the Anglo-Boer War

Tales from the 'Last of the Gentlemen's Wars'

Rob Milne

RJWM Publishers

Helion & Company Ltd

First published in 1999 by Covos Books (ISBN 0-620-25439-4)

This second edition co-published in 2013 by:

RJWM Publishers
P.O. Box 3940
Dainfern 2055
South Africa
website: www.robmilne.com

and

Helion & Company Limited
26 Willow Road
Solihull
West Midlands
B91 1UE
England
Tel. 0121 705 3393
Fax 0121 711 4075
email: info@helion.co.uk
website: www.helion.co.uk

ISBN (South Africa) 978-1-920143-69-5
ISBN (UK) 978-1-908916-25-9

Copyright © Rob Milne, 2013

Designed & typeset by SA Publishing Services, South Africa (kerrincocks@gmail.com)
Cover design by SA Publishing Services, South Africa

Printed in UK by Lightning Source Ltd, Milton Keynes, Buckinghamshire
Printed in South Africa by Pinetown Printers, Durban, KwaZulu-Natal

British Library Cataloguing-in-Publication Data
A catalogue record for this book is available from the British Library

All rights reserved. No part of this publication may be reproduced, stored, manipulated in any retrieval system, or transmitted in any mechanical, electronic form or by any other means, without the prior written authority of the publishers, except for short extracts in media reviews. Any person who engages in any unauthorized activity in relation to this publication shall be liable to criminal prosecution and claims for civil and criminal damages.

*To my wife
Bronislava
"С любовью и нежностью"*

Rob Milne was born in Johannesburg in 1953 and educated at St. David's Marist College and the University of the Witwatersrand. From an early age he spent most of his free time in the veld exploring the South African battlefields with his father, developing a keen interest in the Second Anglo-Boer War, archaeology and geology. He served in the South African Air Force in 1972 and saw active service in South West Africa and Angola, which further stimulated his passion for military history. In over 50 years of tramping the battlefields, skirmish sites and cemeteries of the Anglo-Boer War, as well as interviewing descendants of those involved in the war, Rob has developed an insight into what really happened over 110 years ago. He is the chief financial officer for a large group of companies in the timber industry and lives in Johannesburg.

Contents

Maps	7
Glossary	10
Foreword *by Patricia Glyn*	11
Author's note	13
The origins and conduct of the Anglo-Boer War	14
THE ANECDOTES	22

A perspective	22	Demotion	48
A scout dies	22	Depression	48
A shot in the head	22	Devotion	50
Advancing with the enemy	24	Dirty ending	52
Aerial warfare	25	Disgrace	52
Alcohol	26	Divine message	54
American Scouts	28	Doubtful hospitality	54
Ammunition	29	Drill	54
An American dies	29	Earthquake	54
An angel smiles	29	Eggs	55
Atrocities	30	Escape	55
Attraction	30	Executions	57
Baggage	30	Exposure under fire	60
Battle of the Loop	30	Fair warning	60
Betrayal	32	Father and son	61
Biblical	32	Fire	61
Bitter victory	32	First command	62
Boer qualities	33	First words	62
Bombardment	33	Flight	62
Books	34	Football	62
Campfire story	34	Forgotten	64
Campsite	36	Forts	64
Civilian bravery	38	Friends	64
Coffee breaks	39	Fruitless search	64
Communication	40	Fuel	64
Compassion	42	Funerals	65
Concentration camps	42	Futile loyalty	65
Confusion	44	Ghosts	65
Cricket	44	Gifts	68
Crossfire	45	Government in exile	70
Cruelty to animals	46	Grave under a toilet	72
Deception	46	Graves of unknown soldiers	72

Gross negligence	73	Lucky shots	101
Hand grenades	73	Masquerade	101
Hand-shaking army	73	Matters medical	102
Hard of hearing	73	Military advice	104
Hats	73	Mistaken identity	104
Headless	74	Mixed loyalties	105
Hiding	74	Money	105
Hijack	74	Monuments	105
Holding hands	76	'Moses' stories	106
Hoodwinked	76	Music	106
Horseracing	78	Natural interventions	108
Horses	78	Naval warfare	108
Ian Hamilton's revenge	79	Near-fatal assumption	109
Ill-prepared	82	Nicknames	109
Immobilizing the horses	83	Nicotine	112
Impossible odds	83	No escape	113
Inaccessible treasure	83	No quarter	113
Incomplete burial	84	No surrender	114
Irish courage	84	O.K. Corral	114
Jewish courage	84	Obedience	114
Just desserts	84	Opportunities lost	116
Keeping informed	86	Order of the Bath	118
Kindness to the enemy	86	Owning up	118
Knowledge	87	Peace	120
Kruger Millions	87	Pets	120
Krugersdorp statue	88	Picking up pebbles	120
Ladies of the night	90	Porridge	121
Lady Airlie	90	Pot plants	121
Lady Roberts	92	Practical joke	121
Last casualties	92	Premonitions	121
Last words	92	Prophecy	122
Lightning	96	Queen's birthday	122
Locust-screen	96	Queen's touch	122
Looking a gift-horse in the mouth	96	Quick answer	124
Lone sniper	97	Railway warfare	124
Lost treasure	98	Religious service	126
Love letters	100	Remains and controversies	127
Lucky escapes	100	Remembrance	127

Reprisals	127	The generals	139
Research in reverse	128	The legend of the flowers	142
Restraint	128	Theft	146
Rock art	128	Too many chiefs	147
Saluting the throne	128	Torture	147
Schoolboy warriors	128	Trafalgar	147
Secret messages	130	Traitor's Nek	148
Sense of humour	131	Treasure found	148
Shaving	132	Trenches	148
Signs in the sky	133	Tribute	150
Silence	133	Underwear	150
Smokescreens	134	Unfortunate decision	151
Snakebite	134	Unidentified flying objects	151
Socialism	134	Uniforms	151
Sporting chance	134	Unique souvenir	152
Stampeding cattle	135	Unwanted gratitude	152
State of undress	135	Useless booty	152
Staying cool	135	Vegetables	154
Storming a blockhouse	136	War graves	154
Straight-shooting	136	Warrior women	156
Strategic withdrawal	138	Water	156
Tactical changes	138	What if?	158
Tainted reputation	138	White flag	158
Tears	139	Wild animals	158

Appendix 1	The Jameson Raid: military conflict and aftermath	160
Appendix 2	The development of the British blockhouse system during the Anglo-Boer War	166
Appendix 3	Battlefield guide: chronology of major battles (date sequence)	171
Appendix 4	Battlefield guide: chronology of major battles (name sequence)	173
Appendix 5	GPS locations of battles and important skirmishes (alphabetical order)	175

Bibliography	177
Recommended 'Top Ten' books on the Anglo-Boer War	180
Notes	181
Index	186

SOUTH AFRICA 1899

BATTLEFIELD SITES UP TO BLACK WEEK

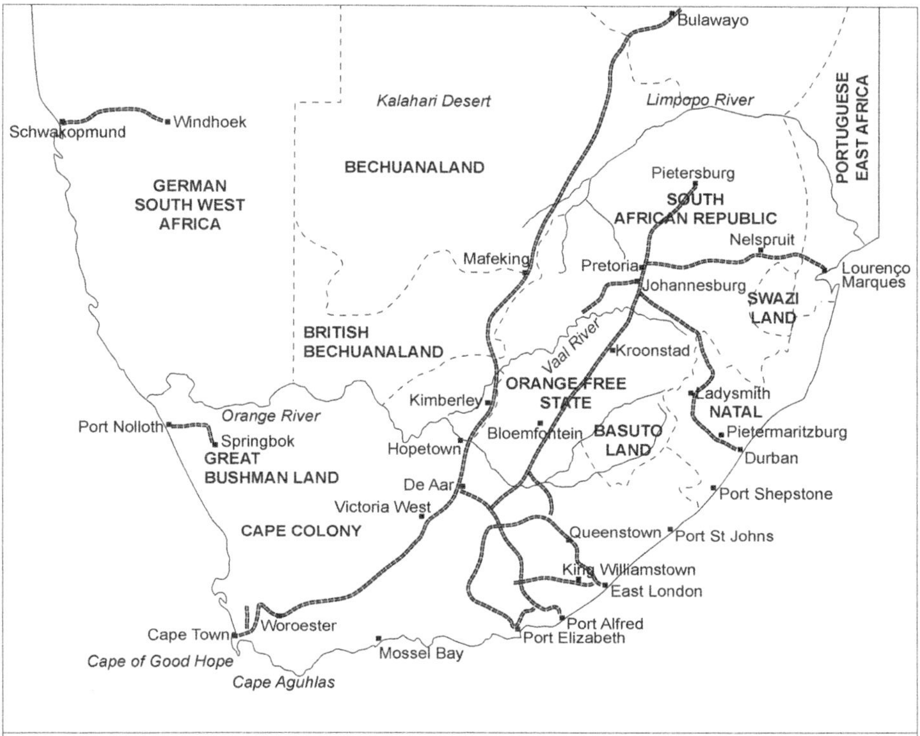

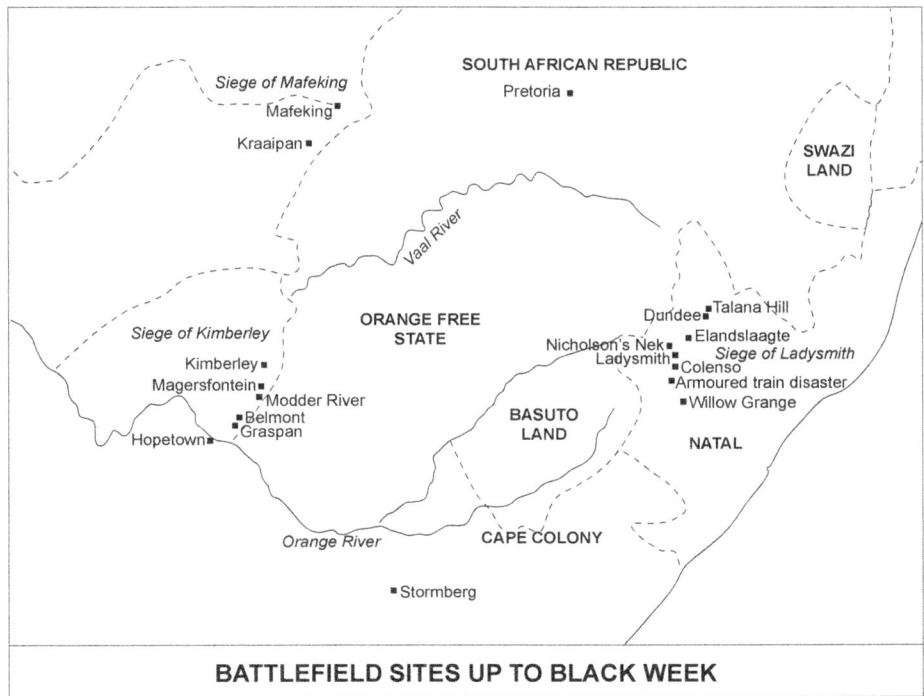

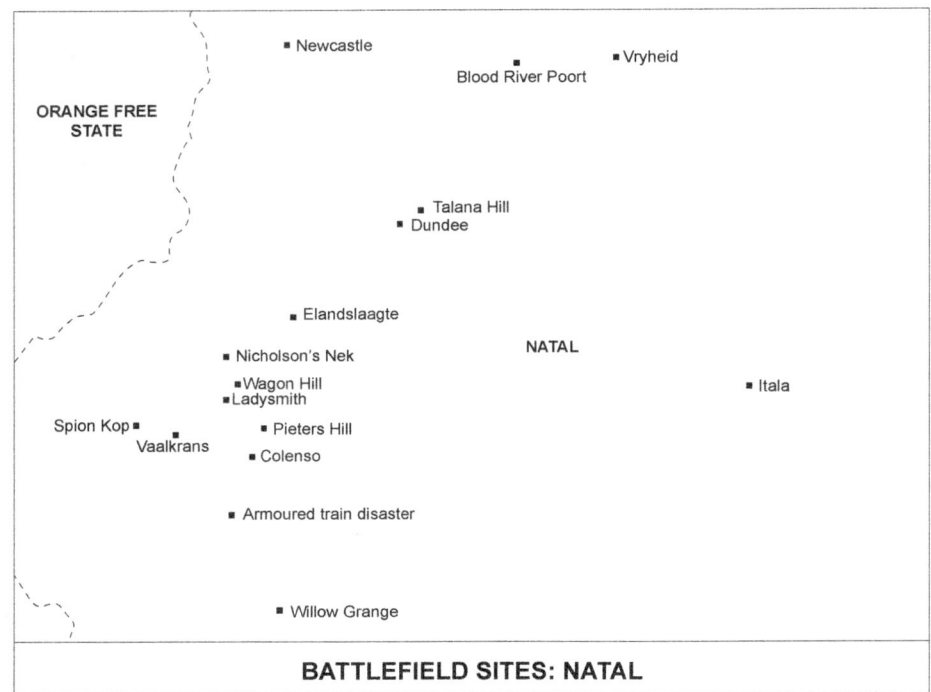

BATTLEFIELD SITES: NATAL

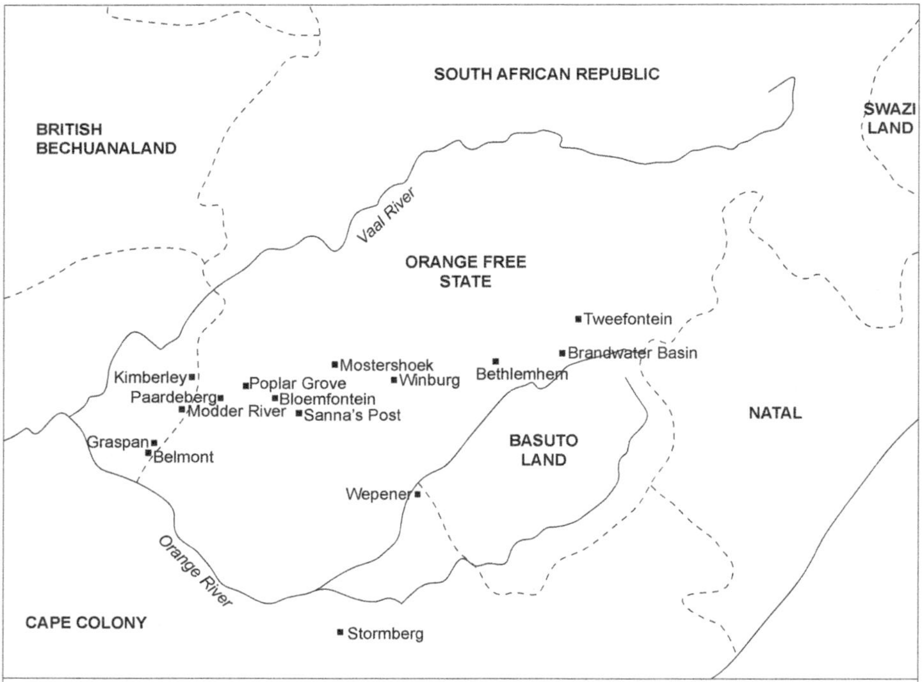

BATTLEFIELD SITES: ORANGE FREE STATE

BATTLEFIELD SITES: EASTERN TRANSVAAL

BATTLEFIELD SITES: WESTERN TRANSVAAL

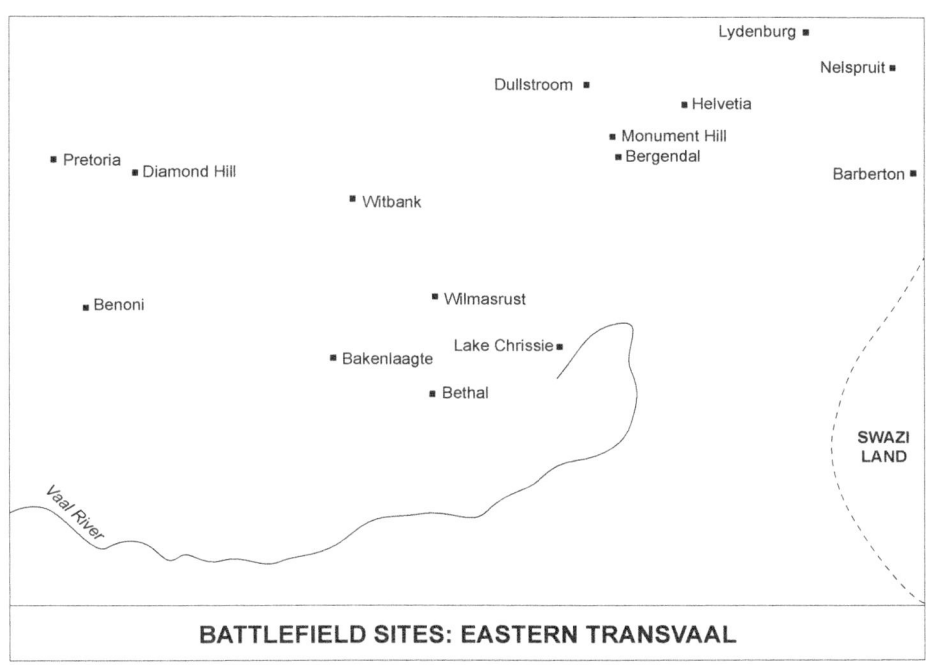

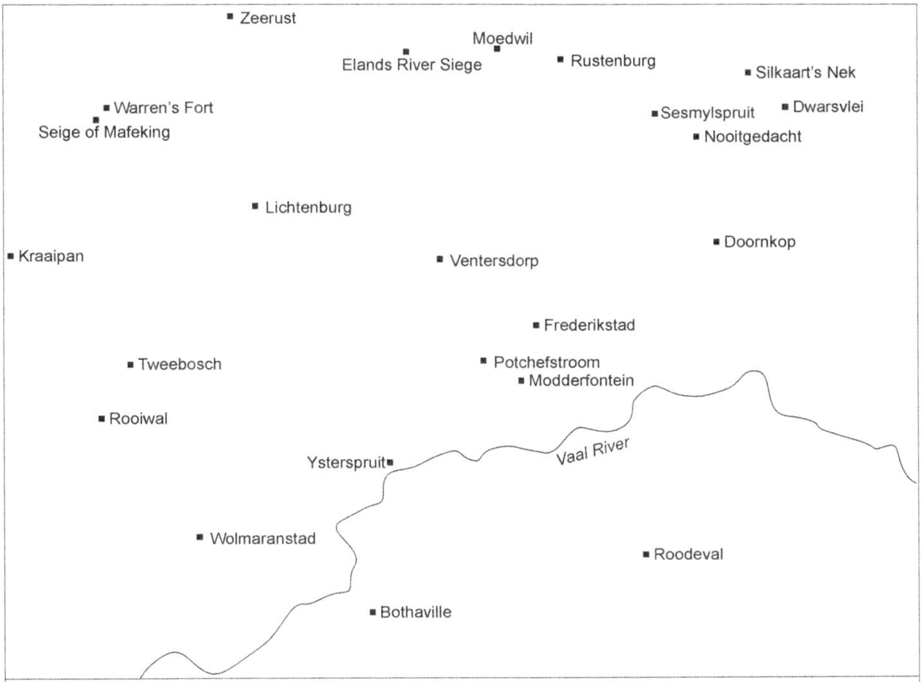

Glossary

agterryer	an attendant on horseback
burgher	a citizen of the Boer republics
dop	a small drink of strong alcohol such as brandy, a dram
dumdum bullet	a soft-nosed small-arms bullet that expands when it hits a target and causes a gaping wound
hartebeeshuis	a simple thatched house, usually with only one or two rooms
inspan	to harness draft animals, usually oxen, to a yoke
kappie	a cloth bonnet worn by Boer women
kraal	a rough stone wall enclosing a cattle or sheep pen
krans	a high perpendicular rock
Krijgsraad	Council of War
laager	a ring of wagons drawn together in a defensive circle
laagte	a shallow valley
nek	a saddle between two hills or mountains
riempie	a strip of cured animal hide used to make whips or interlaced together to make the seat of a simple chair
schanz	a cliff
takhaar	a backveld Boer, the equivalent of an American redneck
trek	journey by ox wagon (past tense trekked)
Trekboers	migrant farmers who lived in their wagons and moved around in search of grazing for their livestock, as well as following the game which they hunted
uitlanders	foreigners living in the Boer republics
vlei	a shallow swamp
voorloper	a person, usually a servant, who walked in front of an ox wagon
vooruit	with determination

Foreword

Rob Milne inspired many enthusiasts with his particular approach to history when he first appeared on my radio programme 'Patricia's People' (SAfm 104-107) back in February 1999. I think that, like me, listeners loved his small brush strokes on the large canvas of our past, his interest in the intimate stories of love, loyalty, pettiness and cruelty that characterized this (and indeed any) human conflict. Most accounts of this dramatic period concentrate on politics, tactics, firepower and logistics and I believe that many of these tales would have been lost to our archives but for Rob's relentless ferreting in koppie and dorp around South Africa. I congratulate him on the passion with which he has pursued this interest and am delighted that these precious stories are now in print.

PATRICIA GLYN

Author's note

This is a book about the people who fought in the Anglo-Boer War and how this war has touched many lives, even up to the present. It has its origins in stories swapped around campfires, dinner tables and during battlefield explorations. In trying to make sense of this, the 'last of the gentlemen's wars', I met many people whose input, encouragement, and friendship I value deeply. These are people from all walks of life and whose roots stem from both sides of the conflict. During the past 12 years I have been alarmed by the rate at which both war graves and structures have been damaged or have completely disappeared. You will notice that I have included a number of 'before and after' photographs in the hope that this creates an awareness of the importance of preserving our heritage.

Firstly, I thank my wife, Bronislava, for walking with me in every sense of the word during the past eleven years. "Wherever you go, I will go; wherever you live, I will live. Your people will be my people, and your God will be my God." (*Book of Ruth*). Thanks also to my sons, Paul and Simon, who often walked with us in our quest for interesting stories.

During the past few years some of the contributors to this book passed on to Higher Service, notably my friend and mentor David Panagos, and Morris Gough-Palmer, who headed up the British War Graves Commission in South Africa for many years. The passage of time has also had its pleasant surprises. My old school friend, Pedro Buccellato, and I met and picked up our friendship and adventures in the veld after a break of 36 years.

Joan 'Tannie Mossie' Abrahams deserves my special thanks for taking such an interest in this edition and for contributing some really interesting new stories. Thank you for remembering, Joan!

Friends who contributed to this edition include Alistair and Marion Moir, Jasmine and Ferdie Coetzee, Louis-John and Judy Havemann, Chris 'Bulldog' Ash, Rita Britz, Rob Hall, Edmond Furter, Ockert Botha, Peter Burmeister, and Naum and Tania Rousine. Thanks also to Pedro for creating and maintaining my website. A special thank-you to Chris and Kerrin Cocks for the editing and final production of this edition, and to Kerrin for the maps.

I have quoted extensively from published sources and have made every effort to trace the copyright holders. Should any infringements have inadvertently occurred, I apologize and undertake to correct any omissions in future editions.

ROB MILNE
Johannesburg
December 2012

The origins and conduct of the Anglo-Boer War

British aspirations in southern Africa began in 1795 when they invaded the Cape Colony, which was under Dutch rule. The reason for the invasion was to protect his strategic Cape port from France during the war with Napoleon. The Dutch king had fled before the French offensive and a puppet regime was established in Holland. After peace was made in 1803, Britain returned the Cape settlement to Dutch rule. When hostilities with France resumed in 1806 the British again invaded the Cape, which became a permanent colony of the British Empire. In all respects the Cape continued to operate along Dutch lines. The Burgher Senate remained in control of Cape Town and the Roman-Dutch laws endured. The British garrison helped to stimulate the local economy and defended the eastern frontier where the trekboers (emigrant Dutch farmers) encountered the powerful Xhosa. This peaceful arrangement suited both the original Dutch settlers and the British, who wished to minimize administration costs and avoid confrontation.

The Dutch farmers were slowly expanding into the interior in their quest for game and fresh grazing. They were dependent on slave labour and when slavery was abolished in 1838 whole communities migrated, or trekked, northward to be free of British rule. This became known as 'The Great Trek'. The burghers established independent republics in the area between the Orange and Vaal rivers (known as the Orange Free State) and the area north of the Vaal (known as the Transvaal Republic). On 17 January 1852, Great Britain formally recognized the independence of the Transvaal Republic at the Sand River Convention, subject to slavery being outlawed in the Transvaal and that they would not interfere in the Orange River Sovereignty's affairs. The latter was a short-lived political entity that lasted between 1848 and 1854. The Orange River Convention (or Bloemfontein Convention) was signed between Great Britain and the Boer Republic of the Orange Free State on 23 February 1854, recognizing the independence of the Boers in the area between the Orange and Vaal rivers. By 1854 both Boer republics had been guaranteed their independence by Great Britain.

On 17 January 1852, representatives of the Boers, headed by Andries Pretorius, and the British government, represented by W.S. Hogg and C.M. Owen, met here and signed the Sand River Convention the next day, recognizing the independence of the emigrant farmers north of the Vaal River in what became the South African Republic. This monument is on the farm Boskop near Ventersburg in the Free State. The discovery of gold on the Witwatersrand in 1886 changed the whole British attitude toward Boer independence as had the discovery of diamonds in the Orange Free State in 1867.

During the 45 years between the granting of independence to the Boer republics, British expansion into southern Africa was driven by three primary factors: first, the desire to control the trade routes to India that passed around the Cape; second, the discovery of diamonds in the Orange Free State and gold in the Transvaal Republic; and third, the race against other European colonial powers who were establishing new territories in Africa, namely Germany, France, Belgium and Portugal.

The discovery of diamonds in the Orange Free State triggered a diamond rush, attracting people from all over the world. Using the excuse of a land claim by indigenous inhabitants Great Britain proclaimed Griqualand West (the diamond fields) as British territory on 27 October 1871. This territory was later formally annexed to the Cape Colony in 1879. Meanwhile, during the 1870s, the Transvaal Republic was involved in a series of skirmishes between the Pedi in the north and the Zulu in the east. In 1877 Sir Theophilus Shepstone annexed the Transvaal Republic for Britain using a special warrant. The Transvaal Boers objected, but if they took up arms against Britain, they feared an invasion by the Zulu under King Cetshwayo. After the Anglo-Zulu War in 1879 and the defeat of the Pedi by British troops later the same year, the Boers were free to give voice against the 1877 British annexation of the Transvaal. President Kruger led two deputations to London in 1878 to negotiate the return of independence, but these were in vain and the Transvaal formally declared independence from the United Kingdom in December 1880.

This lion sculpture clearly has President Kruger's rough facial features, in a relaxed, naturalistic pose.

The two lion sculptures at the entrance to President Kruger's house in Church Street, Pretoria, were presented to Kruger as a mark of appreciation by the Johannesburg mining magnate Barney Barnato before the Anglo-Boer War. They are both quite different and I am sure that the English donor intended the subtle meanings that they convey. The lion on the right is in a traditional pose while the lion on the left is in a relaxed, naturalistic pose. The British ready to strike and the Boers complacent?

The First Anglo-Boer War began on 16 December 1880 with shots fired by Transvaal Boers at Potchefstroom. The Boers ambushed and destroyed a British army convoy at Bronkhorstspruit and besieged all the British army garrisons in the Transvaal from 22 December 1880 to 6 January 1881. After the ignominious defeat of General Colley at Majuba on 27 February 1881, the

British signed an armistice to end the war. Peace negotiations resulted in the signing of the Pretoria Convention, which was superseded by the London Convention which provided for self-government in the Transvaal under British suzerainty, whereby the Boers accepted the Queen's nominal rule and British control over external relations.

Britain, the Royal Guardian of Justice, protects the weak.

This must be one of the very few wooden mine headgears surviving from the early days of the discovery of gold on the Witwatersrand in 1886. The discovery led to a huge influx of immigrants from all over the world, but principally from Great Britain and her colonies. The immigrants, or *uitlanders*, demanded the franchise which the Transvaal Republic was unwilling to give, as the immigrants would outnumber the local farmer population. Behind the scenes Great Britain wanted to control the richest goldfield yet discovered, just as she had done with the Kimberley diamond fields in the Orange Free State Republic. War between Great Britain and the Transvaal Republic was inevitable, no matter how many concessions President Kruger gave to the immigrants. On the outbreak of the war the Orange Free State joined in on the Transvaal side.

George Walker's grave in the Burgersdorp cemetery, Krugersdorp. In February 1886 he and George Harrison discovered the Main Reef gold series at Langlaagte near to what would become the city of Johannesburg. The discovery of the world's richest goldfield was irresistible to British imperial ambitions and the underlying cause of the Anglo-Boer War 13 years later. After all, the British had cheated the Orange Free State Republic by grabbing the richest diamond fields in the world in Kimberley in 1872. The British eventually won the goldfields at the cost of much suffering and loss of life on both sides during the Anglo-Boer War and both the Transvaal and Orange Free State republics lost their independence. Ironically, the Boers helped the British Empire to win the First World War 12 years later and won the first victory of the war by conquering the Germans in South West Africa. George Walker died a poor man in 1924, spending the last years of his life in the bars of Krugersdorp, cadging free drinks from patrons in return for the story of his discovery. George Harrison sold his free claim soon after the discovery and on his journey to the Eastern Transvaal goldfields, presumably attacked and eaten by lions, he disappeared.

In 1886 gold was discovered in the Witwatersrand, re-igniting British imperial interests. This resulted in a gold rush and the consequent influx of miners (mainly British) to Johannesburg which threatened to swamp the small Boer population of the Transvaal.

The immigrants, known as *uitlanders*, or foreigners, began agitating for the franchise as well as the redress of grievances against President Kruger and his government. With no favourable result in sight and with the backing of Cecil John Rhodes, the Uitlanders decided that violent revolution was their only remedy. The Reform Committee, representing the Uitlanders in Johannesburg, began organizing an uprising and smuggled arms and ammunition into the city. Meanwhile, Dr Leander Starr Jameson assembled troops in Pitsani across the border in Bechuanaland (now Botswana). He then received an appeal from the Reformers, known as the 'Women and children letter', and on 29 December 1895 the invasion began. However, Boer commandos shadowed Jameson's raiders and finally cornered them at Doornkop, near Krugersdorp, where Jameson surrendered on 2 January 1896. The Johannesburg revolt didn't materialize and the Reform Committee were arrested and tried by the Boers. Although Britain distanced herself from the raid, it transpired that many senior members of the government, including Colonial Secretary Joseph Chamberlain, knew about and supported the raid.

Above: War and capitalism, or the changing of human blood into gold.

Left: That pleasant sport, Oom Paul.

Germany's Kaiser Wilhelm II sent President Kruger a congratulatory telegram after the raid, which was received in Britain with huge indignation as it implied that Germany would have come to the Boers' aid had the Kaiser been invited to do so. The telegram read:

> I express to you my sincere congratulations that you and your people, without appealing to the help of friendly powers, have succeeded, by your own energetic action against the armed bands which invaded your country as disturbers of the peace, in restoring peace and in maintaining the independence of the country against attack from without.

Oom (Uncle) Paul: "Can't you see, he now eats out of my hand!" (Chamberlain being fed sugar lumps with his paw on the tiger skin, representing Jameson) Tannie (Aunty) Kruger: "Well, well, don't trust the peace. We still know the beasts!"

"Victoria, Victoria!" (after the extermination of the Khalifa at Omdurman)
"Ha, ha, Oom Kruger, now I also have a telegram."

After the raid the Transvaal Republic started preparing for war, which they could now afford as the mining taxes were rolling into their coffers in a torrent. President Steyn of the Orange Free State Republic visited Pretoria after the raid and renewed an offensive and defensive alliance between the two republics. A fort was built in Johannesburg and four forts were built around Pretoria, and arms were imported, including the four famous 'Long Tom' siege guns. Neither side appeared committed to serious negotiations to avoid the forthcoming war.

On 9 October an ultimatum was sent to the British government: if their troops were not removed from the borders of the Transvaal Republic, a state of war would exist between Britain and the Boer republics. The ultimatum expired and the war began at 5 p.m. on 11 October 1899.

The first blow of the war was struck by the

The emotion of a Boer burgher saying farewell to his wife and baby are aptly captured in this statue by Danie de Jager at the Anglo-Boer War museum, Bloemfontein. The Boer ultimatum demanding the withdrawal of British forces on the borders of the Boer republics expired at 5 p.m. on 11 October 1899. Failure to comply was considered a declaration of war. The woman's bonnet (*kappie*) is hanging on her shoulders to indicate the time: it was not polite to wear one's bonnet in the house after sunset. Her husband is carrying a Mauser rifle, is smartly dressed and wearing a tie. The statue of 'The Bitter Ender' after three years of fighting in the veld tells a different story.

The morning of Waterloo (or its South African counterpart) in 1900 (if not earlier). Oom Paul inspects his Guard of Honour before the battle.

Boers the next day when they derailed a British armoured train and attacked and captured the garrison and railway siding at Kraaipan, between Mafeking and Vryburg in the Cape Colony. Captured booty included British Mark IV ammunition, better known as 'dumdum' bullets. Advancing further, the Boers besieged Mafeking on 13 October and Kimberley the next day. The small garrison and civilians in Mafeking had endured the longest siege of the war: relief only came on 17 May 1900, whereas Kimberley was relieved on 15 February 1900.

The Transvaal Boers invaded Natal shortly after the outbreak of war, and the first major battle took place at Talana Hill on 20 October 1899. The British, supported by artillery, made a frontal infantry attack on a hilltop position occupied by the Boers. They carried the position at the cost of heavy casualties, and their commanding general, Sir William Penn Symons, was mortally wounded. After spending two days trying to secure the water supply for their base in Dundee and, cut off from Ladysmith by the Boers, the garrison escaped at night. They endured a forced four-day march of 103 kilometres before they reached Ladysmith. The Boer generals Lukas Meyer and 'Maroela' Erasmus were severely censured by Commandant-General Joubert and President Kruger for letting over 3,500 British troops get away to augment the main British base at Ladysmith.

On 19 October General Kock occupied the railway station at Elandslaagte, cutting off communications between Ladysmith and Dundee. General Sir George White sent his cavalry commander Major General John French to recapture the station. After a fearsome infantry engagement, General Kock was killed and the Boers retreated. French captured two Boer field guns which had originally been taken from Jameson four years before at Doornkop. As the Boers were retreating across the open plain General French unleashed his cavalry, and the 5th Lancers and 5th Dragoon Guards cut down many of the burghers. This charge caused much bitterness among the Boer commandos as some of the wives who had accompanied their husbands on campaign were slaughtered, and no quarter was given to those burghers who tried to surrender.

Meanwhile, the Boers started to encircle Ladysmith and General White sent a large force north toward Nicholson's Nek on 30 October 1899. They were soundly beaten with the loss of over 400 killed and wounded, and 800 taken prisoner. Instead of pursuing the troops who were fleeing to the safety of Ladysmith, Commandant-General Joubert held back his commandos saying, "When the Lord stretches out a finger, don't take the whole hand." His second strategic mistake was his refusal to advance to Durban, deciding to besiege Ladysmith instead. There were very few British forces between Ladysmith and Durban and, had Joubert reached Durban, an early peace could have been the outcome.

The conventional or set-piece phase of the war had begun and this was to endure until the capture of Bloemfontein on 13 March 1900. Only three set-piece battles took place after March: Doornkop (the battle for Johannesburg) on 29 May 1900, Diamond Hill (north of Pretoria) on 11 June 1900 and Bergendal on 27 August 1900.

General Sir Redvers Buller V.C. arrived in Natal at the end of October 1899 as commander of the British Field Force. His first task was the relief of Ladysmith which had been under siege since 2 November 1899. After crushing defeats at the battles of Colenso, Spion Kop and Vaalkrans he finally won through at Pieter's Hill and relieved Ladysmith on 28 February 1900. However, dissatisfaction with his performance had resulted in the appointment of Field Marshal Earl Roberts V.C. as overall commander in South Africa, while Buller was appointed second in command. The military strategy was to follow the main railway lines from the northwest Cape Colony to Bloemfontein and then to Johannesburg and Pretoria, and from Ladysmith in the southeast to Vereeniging on the Vaal River, and thence to Johannesburg, Pretoria and east to the Mozambican border at Hectorspruit.

In the Western theatre Lieutenant-General Lord Methuen advanced steadily along the railway toward Bloemfontein and late in November achieved minor victories at Belmont and Graspan, but was blocked at the inconclusive Battle of Modder River on 28 November 1899. To the east of Methuen's advance Lieutenant-General Gatacre was advancing along the railway line from Queenstown to Molteno and arrived in the area to discover that the Boers had occupied the important junction at Stormberg. During the ensuing battle on 10 December 1899 the British suffered a crushing defeat, the first of three defeats in what became known as 'Black Week'. Ninety-four men were killed or wounded and 696 were captured at the cost to the Boers of eight killed and 26 wounded. The next day, farther to the west, Methuen was soundly defeated south of Kimberley at the Battle of Magersfontein. A brilliant junior officer attached to General Piet Cronjé, Koos de la Rey, conceived the idea of digging trenches in front of Magersfontein koppie instead of defending the summit, as the British would expect. After shelling the hills for a number of hours with 29 guns on 10 December, the Highland Brigade moved forward at night and attacked at first light in a densely packed quarter-column formation. The Highlanders tripped an alarm wire only 370 metres away from the camouflaged Boer trench and the Boers opened fire. Of the British total of 895 casualties that day, more than 700 occurred during the first five minutes of battle. Among the first to fall was the commander of the Highland Brigade, Major-General Andy Wauchope. In this battle, the second of 'Black Week', the Boers suffered 255 casualties.

Four days later, on 15 December 1899, General Buller suffered a worse defeat in Natal at the Battle of Colenso. His losses were 1,138 men against Boer losses of only 50 burghers.

In addition, he suffered the humiliation of losing ten guns and Lieutenant Freddie Roberts, the son of the Commander-in-Chief, was killed trying to save the guns. This was the final British defeat of 'Black Week'. Spion Kop was the next British defeat on 24 January 1900 where Buller lost 1,185 men against Boer losses of 198. After Buller's next defeat at Vaalkrans between 5 and 7 February, the fortunes of war started favouring the British.

Kimberley was relieved on 15 February 1900, and the Boers suffered a humiliating defeat at Paardeberg near Kimberley on 27 February 1900: 'Majuba Day'. General Piet Cronjé was trapped in his laager on the banks of the Modder River and surrendered with over 4,000 burghers after sustaining losses in killed and wounded of 850 burghers. British losses were 1,620 men. The following day Ladysmith was relieved by Buller's forces after the Battle of Tugela Heights. In the west Lord Roberts defeated the Boers at Poplar Grove on 7 March and captured the capital of the Orange Free State Republic on 13 March 1900 after the Battle of Driefontein three days before. Lord Roberts spent three weeks in the capital to rest and re-fit his army before moving north toward Kroonstad and the border of the Transvaal Republic on 3 May 1900.

At an important joint Council of War at Kroonstad the Boers decided to abandon their cumbersome wagons and employ mounted mobile commandos. This heralded a new phase of the war: guerrilla warfare. The new Chief Commandant of the Orange Free State, General Christiaan de Wet, granted his men leave of absence and they regrouped at Sand River on 25 March, imbued with fresh courage. On 31 March 1900 de Wet ambushed General Broadwood's column at Koorn Spruit, near the railway station Sanna's Post, 28 kilometres east of Bloemfontein, in the first guerrilla action of the war. British losses were 159 men against Boer losses of only 13 men, and the Boers captured 116 British supply wagons as well as seven guns. General de Wet followed up his success at Mostertshoek near Reddersburg on 3 April and then besieged Wepener from 4 April to 21 April 1900. Although de Wet was forced to abandon the siege when British reinforcements arrived, British casualties numbered 178 against the Boer's thirty-six.

Mafeking was relieved on 17 May 1900, and Lord Roberts's army continued their advance on the Transvaal Republic. Johannesburg was captured on 29 May 1900 after the Battle of Doornkop to the west of Johannesburg. This was fought over the same ground where Jameson had surrendered on 2 January 1896, a point of attack deliberately chosen by Ian Hamilton in order to avenge this past humiliation. Pretoria fell soon after the Battle of Ses Myl Spruit, after which the Boers under General Botha decided not to defend the capital city. After resting in Pretoria for a week, Lord Roberts advanced eastward along the railway line and defeated Botha at the Battle of Diamond Hill on 12 June 1900. He then joined General Buller's army at Belfast and broke through the Boer defences at Bergendal on 27 August 1900, the last set-piece battle of the war.

Behind the British advance the Boers waged guerrilla warfare in earnest: General de

Wet overcame the British at Roodeval on 7 June, and General de la Rey defeated the British at Silkaatsnek, west of Pretoria, on 11 July 1900 at the cost of 178 British casualties. The Boers captured two field guns, a machine gun, as well as rifles and ammunition which were sorely needed to re-arm burghers who had returned to duty. The Battle of Dwarsvlei, near Krugersdorp, took place on the same day that Fighting-General Oosthuizen attacked a column under General Smith-Dorrien. Captains Gordon and Younger each won the Victoria Cross for their efforts to save two guns, and General Oosthuizen (who had captured Winston Churchill in Natal the previous year) died of his wounds three weeks later.

Lord Roberts realized that he had to counter the Boer guerrilla tactics and on 16 June 1900 issued a proclamation dictating that farms in the vicinity of destroyed rail and telegraph connections were to be burned down. Thus began the British 'scorched earth' policy, which was later expanded under Lord Kitchener, Roberts's successor, to the burning of farms, destruction of crops, and killing of all livestock. The homeless women and children were taken to concentration camps, which were introduced by the British in July 1900. The Boers were eventually forced into giving up their independence by signing the Treaty of Vereeniging on 31 May 1902 due to the large-scale deaths in the concentration camps, as well as their own starvation and lack of clothing. However, after the last set-piece battle of the war at Bergendal, the Boers still had a lot of determination and fight left in them, and no more than 30,000 burghers kept half a million British and colonial troops in the field for another 18 months before they were forced to surrender. After Bergendal there were at least 13 significant, and mostly successful, guerrilla attacks on the British and colonial forces and scores of minor attacks. Although the Boer republics lost their independence, the terms of the peace agreement were generous: among other concessions, Britain made £6 million available for the reconstruction of the two republics. Twelve years later Boer and Brit fought side by side in the First World War, with South African forces giving the Allies their first victory of the war by conquering the German colony of South West Africa.

THE ANECDOTES

A perspective

This book is mainly concerned with the Second Anglo-Boer War, although I do sometimes touch on other events between the First Anglo-Boer War and the Second World War. Herman Charles Bosman, the famous South African short-story writer, gave this perspective on the difference between the First and Second Anglo-Boer wars: "Exciting times followed. There was a great deal of shooting at the leopard and a great deal of running away from him. The amount of Martini and Mauser fire I heard in the krantzes reminded me of nothing so much as the First Boer War. And the amount of running away reminded me of nothing so much as the Second Boer War."[1]

I should immediately say that I give this anecdote as a humorous introduction and not a deprecation of the Boer efforts, for I have nothing but admiration for the two small Boer republics that held out against the might of the British Empire for three years. Bosman laughs at his people and himself, and indeed you will find in this collection that, apart from stories about the crazy antics of the British generals, the Boers themselves initiated many of the humorous exchanges that took place during the war.

A scout dies

Danie Theron, who formed and led the Boer Scouting Corps, died alone in a barrage of British artillery fire on a ridge near Fochville. What drove him to such recklessness to single-handedly engage a whole British column? The answer goes back to 1893, when he set up a successful legal practice in Krugersdorp and courted a young lady called Johanna Neethling whom he intended to marry. Every weekend he cycled from Krugersdorp to Eikenhof and back, a distance of 26 miles, to be with her. In August 1898 she caught a chill, which developed into pneumonia, and she died on the 28th, in the same bed and on the same day as her sister, Henrietta. "There can be little doubt that her death was a great blow to Theron, who never married."[2] It was just eight days after the second anniversary of her death, on 5 September 1900, that Theron came to grief in his final act of defiance. His comrades, aware of the tragic motivation for his rash bravery, arranged for his reburial after the war. Danie Theron now rests in peace beside his beloved Joanna in the small cemetery at Eikenhof.

A shot in the head

The high-powered Boer Mauser rifles inflicted clean wounds with their flat trajectories, and there are numerous reports of British soldiers recovering from chest wounds after just a few days' convalescence. In some cases the Mauser bullet improved performance. "Captain Dibley was almost on top of the hill [Talana] when hit. He had a dim recollection of the gallant Adjutant of the Royal Irish Fusiliers racing up almost alongside him and within a few paces of the summit, when he suddenly saw an aged and gray-bearded burgher drawing a

The graves of lieutenants Grover and Crowle at Sanna's Post cemetery in 1999 after the school children had paid their respects to the Anglo-Boer War centenary.

In 1999 I was very impressed by the wreaths and pebbles left on the graves of the British soldiers by Afrikaans school children at Sanna's Post to celebrate the war's centenary. Here, the teacher who arranged the tributes, Joan Abrahams, revisits the graves 13 years later.

The famous Boer scout's final resting place next to his beloved Johanna who is buried with her sister in the elaborate grave to the right of Danie's grave.

Danie Theron's memorial near Fochville on the ridge where he died alone in a barrage of British artillery fire. The brass shape on top is in the shape of a trigger-guard of a Mauser rifle.

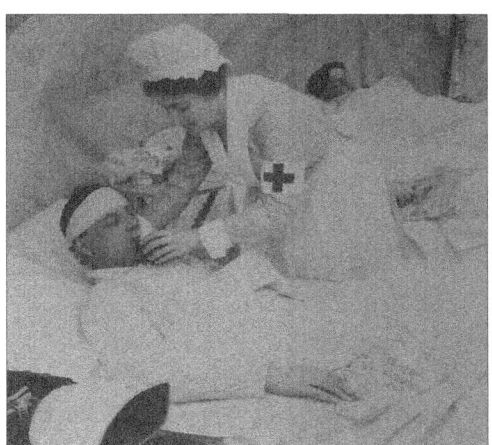

In a field hospital on the Tugela River near Ladysmith, 1900. At the start of the Anglo-Boer War the Army Nursing Service had less than 100 trained nurses. By the end of the war, over 1,400 trained nurses had deployed to South Africa. Usually the volunteer nurses were "single and of good character" but the nurse in this photograph is wearing a wedding ring. The soldier receiving her attention is harbouring a copy of the *Punch Almanac*, demonstrating that his sense of humour survived his head wound which was most likely caused by wearing the white pith helmet (beside his bed) in the face of Boer snipers.

bead upon him at a distance of only a few paces. He snapped his revolver at him, only to fall senseless the next moment with a bullet through his head. Marvellous though it seems,,, he made a comparatively speedy recovery, and was able to ride into Ladysmith, at the head of his company, in the following February, having been in the hospital in the besieged town in the interval. Evidence of the temporary nature of the discomfort caused by a bullet through the head is afforded by the fact that he is today one of the best bridge players in the Regiment."[3]

During the siege of Mafeking, a railway guard serving in the Railway Volunteers was shot in the head, the Mauser bullet entering one temple and exiting the other. He felt no ill effects and was quickly discharged from hospital.[4]

On 4 June 1901, Lord Metheun's column was attacked as it was leaving Jacobsdal. "On our side Lieut. King, of the General's escort, was shot through the brain and two others were also wounded. Though Lieut. King's brains actually protruded from the wound he eventually recovered."[5]

Advancing with the enemy

During the attack on the British camp at Lake Chrissie a Canadian scout, sent by General French with a dispatch to General Smith-Dorrien, arrived at 3 a.m. and found himself in the midst of the Boers who were about to commence their attack. He lay low and as the Boers advanced he followed and ended up in the camp where he delivered the message and "... saluting, handed me the dispatch with as much unconcern as though it had been an Aldershot field day". At one stage during the advance he noticed a Boer looking at him with some interest, so he pushed the muzzle of his carbine into the Boer's back and pulled the trigger, reasoning that "dead men tell no tales".[6]

Jan 'Tweefontein' van der Merwe made a habit of exchanging horses whenever his commando entered a part of the country to which they were not accustomed. Delayed in one of these swaps, he was in a hurry to catch up with General de Wet and his commando, who were on their way to the Orange River on their first attempt to invade the Cape Colony. In haste, and with the setting sun in his eyes, he overtook a number of horsemen at the tail end of his commando. However, he actually found himself riding in the midst of the advance guard of a British cavalry force, who in their turn assumed that he was a Boer 'joiner' acting as a scout. Unsure how to proceed, he continued riding with the enemy until some long-range Boer shells started exploding among the cavalry and stampeded a number of horses. Seizing his chance, he caught a beautiful black stallion and changed mounts. He was about to turn and ride away when more of the enemy came up from the rear and he was forced to mingle with them. Since he was riding one of the enemy mounts his chances of immediate detection were much rosier, so he quickened his pace and moved up the column. He slowly passed the leaders and was about 100 yards in advance of the British when one of them shouted to him. Going into a dip he suddenly dug his heels into his newly acquired horse and dashed off in the direction of his commando. "The Boers saw the lone horseman disappearing into the laagte leaving behind him a cloud of dust and wondered what it meant. As he came into view again about eight hundred yards away, General de Wet, who was with the rearguard said, 'Don't shoot, I want to see what he wants.' Just then Jan waved a handkerchief above his head; but it was only when he was about 30 yards from the commando that they realized it was one of their own men." Five minutes later, after hearing the story, General de Wet laughed heartily for a long time, remarking, "This is the best joke of the war!"[7]

Aerial warfare

The Royal Engineers arrived in South Africa with 20 balloons, which proved to be largely ineffectual due to the fact that they were graded for a height of 4,000 feet at Aldershot, at sea level. Ladysmith, for example, is at an altitude of 3,500 feet; therefore the balloons could go no higher than 500 feet. The balloons were heavy because the fabric was made from rubberized sailcloth. The journalist J.B. Atkins commented that, "I hope the aeronauts will manage to get it up by relieving it of the cradle and sending up some light, acrobatic observer in the ropes. Otherwise I fear that when we get to a still higher place in the hills the balloon will try to go through the ground!"[8] His observation was quite shrewd as the Transvaal Highveld is at an altitude of 6,000 feet.

During the siege of Ladysmith the Royal Engineers operated a total of eight observation balloons. The balloons were khaki in colour, each balloon being filled with 11,000 cubic feet of hydrogen gas, under which hung a wicker basket that carried two men. They were fixed to the ground by ropes and communication was via a telephone link. The Boers realized that it was futile to try to shoot them down with artillery when they were in the air, so they worked

The Royal Engineers brought 20 balloons to South Africa but they proved ineffective as they were too heavy and could not attain sufficient height in the high altitudes where they were most needed. This war balloon is being transported on the march from the Vaal River to Johannesburg. Note that it is inflated to give some relief to the oxen pulling the wagon.

out the exact launch position, and shelled them when they descended.[9] By the fourth day of the siege, two balloons had been lost to shellfire and one in a storm.

During the Battle of Magersfontein a war balloon was kept in the air for most of the day but the spotters directed the naval gun to shoot over the back of the hill instead of shelling the Boer trenches: "… to the present-day the ground at the rear of the hill is strewn thickly with the bones of hundreds of horses, the effect of the naval pills."[10]

A Boer officer, Captain J.J. Naudé, gave an interesting explanation for the British defeat at Nicholson's Nek. Prior to the British attack the British had observed the Boer positions from a war balloon, but the Boers had purposely deployed their forces very thinly in the centre. After the balloon came down, the evening before the early-morning attack, Joubert redeployed forces into the centre, thus beating the British back in a near rout.[11]

Baron H. von Zeppelin, leader of the Hollander Volunteer Contingent, who died of wounds received at Elandslaagte, was a relation of the German airship designer. After the war he was reburied in the Kloof cemetery, Heidelberg.[12]

Alcohol

General Buller had to have a constant supply of French champagne to sustain him in the field, which goes a long way to explain his oft-irrational decisions. At one time he was anxiously awaiting an order of 50 cases of champagne from his wine merchant in England, to whom he had given the strictest instructions to label the consignment 'castor oil'. In reply to an inquiring signal to his military base, an officer replied, "Regret exceedingly no cases as described have yet reached us, but this day we have procured all the castor oil possible (twenty cases), and have dispatched it without delay, as you desired. We trust this unavoidable delay has caused no serious inconvenience."[13]

After General Viljoen's successful attack on the British forts at Helvetia, the British prisoners filled their water bottles with rum looted from their own stores. As they were being marched back to the Boer camp near Dullstroom, Schikkerling watched a prisoner riding on one of the Boer horses, periodically handing his water bottle down to his meek captor. "The latter once more looked up appealingly and the prisoner said, 'No more left.' The captor's meek and appealing attitude now suddenly changed and he shouted: 'Then get off that bloody horse!'"[14]

Jack van den Heever and his brother Gert lay exposed for many hours in the hot sun near Val station, waiting to blow up a goods train. Their expectations were not in vain, as the train which was disabled contained "fat plunder", and was afterward known as the 'whisky train'.

In the foreground is a section of the remains of the Boer trench at Magersfontein. Lieutenant-General Lord Methuen undertook a night march with 12,000 men to attack the Boer centre at first light. The positioning of the Boer trenches at the foot of Magersfontein koppie was a total surprise as previous Boer tactics dictated that the commandos entrench themselves on top of hills. The unsuspecting front ranks were decimated by Boer fire before they could dig cover for themselves. The surviving troops were pinned down for the rest of the day and the Scots suffered from terrible sunburn on the backs of their legs. Note the flatness of the terrain in front of the Boer trenches: a perfect killing-ground.

A contemporary photograph of the 'Whisky Train' burning after being wrecked and looted by the Boers on 29 December 1901.

The remains of the old railway culvert between Greylingstad and Val where the British 'Whisky Train' was ambushed on 29 December 1901. Rita Britz arranged for a monument to be erected at this culvert which was unveiled on 3 November 2012.

Headstone of Baron H. von Zeppelin in the Kloof cemetery, Heidelberg.

My great-uncle Archibald Wilson served with the Royal Field Artillery during the Anglo-Boer War. He began a life-long correspondence with my father who was serving with the SAAF in Egypt and Italy during the Second World War in which he recalled his interesting experiences during the Anglo-Boer War.
Source: Ewen Isdale

Jack was so thirsty from exposure that he drained many bottles of different types of alcohol, and afterward had to be taken back to camp on the back of a mule cart.[15]

Words of wisdom from my great-uncle, a gunner who served with the Royal Field Artillery during the Anglo-Boer War, written in 1963: "Alcohol is a good friend but a bad master."

Dietlof van Warmelo, a Boer commando, recommended alcohol as an antidote for snakebite, provided that it is taken immediately and in sufficient quantity that it goes to the head. A good quantity of brandy should be taken on commando as it is also a good remedy for insect bites, although van Warmelo notes that some Boers regularly 'took a dop' even for a mosquito bite.[16]

A young Free State burgher, Izak Liebenberg, was hanged on 11 January 1902 in Aliwal North as a result of his intoxicated bragging in a bar in Smithfield. Lieutenant Liebenberg was captured by the British on 8 June 1901 on the farm Paardefontein near Pietersburg, while hiding in a barn. He went on trial in Aliwal North as a result of his drunken boast that he had shot a policeman, Leopold Niemeyer, a Free State traitor who was fighting for the British. Izak was convicted of the crime by the British and was wrongfully hanged, but that is the price one pays for drinking and bragging. The last hymn that he sang before his execution was 'Closer my God to Thee', but his execution went horribly wrong. After the gallows lever was pulled, he dropped and ended up standing on his feet, unharmed. Either the structure was too low or the troops had forgotten to dig a hole under the gallows. So a hole was dug and his 'second execution' was successful.

American Scouts

Americans made up approximately 300 of the 2,675 foreigners fighting for the Boers. They attached themselves to various commandos but after the Natal campaign, Captain John A. Hassell, an American who had served with the Vryheid Commando, organized the American Scouts: "… probably was the strangest body of men in the war". One of the American Scouts was John N. King from Reading, Pennsylvania. He and his best friend had spent time in gaol in America before immigrating to South Africa, he for participating in the lynching of an Italian who had robbed the dead after the Johnstown flood and his friend for larceny. "When war was begun King was employed on a Johannesburg mine, and when his best friend determined to join the British forces he decided to enlist in the Boer army. Before parting the two made an agreement that neither should make the other prisoner in case they met. At Spion Kop, King captured his friend unawares and, after a brief conversation and a farewell grasp of the hand, King shot him dead."[17]

Ammunition

It became regular practice for the Boer commandos to replenish their ammunition by following British columns. The British did not trouble to pick up cartridges which fell from their bandoliers, which could be easily replaced at camp. Reitz commented that, "… I doubt if the British ever realized to what an extent the Boers were dependent upon this source of replenishment."[18] Even today, a century after the war, it is surprising how many unfired cartridges can be found in the veld.

An American dies

On 15 July 1901, an Irish-American called Walter Wilson, fighting on the side of the Boers, was badly wounded in a skirmish. The British allowed Chris, his countryman and messmate, onto the battlefield to hear his dying words. Wilson said: "Say good-bye to the boys, and tell them we will meet at the Great Divide."[19]

An angel smiles

There simply has to be an interesting story behind the two graves of Sergeant Woodward in the Kloof cemetery, Heidelberg. On his cast-iron cross his date of death is recorded as 8 August 1900; his engraved stone memorial is two graves away. The story, recorded in the papers of the late Jurie Swart on 20 January 1949, stems from the evidence of two witnesses, a priest and a local woman. Woodward, an Englishman, was apparently sent on a dangerous mission, but never returned. Sometime later a British unit came across his skeleton in the veld and identified him from papers on the carcass that were still legible. His remains were brought to Heidelberg and he received a funeral with full military honours. Some time later, a different reconnaissance group interviewing farm workers and Boer prisoners of war in another area, heard a different account of his death. Farm labourers reported that they had seen two Boers bludgeon Woodward to death with an axe and a pick handle, and had then seen them burying his remains on a hill. Eventually Woodward's remains were recovered from the hill and he was again buried with full military honours by the new British garrison who had no idea of his earlier burial. Having been a bagpipe player of note, he was dressed in full Scottish uniform, bagpipe and all, so that he would be fully equipped for the Resurrection. It was a very emotional funeral, with bagpipes playing and the women weeping.

Many years later it was rumoured that the second set of Woodward's remains were actually those of a Suikerbosrand farmer's pet baboon: the farmer killed it before he fled from the advancing British army. Someone asked the priest: "And what will happen on the Final Day when, amid trumpet calls, the baboon appears among the English soldiers?" The embarrassed priest replied: "What they will do to the baboon I don't know, but this I know full well: if he appears in the company of English soldiers in full Scottish regalia with bagpipes under his arm, even the Angel in charge won't be able to suppress a smile."[20]

Atrocities
After the armoured train was captured near Chieveley, a rumour went around that the Boers had buried one of the Dublins alive. Next to the mass grave is a solitary grave in memory of an unknown soldier. "A poor fellow of the Dublins had his leg shot off and it is supposed he crawled away and the Boers buried him alive, for afterward he was found with his other leg out of the ground. And when we dug up his body he was found to be clutching the ground with both hands. Our doctor said he could not have lived, and the Boers doubtless thought him dead, so we don't blame them for it."[21]

Attraction
While on commando in September 1901, Schikkerling was attracted to a young lady of about eighteen. "In the religion of love, I have, in these peaceful days, reason to believe that I am not entirely an atheist."[22]

Baggage
Lieutenant Fuller's field kit was not supposed to exceed 50 pounds and he was a somewhat perturbed to discover that he had no less than 14 different boxes and bundles. However, he observed that he was not as bad as his colonel, who carried with him a one-roomed corrugated-iron house "... for this was a gentleman's war."[23]

Lord Basing's cavalry column, the Royals, did itself proud as each officer had his own Cape cart. "When this column halted and outspanned near the Bothaville drift, what with the cracking of whips, the yells of the voorloopers, the smoke of the fires, the galloping of horses and the erection of tents, the scene must have closely resembled the Israelites entering the Holy Land. I have never witnessed anything quite so immobile in my life."[24]

Winston Churchill observed that "The vast amount of baggage this army takes with it on the march hampers its movements and utterly precludes all possibility of surprising the enemy." And also: "It is a poor economy to let a soldier live well for three days at the price of killing him on the fourth."[25]

Battle of the Loop
One dark night, close to the blockhouse lines near Bothaville, a remarkable action was fought. The Cork Militia sent out a patrol along the railway line but it got lost. A second patrol was ordered to search for it. Searching for the rails of the main line that had been pulled up by the Boers, the first patrol struck a large loop near the line used for turning trains. They wandered round and round in circles, thinking that they were following the main line. When they felt that they had done enough, they turned to head back to their blockhouse, but presently

Sergeant Woodward's two graves at the Kloof cemetery in Heidelberg. His cast-iron cross is on the left of the regimental memorial and his headstone is on the right. One of these graves contains the remains of a baboon.

The mass grave of the British soldiers killed during the ambush of the train on which Winston Churchill was travelling near Chieveley station on 15 November 1899.

This corrugated-iron building in Belfast, Mpumalanga, was erected by the British army during the war. Now it serves as the Pig & Pickle Country Tavern for those in need of refreshment when on their way to the trout fishing in Dullstroom.

A contemporary photograph entitled 'Crossing the Valsch River Drift, 12 May 1900'. Movement of combatants on both sides was often hampered by flooding in summer.

Graves of troopers Beck and Nell, National Scouts, in the Kloof cemetery, Heidelberg. Boers who changed sides and fought for the British were organized into units of 'National Scouts'. After the war these traitors were ostracized by their countrymen. On a recent visit to this cemetery I noticed that these two metal crosses are now missing, ripped out of their concrete plinths.

heard a noise in front of them – it was the second patrol which had also somehow got itself entangled in the loop. Both patrols opened fire on each other. "So the battle was waged round and around the loop, lasting until dawn [and] revealed the entire militia of Cork standing to arms in the Wolvehoek defences a few hundreds of yards off. Needless to say this battle, like most others in this war, was entirely bloodless."[26]

Betrayal

Troopers John Beck and Frederick Nell, among other National Scouts, were killed in action by their former comrades of the Heidelberg Commando on 24 July 1901 at Braklaagte. They are buried next to each other in the Kloof cemetery, Heidelberg.

During the same action Scheepers, Danie Maartens's brother-in-law, was badly wounded. Scheepers and a group of National Scouts had turned his sister and her daughter out of their house in their nightclothes before burning it. They then drove them in front of their horses into the freezing veld for a kilometre before abandoning them. Danie found his wife and child the following morning in a critical condition from the cold. After the Braklaagte action, Danie demanded to see the wounded Scheepers who was under armed guard. Scheepers crawled toward his sister's husband, begging for mercy. Danie told him that he wouldn't hear any plea but only wanted to shoot him between the eyes. "He aimed, fired, then climbed on his horse and rode away."

Two other turncoats captured during this action, Piet Bouwer and Roelf van Emmenes, were tried and later executed. This was a particularly emotional execution as blood relatives, friends and ex-pupils of the schoolmaster of Heidelberg, Piet Bouwer, carried it out.[27]

Biblical

In Ladysmith it was rumoured that Sir George White was reciting the 100th Psalm to mark the 100th day of the siege.[28] I suspect that his eyes were drawn from verse 2: "Worship the Lord with joy; come before him with happy songs!" to Psalm 102, verses 5 to 7: "I groan aloud; I am nothing but skin and bones. I am like a wild bird in the desert, like an owl in abandoned ruins."

Bitter victory

Of all the Anglo-Boer War battlefields that I have visited, I found Magersfontein to be the most eerie. Sophia Izedinova, a volunteer nurse with the Russian-Dutch ambulance serving with the Boers, observed that, "In general, in spite of the favourable outcome, this battle had left a dark impression on all the Boers I met who had taken part in it. The resolution of the brave Scotsmen who were shot down by an enemy occupying almost invulnerable positions greatly astonished the Boers."[29] Captain Trichardt gave a similar report after the battle: "Our people are calm and quiet and do not exult in the enemy's great loss, but they are determined not to let the enemy pass through them so long as any survive. I cannot describe the battlefield as anything else but an awful slaughter place."[30]

Boer qualities

"The Boer has three rare qualities, hospitality, bravery, and a sense of humour. He is the most vigorous, resourceful, and intelligent peasant in the world. There is an old-time courtesy and chivalry about him, due to his birth, which takes off his hat when he salutes you; yet, at the same time he will not pamper idle women, nor follow the vagaries of a society that less readily forgives an offence against etiquette than an act of dishonour. He is law-abiding and has a reverend regard for custom, and certainly has the best blood in the colonies."[31]

A Boer commando was never seen to exult over a victory, his hand being better adapted to the stem of a pipe than to the stock of an army rifle. "He did not go into battle because he had the lust of blood, for he abhorred the slaughter of men, and it was not an extraordinary spectacle to see a Boer weeping beside the corpse of a British soldier. On the field, after the Spion Kop battle, where Boer guns did their greatest execution, there were scores of bare-headed Boers who deplored the war, and amidst ejaculations of 'Poor Tommy' and 'This useless slaughter', brushed away the tears that rolled down over their brown cheeks and beards."[32]

Bombardment

British artillery support during the Battle of Spion Kop was of more help to the Boers than the British, with the shells falling short and onto the British positions. General Botha reported that some of the Tommies ran across to the Boer positions to escape their own shellfire.[33]

As the war progressed the British developed the creeping artillery barrage, whereby their infantry would advance behind the cover of bursting shells. The key to the Boer positions at Bergendal was a rocky ridge held by 74 men of the Johannesburg Police. "Against this little ridge, not ninety yards in length and held by about seventy-five men, nearly 100 cannon were directed, while the English infantry were advancing under fire of their rifles. I thought everything human had perished, even to the lizards and insects in the rent and battered rocks."[34] Both sides were astounded that there were still men alive to resist the final infantry charge; in fact 32 survived the bombardment and charge, and escaped over open ground to the rear Boer positions. "On our right stood the farmhouse and from behind it dashed a few mounted Boers; they had to ride through a heavy fire, but as we had been running hard it was rather shaky and did not stop many of them."[35]

A British general ordered his guns forward to shell a koppie which was occupied by Boers. As the guns were being brought into action an officer galloped up to the general to warn him that the Yeomanry had just occupied the hill. "Occupied the hill!" exclaimed the general. "Damn it, man, tell them to get off. How do you expect me to capture it without a bombardment?"[36]

Buller, probably affected by too much sun and champagne, studied the Boer positions from Hussar Hill, which he had ordered Lord Dundonald to capture for observation purposes. He decided that, in order to take Hlangwane, he would first have to take Hussar Hill (on which he was already standing). He accordingly withdrew his force and issued orders for the next day: "It is intended to seize Hussar Hill tomorrow, and the spurs to the east of it north of Moord Kraal, and to occupy this position with artillery."[37] On 14 February 1900, Dundonald duly recaptured the hill. What a pity Buller did not survive to the 1950s when he could have contributed to 'The Goon Show'. Incidentally, Winston Churchill's younger brother, John, was shot in the foot during the evacuation of Hussar Hill on 12 February 1900.[38]

Books

Many participants in the war carried the Bible with them, which was their constant companion. Fuller describes the library which he took to South Africa: "It consisted of Shakespeare in six minute volumes, the Bible, d'Aguillar's *Maxims of Napoleon*, *Omar Khayyam* and *A Guide to Paris*, which book very soon went through the porthole of my cabin. I read the works of Shakespeare, Tennyson and the Bible from cover to cover, and when at Leeuwpoort Halt, for some reason which I no longer remember, I learned *Omar Khayyam* by heart."[39] Coincidentally, my father read *Omar Khayyam* daily in the Western Desert and Italy during the Second World War, and told me that "it was an appropriate philosophy at the time".

By late 1901 General de Wet's mobile library was reduced to *Krieg und Frieden* (a German translation of Tolstoy's *War and Peace*), *Anna Karenina*, a biography of Savonarola, some poetry and theological works, extracts from *Seneca*, a book on physics, and a history of the American Civil War.[40]

Campfire story

The Boers were, and still are, accomplished storytellers. During the trek north through what is now the Kruger National Park to commence waging guerrilla warfare, this is one story told around the campfire: "A transport rider was disturbed one night by lions worrying his donkeys which were tied to the wagon. He decided to hurry away at once and, with his natives, quickly harnessed the animals to the wagon and started forward. As it became light, he noticed to his surprise that in the darkness and confusion a lion had been inspanned and was quietly moving with the team. While thinking furiously they passed some travellers, who shouted to know how he had inspanned the lion. 'Don't ask me,' he replied, 'tell me rather how I can outspan the beast.'"[41]

The remains of a portion of the Boer trench at Magersfontein, south of Kimberley.

Over 40 big British guns were served at this spot in the foreground and bombarded Bergendal koppie (where the present monument is situated in the distance) for three hours. The guns consisted of 21st Royal Field Artillery Battery, 61st Howitzer Battery and naval 12-pounders, 5-inch guns and 4.7-inch guns.

This small area at Bergendal farm was held by 74 men of the ZARPs (Johannesburg Police) under Commandant P.R. Oosthuizen and bore the brunt of the British attack on the Boer positions on 27 August 1900. After a three-hour bombardment of over 40 big guns and the subsequent attack by 1,500 infantrymen of the 7th Brigade, Lyttleton's 4th Division, observers were totally amazed that soldiers could live and continue fighting after taking such punishment.

The two lion sculptures at the entrance to President Kruger's house in Church Street, Pretoria, were presented to Kruger as a mark of appreciation by the Johannesburg mining magnate Barney Barnato before the Anglo-Boer War. They are both quite different and I am sure that the English donor intended the subtle meanings that they convey. The lion on the right is in a traditional pose while the lion on the left is in a relaxed, naturalistic pose. The British ready to strike and the Boers complacent?

Left: The British trench on the western side of Spion Kop. The soldiers who died in this trench were relentlessly shelled at short range from Conical Hill to the north.

Campsite

The remains of the British campsite on the hill above the town of Greylingstad can still clearly be seen today. When the veld has burned, one can make out the tent lines with their protective wall and ditches, the kitchens, the stables, and even the parade ground and the sentries' pathways. Having mapped the whole site, including kilometres of fortifications, I have learned how precisely the camp was laid out. I therefore fully appreciate Fuller's comment about the erection of a similar camp at Kroonstad: "Then I had to supervise the pitching of the camp, which was not done with any care for comfort but with a geometric exactness which all but demanded a knowledge of logarithms."[42]

A certain Private Tucker, based at Greylingstad for some months from 2 July 1900, continually complained about the fortifications his unit were ordered to erect. After measuring those kilometres of stone walls in extreme Highveld weather conditions, I share his sentiments. On 17 July 1900, his diary recorded, "Wall building again. We are making this hill like Gibraltar." On 20 July, "Wall building." On 2 August, "Every day, when not on duty, we are employed wall building or road making from 2.00 p.m. until 5.00 p.m."[43]

In the 1950s Morris Gough-Palmer was taken on a tour of the campsite by a veteran of the Scottish Rifles who had been based there. Shortly before his passing, Morris took me on the same tour. I often go there to record the many ancient rock engravings that my Anglo-Boer War research led me to find on that koppie and always feel a close connection with the soldiers who served there.

The Scottish Rifles building defensive walls in their camp above Greylingstad.

Boer prisoners in the Scottish Rifles camp above Greylingstad from a contemporary photograph album. The photo was taken between the tent lines looking toward the mess tents, and this spot is still easily recognizable today.

The well-preserved gun piquet no. 1 constructed on Greylingstad koppie by 'A' Sub of the 16th Battery Southern Division of the Royal Garrison Artillery on 7 July 1900.

Established on 9 January 1900 by Colonel Porter, this is the British camp at Slingersfontein, 15 kilometres southeast of Colesberg. Above the camp is New Zealand Hill which was attacked on 15 January by Fighting-General de la Rey together with 300 Boer commandos. The attack on the sangars of the New Zealand Mounted Rifles and the Yorkshire Regiment was eventually beaten off. The lack of permanent fortifications is obvious; this over-confidence was corrected when establishing new camps such as Greylingstad where many kilometres of walling and fortifications still stand today.

The British campsite on the hill above Greylingstad with the modern track passing through the old tent lines, now just orderly rows of stone circles. Stones were placed around the bell tents to anchor the flaps as well as serving as protection from enemy fire. The officers' tents are on the left-hand side of the main camp with its trench and defensive walls. Exploring the well-preserved campsite is like going back 112 years in time.

A contemporary photograph of a 4.7-inch naval gun in gun piquet no. 1, Greylingstad koppie. This gun replaced the original 5-inch BL gun which was destroyed on 23 December 1900 when a shell exploded prematurely in the breech. Two gunners and a private in the Scottish Rifles were killed and five gunners were seriously wounded in the explosion. During the war many guns were successfully repaired at railway or engineering workshops, however there was a serious problem with the gradual wearing-out of guns that were used for heavy firing. The problem was partially overcome by exchanging guns between batteries and placing the worn guns in positions where they were infrequently used.

This contemporary photograph is entitled 'Colesberg 10 January 1900, firing on a Boer Patrol'. The British soldiers are sheltering behind a sangar, a temporary stone fortification of which many thousands still survive 112 years later in and around the battlefields and campsites.

Civilian bravery

On 26 August 1900, the Boers laid dynamite charges on the tracks to ambush the train running from Greylingstad to Heidelberg but the dynamite exploded after the train had passed. The Boers nevertheless opened fire, killing the stoker and wounding the driver, P. Pickering. In spite of his wounds the driver took the train safely to Heidelberg. Mark West, a dispatch rider with Thorneycroft's Mounted Infantry, was moved by this to write this poem:

T'was on the Traansvaal-Natal Railway
our soldiers lie camping by,
and their white-bleached tents form a cordon,
reaching out to the sky.
T'was after the Boer was beaten
and the winter was dying out,
yet the nights were dark and stormy
and foes assailed the rout.
And often a rail, bridge, or culvert
would be blasted or torn away.
And a driver of courage was needed
to run the first train of the day.

But Driver Phil was ready
to run the first train through.
His hand on the lever was steady
his eye on the line was true.
No thought had he of surrender
when alone and wounded sore.
A gallant and true defender
and a Briton to the core.

He runs through the hills of Greylingstad
he climbs the rise beyond,
and he handles his engine fondly
and well does she respond.
His mate piles on the fuel
as Sugarbosh Rand he nears,
when "halt" rings the startling challenge
and the foe in force appears.
But Driver Phil gripped his lever

and full power on he threw,
he boldly runs the gauntlet
and he runs the first train through.

In the early dawn came the Dutchman
to capture the first train through,
but Driver Phil was on them
ere their fell work they do.
Then in baffled range they volley
on the dauntless unarmed man,
and he and his mate fall wounded
Phil tending his mate as he ran.
With his teeth he slows up his engine
his senses fast ebbing, and weak,
and when on to the platform he staggers
"my mate" is all he can speak.

But Driver Phil was ready
to run the first train through.
His hand on the lever was steady
his eye on the line was true.
No thought had he of surrender
when alone and wounded sore.
A gallant and true defender
and a Briton to the core.

West added the following: "With reference to the facts of this story, see the papers of the day, how P. Pickering, an engine driver, drove the train through from Standerton to Heidelberg, in the face of a strong Boer force that tried to intercept him and rob the train. But pluckily he ran the gauntlet and got through although badly wounded, and shot through both his arms, slowing up his train at Heidelberg with his teeth and then falling fainting on the station platform. His foreman was fatally wounded and died. I saw the place of the hold-up a few days afterward, while running dispatches."

Coffee breaks
After destroying the farm of Commandant Fourie, the English officers demanded coffee from his daughter. She brewed it and served it herself, and when asked why she did not use her servant, replied: "Because I know that when our people hear that I served you coffee in the ruins of the property, you will pay with an extra life for every cup I have poured."[45]

Schikkerling and his commando took pity on the recently released British prisoners of war making their weary way from Nooitgedacht to Waterval Boven, as the Boers were retreating down the railway line. "We made many kettlefuls of coffee for distribution, and handed them out as they passed. The Tommies relished it greatly, some of them even lapping up the grounds."[46]

Communication

The first time that radio was used in military operations was during the Anglo-Boer War. Ironically, the six radio sets ordered by the Transvaal Republic were intercepted by the British and used by the Royal Navy in their blockade of Delagoa Bay. The equipment had been ordered to link the forts surrounding Pretoria, because the cost of laying underground telephone cable was prohibitive. The British experimented with the wirelesses in the Northern Cape, eventually establishing wireless contact between the Orange and Modder rivers to provide early warning of possible Boer attacks. However, atmospheric conditions made reliable communication impossible, and by March 1900, five sets were installed on the Royal Navy cruisers blockading Delagoa Bay. Thus the cruiser *Thetis* became the first ship to be fitted with wireless under wartime conditions. The maritime experiments were successful and, by the end of 1900, it was decided to equip 42 ships and eight shore stations around Britain with radios.[47]

The British prisoners of war held in the State Model School, Pretoria received the war news at the same time as President Kruger, via a Mr Patterson in the telegraph department and a Miss Cullingworth who communicated it from her house to the signalling officer in the school.[48]

Dr O'Reilly left carrier pigeons with his patients' families on his rounds of the farms near Heidelberg, so that he could be kept informed of their progress. This practice caused suspicion among the British troops occupying Heidelberg and, suspecting that he was passing information to the Boers, he was arrested and deported to Cape Town.[49]

Heliographs played an important role in communications throughout the Anglo-Boer War. These are instruments in which two round mirrors reflect the sun's rays in any selected direction; a Morse code key is used to tilt the one mirror in order to send messages. One of the Boer heliographs was captured from the Jameson raiders in 1896, and this was later found buried with other equipment at the end of the Anglo-Boer War. This heliograph can be seen in the Royal Signals Museum and is marked 'Jameson 1896' on its upper edge. The instrument reached its peak efficiency during the Anglo-Boer War, with speeds of up to 16 words per minute. Depending on the size of the mirror (there were 3-inch, 5-inch and

This 1893 steam locomotive located at the Anglo-Boer War Museum in Bloemfontein is a relic of the war.

Fort Skanskop, together with three other forts surrounding Pretoria, was built after the Jameson Raid in 1896 when it became clear that Britain's ultimate objective was the incorporation of the South African Republic into her Empire. Two German engineers, O.A. von Dewitz and H.C. Werner, designed the forts and, by April 1897, Fort Skanskop was the first completed and handed over to the government. The garrison at Fort Skanskop consisted of one officer and 30 other ranks of the Transvaal Staats Artillerie and was built to guard the Johannesburg-Lourenço Marques (now Maputo) railway and the road from Johannesburg. The planned armament for the fort was two 15.5cm siege cannons, two 7.5cm cannons and two 3.7cm Maxims. The fort had its own electricity supply – a paraffin engine connected to a dynamo – as well as its own water-storage tank. Besides overhead telegraph wires and heliographic communication with Pretoria, the recently discovered wireless telegraph system had been ordered from Berlin. The wireless sets never arrived; they were confiscated by the British in Cape Town.

The heliograph station situated in the small Royal Engineers camp above Greylingstad. Messages were relayed via a series of heliograph stations from Durban via Standerton in the south to Johannesburg via Balfour to the north.

Damage from Boer shells fired at Silkaats Nek on 11 July 1900 can still be seen on the rocks above the location of the British camp. Silkaats Nek was also known as Uitval Nek which entered the British records as Nitrals Nek due to a British signaller's error: during the battle an officer wrote a signal in cursive and referred to the farm name 'Uitval'. Due to his bad handwriting the signaller interpreted the 'U' as an 'N' and the 'v' as an 'r'.

10-inch mirror heliographs in service with the British army), the heliograph had a range of nearly 100 miles. In 1935 a South African record was reached by a South African artillery unit when, using a 5-inch heliograph, they sent a signal 96 miles, from Massamnekop in Bechuanaland (Botswana) to Pilansberg in the Transvaal. Heliographs were used during the First and Second World Wars, and the last recorded use of the heliograph under active service conditions was in 1941, at the siege of Sollum Hayata in the Western Desert.[50]

One of the causes of the British defeat at Spion Kop was the lack of communication between the Kop and General Warren's headquarters. One of the two heliographs on the summit was smashed by a bullet early in the fight and the other was in too exposed an area to be used. Flag signals were almost impossible to read due to the smoke on the summit, and someone had forgotten to run a telephone line between headquarters and the Kop, although the equipment was available. In contrast, General Botha was well briefed on the situation, as his heliographer had set up his equipment below Aloe Knoll as soon as the sun broke through the morning mist.[51] At night, the British could not signal from Spion Kop with their lamps because the oil had either run out or not been brought at all.[52]

The first ever use of the telephone to direct a battle took place on 6 January 1900 during the Boer attack on Wagon Hill. The main headquarters at Ladysmith was connected with the headquarters of each defence point and these were in turn connected to the outlying pickets.[53]

Compassion

When General Botha heard that Major Doveton was dying in Ladysmith, he sent an ambulance cart and an escort to fetch Mrs Doveton to see her husband. She arrived before he died and was with him at the end.[54]

Seventy years after the war when Mr Prinsloo, who fought for the Boers, was asked to recall what happened when the British crossed a single pontoon bridge across the Tugela, under heavy Boer fire, he said: "Now then, I must go slowly, so that I don't cry; so that I don't cry. That was a very sad business, a cruel affair."[55]

Concentration camps

The Boer remedies for illness exacerbated the horror of the concentration camps. "It was to this hospital that in July last the unfortunate children were brought, whose mother had painted them with common green oil paint as a remedy for measles. There were three of these children, one died in the tent; the other two were brought into hospital, but their lives could not be saved. They died from the effect of arsenic poisoning. Not content with painting their bodies, the mother had, in the case of one child, added a plaster of American cloth thickly

Mount Alice and the Tugela River from the summit of Spion Kop.

According to the contemporary caption to this stereoscopic photograph, this is a British telegraph operator telegraphing news of the British victory at Klip Kraal Drift on 13 February 1900. Actually, Commandant Lubbe's commando had retired across the drift which was only secured on 17 February 1900. However, the British public was desperate for good news.

One of the brass panels on the Women's Memorial, Bloemfontein, depicting the suffering of Boer women and children in the British concentration camps. As opposed to the short bonnet depicted in the statue 'The Farewell', the women are now wearing long bonnets in order to protect their shoulders from the elements.

This is the gun that saved Ladysmith when it was under siege by the Boers. It is a long-range 12-pounder quick-firing gun with a range of 8,500 yards. Four of these guns were taken off the HMS *Powerful* and HMS *Terrible* and arrived in Ladysmith just before the siege commenced. They had to be transported across difficult terrain during the final stage of their journey; one account is that a gun had to be carried by sailors for two miles after one of its carriage wheels collapsed. The annual Royal Navy Gun Run competition, held from 1902 to 1999, originated from the siege of Ladysmith.

Another brass panel on the Womens' Memorial, Bloemfontein, capturing the despair of the Boer women in a concentration camp. The women and children are shown with their dominant feet forward, meaning *vooruit* or 'with determination'.

daubed with the same paint. The nurses told us that it was very common among the Boers to tar a patient's feet as a remedy for fever. Dog's blood was recommended for fits and so on. The nurses spoke of one case where a child in a tent was in a high fever (temperature 104) from measles. The mother utilized the heat thus generated by putting the bread, which she had just made, inside the child's bed to cause it to rise."[56]

Petrus Jacobs, who had surrendered before the guerrilla phase of the war, escaped from the Turffontein concentration camp in Johannesburg and delivered a letter from another camp inmate to his cousin who was serving with the Heidelberg Commando.[57]

The myth that civilians were imprisoned in the concentration camps still persists today. Evidence from the British command papers disproves this. "A good many people have obtained permission to live in town with their relations."[58] "The camp people also come into Krugersdorp and spend money in the shops there. In one very good tool shop which we visited the man spoke bitterly of the camp women coming in and spending 'money by the sovereign'."[59]

Walter Mears of the Scouting Corps (who succeeded Danie Theron as Commandant) used to visit his fiancée in the Pietermaritzburg concentration camp, disguised in British uniform.[60]

A visit to the concentration camp at Krugersdorp resulted in some interesting observations. "In one very smartly furnished tent with carved oak and red velvet chairs the woman had chickens and guinea pigs inside, the latter of which she was feeding on raw carrots. She was very cheerful and conversational, and said she had plenty of chickens when she first came to camp, but '… though they only had two feet to start with, in camp they quickly got four'."[61]

Confusion
When Veldkornet Slabbert fell off his horse, he was dragged along the ground at a gallop for 200 yards, his foot caught in the stirrup. On being asked whether he was still conscious, the first man on the scene replied: "He don't know his arse from a hole in the ground!"[62]

Cricket
As Lieutenant Egerton was directing the fire of his 4.7-inch naval guns at Ladysmith, a shell came through the battery's earthworks and hit the young man across both his legs. His comment was; "This will put a stop to my cricket, I'm afraid."[63] This put a stop to more than his cricket as he died later that day, after having both his legs amputated.

When a Long Tom shell narrowly missed the gun-trail of a 12-pound naval gun at Caesar's Camp a naval gunnery lieutenant remarked, "They've put on a new bowler."[64]

On the 101st day of the siege the Boers heliographed a message to Ladysmith: "101 not out." The Manchester Regiment promptly replied: "Ladysmith still batting."[65]

Crossfire

The Boers became adept at guerrilla tactics, one of their favourites being a night attack. Almost without exception the proportion of British casualties was much greater than that of the Boers; however, things went wrong during the night attack on Colonel Park at his temporary camp near Dullstroom on 19 December 1901. The plan was that Commandant Groenewald would fire on the enemy from a good position to the east, while Commandant Trichardt would take a position to the west on the top of the mountain. Assistant Commandant-General Muller would set up his pom-pom to the south and fire into the camp. The commandos were ordered not to storm the position unless an appropriate opportunity arose. Only then could all the burghers charge from the same direction. In his eagerness Trichardt and his Middleburg commando stormed the camp and were caught in crossfire from the other two Boer positions, which resulted in eight Boers killed against the British tally of nine.[66]

Today the small cemeteries can still be seen on opposite sides of the road between Dullstroom and Lydenburg, the British on the northern side and the Boer cemetery on the southern side of the road.

About 16 years ago flowers appeared in the British cemetery together with a copy of Rudyard Kipling's poem 'Recessional'. Standing in the small and lonely British cemetery, one recalls the first two verses of the poem:

> God of our fathers, known of old –
> Lord of our far-flung battle line –
> Beneath whose awful hand we hold
> Dominion over palm and pine –
> Lord God of Hosts, be with us yet,
> Lest we forget – lest we forget!
>
> The tumult and the shouting dies –
> The Captains and the Kings depart –
> Still stands Thine ancient sacrifice,
> An humble and a contrite heart.
> Lord God of Hosts, be with us yet,
> Lest we forget – lest we forget![67]

Cruelty to animals

The British destroyed captured enemy livestock by bayoneting them, and some of the soldiers learned to enjoy this terrible task. After they were ordered to stop killing sheep, a British soldier was caught by his officer standing over a sheep that he had just bayoneted. "Under the officer's eye he looked severely at the prostrate beast, and remarked: 'I will teach you to attempt to bite a British soldier!'"[68]

Deception

Even though the British force based at Dundee had just won the Battle of Talana Hill, they realized that they would have to escape the encircling Boer forces by means of a four-day forced march to Ladysmith. The 4,000 men under General Yule left camp undetected on the night of 26 October 1899, having left lighted candles in their tents.[69]

Colonel Baden-Powell built a system of 60 sandbag forts to defend his eleven-kilometre perimeter. Hundreds of mines (small black boxes) were placed in the front lines and connected by wires to his observation post. A mine was publicly exploded, with impressive effect, but no one suspected that the other boxes were filled with sand.[70]

Colonel Knox sited a battery of guns near the racecourse in Ladysmith, which the Boers repeatedly shelled. The guns never replied as they were made from wood and canvas.[71]

The Boer women of Heidelberg were determined that the British troops about to occupy their town should not drink water from the town spring, so they built a Dutch oven over it. During the British occupation they baked bread in the oven daily, and the British never suspected that the oven concealed a spring. The long stone oven can still be seen in the park at the corner of H.F. Verwoerd and Fenter streets.

During the night attack on Lombard's Kop near Ladysmith, which resulted in a Long Tom being disabled, the British were challenged near the summit by a Boer sentry. At the loud "Fix bayonets!" command, the Boers below the summit ran away. The soldiers did not in fact have bayonets, and had tapped their rifle butts against rocks to imitate the dreaded sound.[72]

The British were often misled by white flags and false bugle calls. Before the Battle of Spion Kop, Buller warned his troops to be on their guard for this type of deception.[73]

Commandant Mears and Veldkornet Kamffer moved into position one night for a dawn attack on a mission station at Beerlaagte. In order to be mistaken for cattle if detected by the enemy, the men draped wildebeest skins over themselves and lay down next to their horses, holding the reins in one hand.[74]

Of the thousands of Krugersdorp concentration camp graves in the old Bugershoop cemetery, only one has a name: Susanna Kruger. There must be an interesting story behind this as the family went to the trouble of tracing the location of a single grave and placing a memorial on it.

Neat rows of hundreds of cast-concrete grave markers at the Burgersdorp cemetery, Krugersdorp, bear testimony to the terrible loss of civilian lives in the British concentration camps. There were a total of 35 concentration camps for whites by September 1901, holding an estimated 110,000 inmates. After the war, the official number of deaths was determined at 27,927 of which 26,251 were women and children (with over 22,000 who were under 16) and 1,676 men over sixteen. In the 66 concentration camps for black and coloured families there were also well over 100,000 inhabitants, the final official number of deaths in these camps totalling 18,003: in all, just under 46,000 deaths.

The Mafeking Museum in the old town hall. The stone pillars in the foreground replaced 'imitation' Long Tom shells fired during the siege, which were joined by a chain to keep cars off the lawn. According to the late Audrey Renew, after parties and celebrations in this building, the none-too-sober guests used to reverse their cars into the 'imitation' shells and generally knock them about. After many years, an explosives expert examined the shells and pronounced them to be genuine and very much live. They were removed and exploded in the veld.

This 94-pound 'Long Tom' shell was found in the basement of the Mafeking Museum by the curator, Audrey Renew, in the early 1960s. With some help, having dropped the shell a few times, she put it on display in the museum. A few years later a munitions expert visited the museum and discovered that it was in fact still live. The shell was subsequently exploded in the veld and Audrey patiently gathered all the pieces and glued them together to put the shell on display again.

Demotion

Commandant Jan Weilbach, who led the Heidelberg Commando into Natal, was removed from command in June 1900 after repeated cowardice. He had failed to support the attack on Dundee on 20 October 1899, ignored an order to assist General Lukas Meyer before the Battle of Nicholson's Nek on 27 October 1899 and was temporarily suspended for failing to protect the Long Tom on Lombard's Kop (Ladysmith) which was disabled by the British during their successful night attack on 7 December 1899. At Brandkop, the last defensive position before Bloemfontein, Weilbach abandoned his position before even trying to engage the Greys under Major Allenby. Weilbach was finally dismissed after prematurely abandoning his positions at Irene during the Battle of Ses Myl Spruit, which led to the surrender of Pretoria.[75]

Depression

Cornelius 'Cor' Vincent van Gogh, brother of Vincent, the famous painter, is presumed to have committed suicide on 12 April 1900 while in a temporary military hospital in Brandfort. He had served with the Boers in the 'International Legion' which was made up of volunteers from all parts of the world.[76] On the occasion of Cor's wedding to Anna Catherine Fuchs before the outbreak of the war, Vincent sent the couple ten of his paintings as a wedding gift. When the advancing British army captured Pretoria on 4 June 1900, they ransacked Cor's house and the paintings disappeared. It is an interesting thought that one day the missing Vincent van Gogh paintings may be rediscovered in a dusty barn or attic somewhere in South Africa.

During the course of his research into the Battle of Bergendal, my friend Huffy Pott visited the military cemetery near Airlie station in the Elands Valley. After complaining about the overgrown state of the cemetery to the National Monuments Council, Huffy later visited the manager of the farm, Geoff York, at Ryton Estates to find out exactly where the Nooitgedacht prisoner of war camp had been. Unknown to Huffy the National Monuments Council had written to Geoff and asked him to clean up the cemetery. Geoff showed him the letter and then told him a 'ghost story'. The last grave in the cemetery records that Major R.L. MacGregor, 1st Battalion the Royal Scots, died there on 2 April 1901. Geoff and his wife Anita walked down to the cemetery to ensure that it had been cleared properly, and took their Jack Russell terrier with them, which smartly examined each grave, sniffed here and there and lifted his leg a few times. When he got to the last grave, he froze, growled menacingly and all the hackles on his neck rose. Geoff and Anita thought he had seen a snake but the area had been cleared and they could see no reason for his aggressive behaviour. Suddenly he turned and, with tail between his legs, fled. This is when Geoff said, "He must have seen a ghost!"

A few weeks later they saw an elderly couple opposite the cemetery poring over a large book. Thinking they were lost, they asked if they could help. The elderly couple said that

The Dutch oven at Heidelberg built to hide the spring before the British occupied the town.

Louis-John Havemann (left) and the author standing beside the headstone of Major MacGregor near Airlie station in the Elands River Valley between Waterval Onder and Nelspruit.

It is difficult to imagine that a dying bugler would waste his final breath blowing his bugle! It reminds one of the opening scenes in Peter Seller's film, 'The Party'. This posed scene recalls the enormous popularity of Bugler Dunne who was wounded and lost his bugle in a charge at the Battle of Colenso. Queen Victoria later visited him in hospital and presented him with a new one.

Fort Skanskop played no role in the defence of Pretoria. When Lord Roberts captured Pretoria on 5 June 1900 the fort had already been stripped of its guns and its garrison was serving in the field. The Pretoria forts remained crown possessions until 1922, when they were transferred to the Union of South Africa. Forts Skanskop and Klapperkop were proclaimed national monuments in 1938 but were last used for military purposes during the Second World War (in spite of protests from the Historical Monuments Commission).

The original headstone of Major MacGregor which was rescued from the veld together with other British headstones which had been made by the POWs at Nooitgedacht camp. These headstones have now been built into a wall of the Jannie Viljoen MOTH Shellhole in Nelspruit.
Photo: Louis-John Havemann

they had just visited the cemetery and told them that Major MacGregor, in the last grave, had committed suicide. A few months later Huffy's White River friend, James MacGregor, revealed that Major MacGregor was his great-uncle, and he still had correspondence about his death at his home, Lochaber. James had found a letter from Lieutenant-Colonel William Douglas, the commanding officer of the Royal Scots Regiment, explaining the circumstances leading up to the suicide. It revealed that his great-uncle was depressed and being undiagnosed and without help, the Major shot himself. It turned out that there was a history of depression in the family, so we conclude that, through Huffy, the major was passing this message on.

This story has a strange sequel. Huffy was looking for pictures of horses in Wilson's books, *With the Flag to Pretoria* and *After Pretoria: The Guerrilla War*. There are 1,724 pages in these four volumes and, putting Lieutenant-Colonel Douglas's letter to one side, he chanced to open volume 3, page 585. Instead of finding a picture of a horse, he found a photograph of Lieutenant-Colonel William Douglas, whose letter he had just put aside. Huffy had unwittingly become a cog in the supernatural wheel that linked the major with his great-nephew and had thus brought the family history of depression to James's attention.

There was yet another strange sequel to this story 15 years later. I heard that Major MacGregor's grave had been desecrated late in 2011 but could get no further information from the local newspapers. On 17 March 2012, I met my friend Louis-John Havemann from Nelspruit at the grave. Louis-John had spent hours clearing the thick bush before I arrived and we examined the grave together. There were no obvious signs of damage so we took photographs and drove to Louis-John's farm outside Nelspruit to spend the rest of the weekend. On downloading my photographs I noticed that a strange shape, like a ball of cotton-wool, had appeared above and to the right of Major MacGregor's headstone. It certainly had not been there when we had taken the photos, and it only appeared in two of my photographs. I remarked at the time that it could be a message or a warning. Three months later the major's great-nephew, James MacGregor, died suddenly at his home in White River.

Devotion

Every September, since 1901, a package arrived at the post office in Chrissiesmeer (Lake Chrissie) in the Eastern Transvaal (Mpumalanga) addressed to 'The Postmaster' with no accompanying note or even return address. The package contained a sprig of heather, one year bound with a blue ribbon, the next with a pink ribbon. Instructions were passed from postmaster to succeeding postmaster that the heather was to be placed on the grave of Lieutenant Arthur William Swanston of the Inniskilling Dragoons who died in action near Lake Banagher on 18 October 1900 while trying to save the life of Private J. Garlick. My informant, 'Tannie Rensie' Kruger, was postmistress from 1947 to 1957 and had, for ten years, placed the sprig of heather on Arthur's grave. In 1957, just before she left Chrissiesmeer, she received a note with the package which she translated from English with much difficulty.

The sender revealed that she had been Arthur's fiancée and that she had never married, but was now very sick and thought that this might be the last time she could send heather for her beloved's grave. However, the package continued to arrive for the next two years and Tannie Rensie's successor continued the duty. This touching act of devotion over a period of 60 years is all the more remarkable for the trust placed in the Afrikaans-speaking postmasters who, understandably, harbour bitter memories of the British policies of farm burning and concentration camps during the war. Giving credit to the postal services of the time, Tannie Rensie commented, "Not a single flower of heather was ever damaged."

According to a report in *The Star* newspaper on 30 September 1969, and a subsequent article on 14 November 1969, Lieutenant Anderson died of wounds received at Zeekoehoek (Breedt's Nek, Magaliesberg) on 11 July 1901 where Lieutenant-Colonel Allenby had captured 13 burghers in an attack on 10 July 1901. Anderson was buried where he fell but his remains were later re-interred in a very elaborate white marble grave in the old Middleburg cemetery; however, his old headstone remains high in the mountains overlooking Loskop Dam. According to farm workers living in the vicinity of his old headstone, an old woman with white hair used to visit it every year. When the workers asked her where she came from, she said, "From far away across the big waters." Her annual pilgrimage lasted for over 50 years, until the early 1960s and probably only ended with her death. Who was she? A wife, a lover, a sister? No one will ever know.

On 5 March 1901 there was a skirmish between the commando in which Izak Liebenberg served and the Imperial Light Horse on the farm Klein Kalliesfontein near Philippolis in the Orange Free State. The Boers came around a koppie and surprised the ILH patrol, ordering their commander, Second Lieutenant Barker to surrender. He refused and was shot. Out of respect for his courage the Boers buried him where he fell. After the war his fiancée came out from the UK to arrange for the erection of his headstone and to place flowers on his grave. She returned to his grave for a few years after her first visit. The devoted fiancée, whose name is unknown, set up a trust fund to provide for the maintenance and care of Lieutenant Barker's grave as well as for flowers to be placed on his grave annually on his birthday. She also gave Barker's sword and pistol to the farmer who agreed to take care of the grave. Now, more than a century later the grave is still kept in immaculate condition, flowers are placed on it every year, and the sword and pistol are still in the care of the farmer's descendants. Some years ago Joan Abrahams traced the family of Lieutenant Barker to Great Gonerby, near Grantham in Lincolnshire, England. She met an elderly lady living in the Barker family home who gave her the only family relic of the Barkers that she had found in a drawer: a doily of Grantham lace. She wrote on the linen centre of the doily, "With grateful thanks for looking after our Lieut. Barker."

Dirty ending

During a skirmish near Belfast in February 1901, a British soldier took shelter from Boer rifle fire behind a tree. His pet monkey, which had followed him, sat above him in a branch of the tree and, being scared and excited, regularly relieved himself on the soldier's head. The soldier was permanently put out of his misery when a powerful bullet passed through the tree and killed him.[77] The letter of sympathy sent to his family must have made interesting reading!

Disgrace

The Boers were the first side to suffer the disgrace of losing their guns to the enemy, when two 75-mm guns were overrun at Elandslaagte on 21 October 1899. However, the gunners had served them to the last and even General Kock (who led the invasion of Natal) was fatally wounded defending them.[78] These guns were later used in the defence of Ladysmith.[79]

At the Battle of Colenso, on 15 December 1899, the British lost ten guns of the Royal Field Artillery under the command of Colonel Long. General Buller placed the blame squarely on Long's shoulders as he had deployed his guns too far forward, and commented that he was "Sold by a damned gunner." The historian Darrell Hall analyzed the remarkable chain of events leading to the loss of the guns and concluded that it was Long who should have said, "Sold by a damned general." Firstly, Buller ordered him to take personal charge of the guns instead of being at his rightful place with General Buller where he could have exercised overall control of the artillery. Secondly, through inadequate reconnaissance, the British were unaware of the Boers' presence at Fort Wylie, a position which enabled them to enfilade Long's position. Long was ordered to shell the Boer positions in the trenches and hills north of the Tugela but ended up expending nearly all of his ammunition in trying to neutralize the rifle fire from Fort Wylie. While Long admitted that he had positioned his guns about 300 yards too far forward, the expected infantry support was not forthcoming. When he ran out of ammunition his surviving men were ordered to take cover in a nearby donga and with the ammunition finally on its way, Buller interfered and ordered it back.

Once he started interfering he couldn't stop and personally directed the attempts to save the guns; he withdrew the supporting naval guns, gave up the whole infantry attack and withdrew the soldiers who were protecting the guns. No orders were given to disable the guns and it was an easy matter for the Boers to cross the river and capture them. General Botha, who directed the Boer defence, later claimed that Long had in fact saved the British army that day because, if the infantry attack had gone ahead, the troops would have been decimated in a carefully planned 'killing ground'. In fact, it was the 7th Battery (well to the right of Long) whose attack on Hlangwane Hill caused the Boers to reveal their positions before the infantry on the British right flank entered the trap.[80]

The author and his wife, Bronislava, at Lieutenant Swanston's grave at Chrissiesmeer.

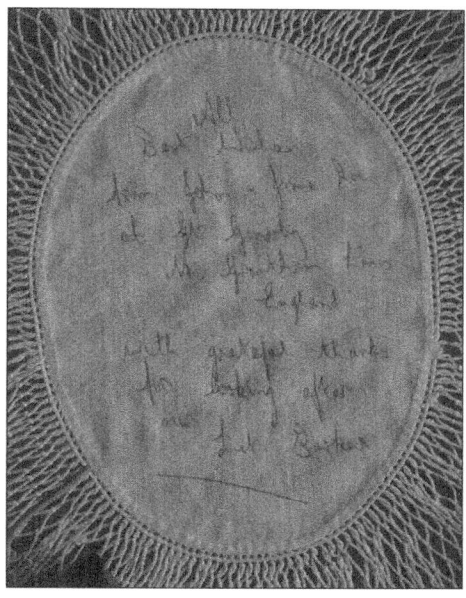

The crocheted linen doily belonging to Lieutenant Edward Henry Barker's family given to Joan Abrahams which reads: "With grateful thanks for looking after our Lieut. Barker".

Lieutenant Anderson's grave in the military section of the old Middleburg cemetery.

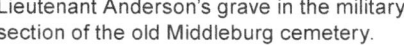

A view of the battlefield at Colenso from General Buller's former headquarters, now the Clouston military cemetery.

The concrete plinths mark the positions of each of Colonel Long's guns which were fiercely defended, but ten of the Armstrong guns fell into the hands of the Boers.

British officers in disgrace were sent to the main base at Stellenbosch in the Cape which gave rise to the expression 'to be Stellenbosched'. Colonel Gough was one of the first to be Stellenbosched as a result of a disastrous reconnaissance mission near Orange River Station. He took it badly and ended up shooting himself.[81] Here is an excerpt from Kipling's poem 'Stellenbosch':

> And it all goes into laundry,
> But it never comes out in the wash,
> 'Ow we're sugared about by the old men
> ('Eavy-sterned amateur old men!)
> That 'amper an' 'inder an' scold men
> For fear o' Stellenbosch![82]

Divine message

In the early morning of 7 February 1901, Maggie Biccard woke up in the concentration camp at Howick to hear an angelic choir singing her husband's favourite hymn. She knew that something had happened to Johnny. Two weeks later she learned that her husband had been killed during the night attack on Lake Chrissie.[83] Coincidentally, Lake Chrissie was named after Maggie's mother, Christina, daughter of the Voortrekker Andries Pretorius.[84]

Doubtful hospitality

A Boer named Pienaar unexpectedly came across two British soldiers in the bush. In his excitement, forgetting the words for 'Hands up' and being a hospitable man, he shouted out, "Come in, come in!"[85]

Drill

General Hart's Irish Brigade fell in for the attack on Colenso at 3.30 a.m., and having drilled them for half an hour, he marched them in parade-ground style to the Tugela River, leading many of them to their deaths.[86]

Earthquake

Before the Battle of Bergendal, both sides experienced an earthquake. According to Jack van den Heever of the Heidelberg Commando, "The tremor was brief, but so violent that some of the stones rolled off the schanzes. It was a new phenomenon to most of us. Although I did not hear it, some of the burghers told me that they had heard a rumbling like thunder in the distance."[87] Deneys Reitz reported that the earthquake occurred during the second day of the British artillery bombardment, 26 August 1900: "It came with a loud rumbling and the ground rocked beneath us like a ship, while stones fell from the works, causing much alarm, for disturbances of this kind are practically unknown in South Africa. We thus suffered a bombardment from above and an earthquake from below at one and the same time, and this remained a topic for wondering discussion months afterward."[88]

Eggs

In August 1900 Lord Kitchener, with cavalry and mounted infantry, was on the left bank of the Vaal River, and Lord Methuen with his column was on the right bank – both snapping the trap shut on the elusive General de Wet. At this time a British patrol called on General de Wet's farm near Venterskroon, where his wife was still living. One of the officers came up to the house and asked Mrs de Wet if she could sell him some eggs.

"He was sitting at the table when she brought in the eggs, and taking them from her he managed after several efforts to place them in a circle on the tablecloth. Mrs de Wet was just about to pass him on her way out of the room when he took half a crown from his pocket, and placed it in the middle of the circle, and looking at her keenly he said, 'You see that half-crown and that circle? That is how we have surrounded your husband. He will not get away this time.' 'You're wrong,' she replied, pointing to the general's photograph on the wall. 'There he is.' And as the officer turned round to look at the photograph, she quickly reached over and removed the half-crown. Then, as he turned back, she asked, 'Where is de Wet now?' 'Madam,' he answered, half abashed, half amused, 'the spoils to the victor. The half-crown is yours!'"[89]

Escape

Both Winston Churchill and Captain Aylmer Haldane, the officer in charge of the train, were captured after the Boers ambushed the armoured train at Chieveley. They both later escaped from the Staats Model School in Pretoria, where they were held prisoner. The details of Churchill's escape are well known, but Haldane had a more interesting (or should I say boring) time.

After Churchill's escape, the officers were advised that they would shortly be moved to a more secure prison. Captain Haldane and a non-commissioned officer hid under a tiny trapdoor in the wooden floor. Unable to stand, and having overestimated the Boers' efficiency in arranging the transfer, they remained there for weeks, being fed by three officers who shared their secret. Eventually the prisoners were moved and, with the building deserted, the two made their escape by rail to Delagoa Bay.[90]

When a Boer called John Logan sneaked through the British lines into Lydenburg in an attempt to free General Viljoen, he stumbled into a sentry in the dark, and in order to be taken for an English officer, he swore most terribly at the soldier for not saluting. The Tommy apologized and Logan escaped.[91]

Cornelius Spruyt was captured on 19 February 1900 during the early phase of the Battle of Paardeberg. On his way to Cape Town by train he managed to untie himself and jumped out of the speeding carriage. Hiding during the day and marching at night, he arrived at Colesberg four days later.[92] Another member of the Heidelberg Commando captured at Paardeberg, Charlie Brink, escaped in Cape Town and boarded a Russian ship which took him to Lourenço Marques.[93]

At Moordenaar's Poort in the Northern Cape, General Smuts took three commandos with him on a recce of the nearby British positions. He returned later on his own, on foot, having escaped an ambush that saw his three companions killed.[94] In hindsight, the British were lucky that he escaped, as in later life he became Prime Minister of South Africa and a staunch supporter of the Empire in both world wars.

During his invasion of the Cape, Smuts's commando was completely surrounded on a plateau, with all the exits guarded. That night, while they were preparing for a last stand in the morning, a local hunchbacked cripple volunteered to guide the commando out of the trap. He led them along a boggy path within earshot of the British sentries and then to a steep escarpment. As Reitz reports, "We now began to descend what was probably the nearest approach to the vertical attempted by any mounted force during the war … At times whole batches of men and horses came glissading past, knocking against all in their course …"[95]

Just after this incident the British cavalry commander General French had a lucky escape. The train, on which he was travelling to control operations on the plateau, passed Smuts's commando in the dead of night. Smuts forbade his men to fire on the train in case civilians were injured, and French raced past in the dark, unaware of the danger.[96]

At his camp at Nooitgedacht, between Rustenburg and Pretoria, General Clements sited his six-ton 4.7-inch naval gun on the hillside facing the valley but neglected to give orders to the artillerymen to clear a field of fire in the bush. When generals Smuts and Beyers attacked the camp from the top of the hill, the gun was found to be pointing the wrong way. While the Boers were looting the camp, the gun's commander, Major Inglefield, tried to rescue the gun with nine of the 16 surviving oxen from his gun team. The oxen refused to climb the hill and Inglefield had to think of something else. "Out of the disaster emerged a kind of comic miracle: Inglefield's gun crew heaved the great gun bodily round in its emplacement; it shook itself free, rose like a great elephant from the mimosa scrub, rolled down the hill, gathering speed, every Mauser levelled at it; now it was travelling fast; it thundered through the camp; and at length Inglefield, the triumphant mahout, roped it up and conducted it safely onwards to Yeomanry Hill."[97]

General Broadwood's column launched a pre-dawn attack on the town of Reitz on 11 July 1901 and succeeded in capturing most of the Free State government. President Steyn was warned just in time by his servant, Ruiter. He fled to the stables, without his jacket and with his nightcap on his head, and hurriedly saddled his horse. "Without bridle or bit, and with only the reim of the halter in the horse's mouth, the President galloped away. A soldier followed and shot at him; but the President's horse was fresh, and gained on the tired steed of the soldier, until he was out of danger."[98]

Executions

On 20 March 1900, General Piet Joubert was sentenced to death at a Council of War in Kroonstad, according to P.J. Pretorius. The Commandant-General of the Transvaal Republic was accused of deliberately letting opportunity slip by allowing General Yule to escape from Dundee unmolested, failing to follow up his victory at Nicholson's Nek when he had the chance to destroy an army of 10,000 men in full flight, and disregarded sound advice to push on to Durban when he had the option, a move which might have forced Britain to sue for peace. After the relief of Ladysmith, Joubert was censured along with eight other generals present at the council of war at Glencoe station because only three generals were present during the retreat: Botha, Meyer and Erasmus.[99] These generals had been fighting for almost a week without a break and their 2,000 men were utterly exhausted. Joubert was asked to send reinforcements but a *krijgsraad* (council of war) had decided that the entire army would retreat to the Biggarsberg. "Joubert could not, or at least would not, send any burghers to the Tugela, with the result that Botha was compelled to retreat and abandon positions which could have been held indefinitely …"[100]

When President Kruger visited Joubert at Glencoe he knew that Joubert had made a grave mistake and he did not hesitate to show his displeasure. "He and Joubert had had many disagreements in their long experiences with one another, but those who were present in the general's tent at that Glencoe interview said that they had never seen the president so angry."[101]

Among the generals present at the Kroonstad council of war, according to Pretorius and de Wet,[102] were Botha, de la Rey, de Wet and of course Joubert. It was General Botha who placed a Mauser bullet and a glass of poison in front of Joubert and told him, "Take your choice!" These words were also heard by two guards outside the tent, Ellis and Swart. Joubert said, "I do not see the opportunity of a bullet," and then requested that his family be kept in the dark as to his sentence. He then stood up, drank the poison and walked back to his chair. As he reached it, he dropped in his tracks and died.[103]

Is this a true account of Joubert's death or just speculation? My fellow historians are doubtful. According to Todd and Fordham, "Piet Joubert, the old and cautious Commandant-General, was taken ill immediately after the council of war and forced to retire to his farm.

There, on 27 March 1900, he died."[104] Trew adds that Joubert left the council of war with a severe cold. Presidents Kruger and Steyn were present at the council of war, at least on 17 March 1900.[105 & 106]

Why does Pretorius not mention both of the presidents' presence at the meeting, unless they left the problem to their generals to sort out (by court martial) after their premature departure? Also, why did the generals never, even in later years, disclose what really happened at the council of war? In 1893 Kruger narrowly defeated Joubert in the presidential elections, but Joubert, the hero of Majuba, was still held in high esteem by the Boers. Was the council of war a means to eliminating a serious rival? What was Kruger's real message at Joubert's state funeral when he said, "He died as he has lived, on the path of *duty* and honour ..."?[107] Kruger also said, "... for the spirit is willing, and the flesh is weak." Later he said, "No success will come, no blessings be given to our great cause unless you remove the bad elements from among us ..."[108]

In my opinion, contemporary accounts point to the fact that there was some skulduggery at the council of war. Various sources quote the date as 17 March, others 20 March. One of the questions settled at the council of war was that it was Joubert's wish that Louis Botha should succeed him as Commandant-General.[109] General Viljoen later wrote: "And if I am not mistaken, this was the first announcement of the important fact that Botha was to lead us in future."[110] The political matter of succession settled (why did politicians and not the senior generals preside at the meeting as was customary?), it seems as though the presidents left the meeting and Joubert was tried, sentenced and executed and his body probably smuggled to Pretoria. It is also interesting to note that Viljoen had put forward a motion at Kroonstad, "That all the Generals be asked to resign, with the exception of one Assistant-General and one Fighting-General"[111]

We will probably never know what really happened at Kroonstad. Viljoen commented that, "Much more was said and much arranged."[112] General de Wet said, "I shall not enter upon all that happened at that meeting."[113] A cover-up?

A final comment about General Joubert: "The majority of the Boers in Natal needed a commander-in chief who would say to them 'Come,' but Joubert only said 'Go.'"[114]

When the commandos in the Eastern Transvaal received the news of the execution of Commandant Scheepers in the Cape Colony, Schikkerling commented that, "This is the sort of thing that makes enemies bad friends."[115]

In August 1901, the Bush Veldt Carbineers shot 12 Boer prisoners of war on the orders of their officers. Five Australian and one English officer were court-martialled and two of the Australian officers, lieutenants Hancock and Morant, were found guilty and executed. Because this was an Australian unit there was a great political outcry in that country.

Kitchener was forced to take extreme action against this kind of indiscipline in his army.[116] Lieutenants Hancock and Morant are buried in Pretoria's old cemetery in Church Street within consecrated ground. This is unusual, as the practice at the time was to bury executed soldiers in unconsecrated ground.

Commandant Groenewald was trying to dislodge some armed black men from a cave in the Steenkampsberg when he was shot in the back. His men were so enraged that they caught the guilty black man and stoned him to death.[117]

After the war a member of the occupying British garrison in Pretoria, Private Letchford, was court-martialled and executed for misappropriating canteen funds. He was buried in the cemetery at Roberts Heights on 20 November 1912 in unconsecrated ground. In subsequent

The memorial stone at the place where Sir Winston Churchill was captured near Chieverly station.

Private Letchford's grave at Voortrekkerhoogte, Pretoria, in 1999.

Private Letchford was buried outside consecrated ground, having been executed in 1912, as was British military practice at the time. His parents later appealed his sentence which was reversed and his grave was consecrated and incorporated into the main military cemetery.

The old wire fence around the military cemetery at Voortrekkerhoogte, Pretoria, has recently been replaced with a concrete palisade fence. Unfortunately, the contractors made a separate fence around Private Letchford's grave (on the right), so he is again separated from his comrades, albeit in consecrated ground.

years his headstone had to be repeatedly repaired because lightning kept striking it. His family took up the case and, with proper legal representation, he was found to be innocent and his name cleared. Letchford's grave was then consecrated and the fence was extended to incorporate his grave into the cemetery.

After this, the lightning strikes stopped.

Exposure under fire

During the fourth attempt to relieve Ladysmith a Royal Artillery officer, Major Caldwell, was calmly directing fire from his deck chair with Boer shells falling all around him. When asked why he did not take cover, he replied, "It's not our way."[118]

Contrast this with the Boer artilleryman's fear of reprisals from the British gunners. Macdonald watched their gunners prepare and load the gun and then retire on horseback a quarter of a mile to the rear. The gunner appointed to fire the gun had a long lanyard and a fast horse. He withdrew about 200 yards, pulled the lanyard and then galloped back to his companions.[119]

Fair warning

An early warning about a planned Boer attack on Ladysmith was taken seriously and every fighting man was put under arms. The warning came in a curiously roundabout way. A Frenchman serving with the Boers got word of the planned attack and, believing that this would lead to the fall of Ladysmith and a devaluation of the pound, decided to invest on the Paris stock exchange. An English stockbroker in Paris bought the information and sent it to his partner in London who informed the War Office who cabled Buller who passed on the warning to Sir George White.[120]

In Mafeking there was an arrangement between Colonel Baden-Powell and General Snyman that no fighting would take place on Sundays. Guy Fawkes Night fell on Sunday 5 November 1899 and the colonel considered it prudent to advise the Boers in advance that the explosions and coloured lights would not signal an attack. The traditional celebrations were then enjoyed without interruption.[121]

Whenever they could the Boers prepared themselves for an attack on the enemy by saying prayers and singing hymns. At midnight on 5 January 1900, the Imperial Light Horse picket on the southern side of Wagon Hill heard the Boers singing hymns but attached no significance to this.

Three hours later the Boer attack on Wagon Point took place.[122]

Father and son

After the Battle of Elandslaagte, a stretcher-bearer came across a dying white-haired old Boer who asked him to try to find his 13-year-old son who had been fighting beside him. He found the son's body close by and brought him to his father. Hugging his son and moaning to himself, the old Boer died.[123]

A 70-year-old Boer and his grandson fought side by side at Spion Kop. Every time the old Boer hit a British soldier, his grandson would remark, "One more Rooinek down, Oupa!" The next day they were both found dead.[124]

As the sun set on 28 November 1899, General de la Rey's 19-year-old son, Adriaan, was hit in the side and the stomach at the Battle of Modder River. Although he himself was wounded, his father carried him into the Boer hospital at Jacobsdal where Adriaan died an hour later.

Two weeks later General Roberts's son, Freddie, was killed at Colenso in an attempt to save Long's guns. These tragedies drew the men together in later years.[125]

Lord Roberts and his son were both awarded the Victoria Cross, the father in India and the son in South Africa.

Prior to the Battle of Bergendal a young artillery lieutenant, F. Rainsford-Hannay, engaged the Boer artillery with two guns of the 21st Battery. Four of his men were wounded by rifle fire and they were running short of ammunition. By coincidence, his father, a colonel, had been given permission to visit his son, and arrived at this crucial time. Without any hesitation he assumed the duties of a lowly No. 6, took off his jacket and carried ammunition to the guns under heavy fire. Such an event is without parallel in the history of the Royal Field Artillery.

At the battle of Koedoesrand on 17 February 1900, 15-year-old Pieter de Jager of the Bethlehem Commando was seriously wounded by a shell while he was conveying his injured father from the field.[126]

Fire

Before the Battle of Bergendal, generals Botha and Viljoen were headquartered near Dalmanutha station, which, during their absence, had been destroyed by a veld fire.

"When we came to the spot that night we found everything burned save the iron tyres of the wagon wheels, so that the clothes we had on were all we had left us. All my notes had perished, as well as other documents of value. I was thus deprived of the few indispensable things which had remained to me, for at Elandslaagte my 'kit' had also fallen into the hands of the British."[127]

In 1964 my great-uncle, gunner Archie Wilson, recalled the Battle of Doornkop in a letter to my father. "The big fight for Johannesburg was at Doornkop where my battery took a prominent part. The veld went on fire, and it was difficult to get some of the wounded removed, but of course these things do happen in war." Corporal J.F. McKay of the Gordon Highlanders was awarded the Victoria Cross for repeatedly attending to the wounded at Doornkop, under withering fire at short range.[128]

First command

Lieutenant Fuller's first independent command was at a place called Jordaan Siding, officially known as No. 2 Cossack Post. "The garrison consisted of one officer and 20 men of the 5th Royal Fusiliers – the officer a mere boy and his men little more than children – 18th Mounted Infantry who presumably were the Cossacks, two signallers, two telephone operators and 27 black nightwatchmen, armed with Martini-Henry rifles, who were dubbed by the soldiery the 'Black Watch'. I walked round my command, almost wept over its inefficiency, bought some eggs at the farm, read a chapter or two of *Les Cent Nouvelles*, which cheered me immensely and then retired to bed to listen to a battle on the railway line between the black watchmen who were blazing away at each other."[129]

First words

Major Gough was the first British officer to enter Ladysmith after the relief. He knew Sir George White who greeted him with the words, "Hello, Hubert, how are you?"[130] Gough's mounted infantry were humiliated by General Botha 18 months later at Blood River Poort, losing 23 officers and men killed, 21 wounded and 241 taken prisoner, including Gough.[131]

Flight

During the terrifying charge of the 5th Royal Irish Lancers through the Boers fleeing the Battle of Elandslaagte, a Boer threw down his rifle, held his wife's hand and shouted, "We surrender!" A Lancer shouted, "Stick those pigs!" and ran the burgher through and then his wife. An officer later ordered the Lancers to bury her; the man who killed her stole her ring.[132]

Football

A Boer shell interrupted a card game as well as a football match between the Gordon Highlanders and the Imperial Light Horse during the siege of Ladysmith. Bella Crow, a nurse, wrote in her diary on 18 November 1899 that a Long Tom shell landed in an unoccupied tent and then buried itself between that tent and the next one, in which a number of men were playing nap. "It scattered dust all over but they never moved, went on playing, so did the footballers."[133] A war correspondent observed that, "Under cover of the smoke the Gordons sneaked a goal and the point as to whether such a contingency is covered by the rules of the game was remitted to English sporting authorities."[134]

The Battle for Wagon Hill took place on 6 January 1900, the only determined attack made by the Boers on the beleaguered garrison of Ladysmith. The main battle took place where the memorials to the Devons and the Imperial Light Horse appear on the skyline as seen from Wagon Point.

Although the British main trench was slightly higher in elevation than Aloe Knoll (just below the arms of the cross in the foreground), this photograph makes it clear that the Boer marksmen on Aloe Knoll could easily pick off the men in their shallow trench.

A view of Wagon Point from Wagon Hill.

This was the right flank of the Boer defences during the Battle for Johannesburg on 29 May 1900 and overlooks the farmhouse where Jameson and his raiders surrendered on 2 January 1896. Although General French had already outflanked the Boers farther to the west, Ian Hamilton was determined to take his revenge on the very ground of Jameson's humiliation four years earlier. He ordered the City Imperial Volunteers and the Gordon Highlanders to charge the Boer positions among these boulders across open ground without adequate cover. The Gordons lost 100 men in ten minutes. This battleground is no longer visible, now covered by low-cost housing.

A contemporary photograph of a gun belonging to the Royal Field Artillery ready for action, possibly at Modder River in November 1899.

Forgotten

When General Yule abandoned Dundee he forgot his secret papers. Their subsequent publication caused Britain acute embarrassment, as they contained plans for the invasion of the Transvaal and the Orange Free State, drawn up in 1896 after the Jameson Raid.[135]

Forts

In the field it is fairly easy to distinguish a Boer from a British fort. "We commenced building a stone fort on an eminence which commands a very wide view. We loosen stones all about and build without mortar or regard to symmetry."[136]

Friends

Two close friends had farms in the neighbourhood of Spion Kop, Mr Pretorius and Mr Spearman. At the outbreak of war Pretorius joined the Boer forces and Spearman the British. After Spearman had left, Pretorius collected all of Spearman's valuables and sold them. At the end of the war they both returned to their farms and greeted each other like long-lost brothers. Pretorius then took Spearman to the veld and unearthed the proceeds of the sale, explaining, "I didn't want either the Boers or the British to rob you."[137]

Fruitless search

Roger Webster heard an interesting story in the town of Magaliesburg about a wooden box unearthed by children in the 1950s in the town of Jagersfontein, Orange Free State. The children had been digging next to their house and found some bullet casings as well as a box containing papers with the name 'J.C. Smuts' written on them. The children's father was angry at the partial destruction of his garden and reburied their finds, forbidding them to dig further. Surmising that the Boer general Jan Smuts had buried his valuable papers in the town before embarking on his invasion of Cape Colony, Roger and I went to the home of the de Jagers in Jagersfontein with a metal detector, prepared to make a discovery of great historic importance. A garage had since been built over the area of the original discovery, but we found that it still had its original earth floor. After four hours of scanning and digging we had amassed a huge collection of old roof bolts, nails and assorted bits of hardware and gave up our search in disgust. A couple of years later we heard a different version of the story from one of the original discoverers. His father had been angry because the children were digging up the old rubbish pit of their neighbour: a lawyer named J.C. Smuts!

Fuel

When Fuller was based at Jordaan Siding he worked out a method of stealing coal from government trains. In order to prevent the theft of coal, an ignorant transport officer had introduced a system of whitewashing each truckload of coal to disguise it. This was a dead giveaway to Fuller's raiding party who waited at a bend in the railway line and, when the train with its load of whitewashed coal was spotted from the bluff, hid in a culvert. As the train passed, two men on one side threw a rope over the train to two men on the other side and in this manner they skimmed two or three hundredweight of coal off the truck.[138] Fuller remarked that throughout the war it was not so much polluted water as a lack of fuel that was the cause of enteric, or typhoid.[139]

Funerals

When General Penn-Symons, mortally wounded at Talana Hill and who died on 23 October 1899 in Dundee a prisoner, many Boers attended the funeral, acting with great reverence; the Commandant-General sent a letter of sympathy to General White in Ladysmith.[140]

While burying the dead after the Battle of Vaalkrans, the British funeral party came under shellfire from the Boers. The minister instructed the men to lie down and calmly and slowly proceeded with the funeral service. One of the soldiers commented afterward, "That knocked the bottom out of any kind of service I had ever been to before, and I don't know as I'm particular anxious to go to another like it either."[141]

Futile loyalty

At the height of the Battle of Spion Kop, when the combatants were shooting at each other at a range of only 20 yards, a Boer's black servant wandered among the rocks looking for the body of his master. In spite of repeated warnings, the servant continued to examine the dead and was soon shot through the brain.[142]

Ghosts

On 28 August 1983, while conducting field research at the Helvetia battlefield, I stayed at the nearby Ye Wayside Inn in Waterval Onder. In conversation with the owner, a Mr Dustin, I asked whether he had heard the story of the ghost of a British officer who meets a nurse under one of the giant gum trees near the hotel. Although he knew the story, he had not heard of any recent sightings. He remarked that it was strange that I had raised the subject, as one of the pub regulars had seen a ghost elsewhere a couple of weeks before my visit. The man had rushed into the pub just after nightfall in a great state of agitation. He had been driving his truck on an old track in the hills at sunset and had stopped to open a farm gate. After exchanging greetings with a well-spoken Englishman who was standing near the gate, he noticed that the man was dressed in an old-fashioned officer's uniform and had a bandage around his head. The officer then disappeared and the farmer drove as fast as he could to the nearest pub, Ye Wayside Inn.

I established from Mr Dustin that the incident had taken place on the Helvetia battlefield, and I was able to identify the officer as Major Cotton of the King's Liverpool Regiment, who had surrendered two of the Helvetia forts at an early stage during the Boers' pre-dawn attack. "The officer in command of Middle and South Hills, deprived of judgement by a severe wound in the head, thought nothing worth saving when the gun was lost, and ordered a surrender."[143] Although Major Cotton survived the war, it would appear that his ghost visits the scene of his humiliation. The British lost eleven men killed, one officer and 28 men wounded, with four officers and 231 men taken prisoner.

During the past 110 years the ghosts of a British army officer and a nurse have been seen meeting under the old gum trees, in the vicinity of Ye Wayside Inn, near the stump of a burned-out pepper tree at Waterval Onder. The officer is reputed to be Lieutenant John Lawlor who died of wounds received sometime after the Battle of Bergendal and who is buried in the small British cemetery nearby. He supposedly fell in love with his nurse, Maria, and they used to meet under the old pepper tree before he succumbed to his wounds on 31 August 1900. Later, Maria was either killed by a Boer shell or committed suicide by jumping over the nearby waterfalls that tumble from Waterval Boven to Waterval Onder.[144] However, the little railway village was not taken by the British until 31 August 1900, which would have given the ghostly couple no time to fall in love and meet under the pepper tree in real life. It seems likely that Lieutenant Lawlor was the mounted officer who was badly wounded by a sniper when he was on his way down the track to take the village the day before he died of his wounds (see 'Lone Sniper'). Had he been wounded at the actual Battle of Bergendal on 27 August 1900, he would have been cared for by the field ambulance adjacent to the battlefield and buried in the small British cemetery there (as was Captain W. Steward who died of his wounds on 30 August 1900). It is interesting that Lieutenant Lawlor's old tombstone records his death on 31 August 1900 but the new headstone has the date of 30 August 1900. Whatever the true story may be, it is highly likely the ghost of some other British officer seen under the gum trees meeting with his faithful nurse.

There is the tale of a ghostly couple who meet on the Bergendal battlefield. During the later guerrilla phase of the war a British soldier on patrol met and fell in love with the feisty daughter of the Boer farmer at Bergendal. They used to meet late at night in the storeroom of the farm, but their affair was soon discovered by the local Boer commandos who then ambushed and killed the British soldier as he arrived at the storeroom for one of his liaisons. His grief-stricken lover then betrayed the Boer commando to the nearby British camp at Belfast who wiped them out. Branded a traitor, the Boer girl lived out her solitary life on the Bergendal farm. Now her ghost is seen to meet the ghost of her British soldier lover on the anniversary of his death around October each year.[145] After a careful examination of all the headstones in the Bergendal family cemetery I have found that the Boer woman might well

British troops manning a sangar, a small temporary fortification built of stone. The term was originally used by the British Indian Army on the North West Frontier and probably derives from the Persian word *sang*, or 'stone'.

Roger Webster searching for the lost papers of General Smuts in a garage in Jagersfontein.

Helvetia cemetery near Machadodorp, Mpumalanga.

The search for the lost papers of General Smuts extended beyond the garage into the driveway where we found a lot more old hardware.

The gum trees at Waterval Onder where the ghosts of a British officer and a nurse are said to appear.

Lieutenant Lawlor's grave in the small military cemetery at Waterval Onder. He was fatally wounded by a lone Boer sniper after the Battle of Bergendal as he rode down the pass to the hamlet. His ghost reputedly appears under the giant gum trees near Krugerhof together with a nurse.

rest there. The Bothas and Potgieters buried in the cemetery either rest beside their spouses or their spouse is mentioned on their headstones. The grave that interests me is that of a single Boer woman, possibly a widow in her early forties at the time of the affair. A woman having her identical maiden name is buried close by, most likely her daughter, born when her mother was 27 years old. The grave in question has a curious epitaph: "Ges. 7.1." This can be taken to mean 'psalm' and not the Gereformeede Church hymn or *gesang* (which can also mean 'psalm') and Psalm 7, verse 1 reads:

> O Lord, my God, I come to you for protection;
> rescue me and save me from all who pursue me,
> or else like a lion they will carry me off
> where no one can save me,
> and there they will tear me to pieces.

These words are appropriate for a woman labelled a traitor after the war and shunned by her own people. Added to this quote are the words in High Dutch, "*Op Bergen en in Dalen*", which means "On mountains and in valleys", a reference to the great highs and lows of her life. I do not mention this woman's name as I have not had the means to research the family history, but it is curious that she died on 10 October 1933 and the ghosts of the two lovers are said to appear in October each year.

There is only one British soldier's grave in the nearby British military cemetery in Belfast about whose death very little is known, except the month that he died. It is that of Driver Thom who died in January 1901. His regimental number, his regiment, the cause of death, and the exact date that he died are not recorded. Could this be the lover who was murdered by the Boers, and were his remains later found in the veld?

Or do the lovers only appear in October? A very strange thing happened when I was taking photographs of the kraal in which the Boer survivors (ZARPs) surrendered to the British after they were overwhelmed at the end of the battle on 27 August 1900. There is a very unusual cut-stone monolith at the entrance to the kraal which stands over 1.2 metres high. It has linear engravings on its white patina and it is chert – unlike the black reef granite that outcrops in the area. A number of my photos clearly show the ghostly figure of a woman in a long Boer dress just above the clear image of a man's face.

Is the mystery British soldier buried here, or did the ghostly lovers decide to show themselves to a curious researcher 111 years later?

Gifts

The British besieged in Ladysmith thought that the Boers would at least respect Christmas Day. However a few shells were fired into the town. These failed to explode and, on

This is the old barn near Bergendal farmhouse where the two lovers met. The British soldier was ambushed and killed by Boer commandos when he was on his way to meet his Boer lover.

This is the final resting place of the Boer woman whose ghost appears with her British soldier lover in October each year. She died on 10 October 1933.

The inside of the barn at Bergendal farmhouse in 1984. The farm was abandoned at that time but a farm worker opened the barn for us and inside was a treasure trove of old wagons and a Fordson tractor.

The inscription on the headstone of the Boer woman whose ghost appears with her British soldier lover in October each year. Her epitaph is Psalm 7, verse 1, which sums up her situation as a 'traitor' after the war. The inscription below that, "On mountains and in valleys", is a play on the farm name 'Bergendal' which means 'mountain and valley'. It also refers to the highs and lows of her life. I have omitted her name as I have no means of verifying from the family the story which I have pieced together after 111 years.

In the Belfast and Machadodorp districts the details of most of the British dead are known and carefully documented. However, the grave of Driver Thom in the Belfast military cemetery only records the month of his death and no other details of the circumstances of his passing are recorded in other histories or official records. I therefore came to the conclusion that he may have been the lover of the Boer woman at Bergendal farm and who was killed by Boers one night on his way to his liaison at the old barn. His remains were most likely later discovered in the veld and laid to rest in Belfast. *Photo: Marion Moir*

investigation, were found to be filled with plum-pudding.[146] One of these shells, a Long Tom, is on display at the Ladysmith Museum inscribed "Compliments of the Season".

By February 1900, the beleaguered garrison in Ladysmith wondered whether General Buller would ever break through the Boer lines and rescue them. At this time a Boer heliograph operator signalled the following message to his counterpart in Ladysmith: "When is General Buller coming over here for that Christmas dinner? It is becoming cold and tasteless."[147]

At the beginning of January 1900, General Schoeman was hard-pressed by General French in his defence of the town of Colesberg, Cape Colony. The commandos occupying the hills along the railway line just to the south of the town woke up one morning to the surprising sight of a long train of trucks without an engine standing stationary about 1,500 yards from their positions. Some burghers thought that this was a trap, but others thought that it was a runaway train as the trucks stood at the bottom of a steep slope away from the junction to the south where the British held their positions. Only three volunteers went forward to investigate: Stefan Pohl, his cousin Pierie Hartman and a man named Fourie. Expecting to be blown sky-high by dynamite at any minute, they approached the trucks very cautiously. They gingerly split up and passed along the entire length of the train without detecting any signs of life. Pierie then entered a truck and gave a surprised exclamation: it was full of chocolate, puddings and delicacies of all sorts! The three gathered as many spoils as they could carry and bolted for the Boer lines. "Their arrival made great excitement and soon all wars were forgotten and loot and looting engrossed all attention." The looting continued until the afternoon of the second day when British shells drove them off. "But even the knowledge that the British had mounted a gun or two on some convenient kopje did not keep the Boers from such a treasure trove, though henceforth, for the better part of a month, their journeys were made at night."[148]

Government in exile

The Transvaal government had to remain mobile during the guerrilla phase of the war. The Treasurer-General was able to load the entire Treasury of paper money ('blue backs') onto a mule at the first sign of danger. And so the wealth of the state that owned the richest mines in the world could be accommodated on the back of a single mule – and there was space to spare for a few sundry tin cans.[149] Contrast this with the wealth of a member of the Fordsburg Commando who accumulated gold at the Glynn Mine, Sabie, by scraping the amalgam off the plates. At this time his wealth amounted to seven ounces of fine gold, 14 pumpkins, biltong, a bottle of lard and some dried peaches. "Now, like one of Napoleon's defaulting marshals, he dare not tempt fortune by going into battle."[150]

In this small cattle kraal just below the Bergendal koppie, seven wounded Boer ZARPs were captured at the conclusion of the Battle of Bergendal on 27 August 1900. The ghosts of the Boer woman and her British soldier lover appeared in some of my photographs of the large white monolith in the foreground in December 2011.

The ghost of the Boer woman in a long white dress of the Boer War era appears in broad daylight above the face of her British soldier lover on the two-metre-high cut stone at the entrance to the Bergendal cattle kraal.

Apparently these are British soldiers resting near Colesberg on 30 December after French's attack. If this was really the case and not posed, the Boer snipers would have been delighted, first picking off the guards standing close to the men.

One of the Boer shells that was fired into Ladysmith on Christmas Day 1899 and which failed to explode. It was filled with plum-pudding and inscribed, "Compliments of the Season".

Grave under a toilet

Early in 1902, Colonel E.C. Knox's column swept across the Eastern Transvaal in a great 'drive' to round up the scattered Boer commandos. On 1 February 1902 there was a skirmish with the Bethal Commando near Witbank in which J. Bryant of the 26th Mounted Infantry was killed. He was buried in the veld where he fell and a metal cross was later placed at the head of his grave. After the war a coal mine was opened in the area, and it was decided to build a railway station near Bryant's grave in the town now called Ogies, after the farm Ogiesfontein or 'the fountain with many eyes' (springs). The railway authorities determined that the tracks would pass over the grave so they decided to disinter the remains and rebury Bryant under the station platform. This became the only military grave in the world located on a railway station.

However, there are curious links to two railway stations in England. There is a plaque between platforms 1 and 2 in Manchester's Victoria station recording that part of the old Walker's Croft cemetery lies under platform 2. In 1988 a grave, thought to be that of Boudicca the Icenic warrior queen, was discovered under platform 10 in King's Cross station, London.

The story of Bryant's grave under the platform at Ogies railway station does not end here. As the station got busier it was decided to build on, and again the grave was in the way. The remains were left where they were but Bryant's cross was moved a few metres along the platform to the east of the new building extension. Now Bryant's remains lie under the new building: the men's toilet.

Graves of unknown soldiers

Surgeon Blake-Knox gives an insight into why some British dead could not be identified. "The identification of soldiers killed in action is very laborious, and quite often impossible. The present identification-ticket is sewn in a special pocket in the soldier's tunic; men often take off their coats in action, and they are temporarily mislaid, or their coats may be taken off to dress their wounds."[151]

Boer commandos were raised by district with family, friends and neighbours serving in the same commando; therefore there was no need for a formal system of identification. If a Boer found himself fighting with a strange commando, he would have a discussion with his neighbours to find out whether they had mutual acquaintances or relatives to ensure that someone would remember him if he was killed.[152]

A week after the Battle of Modder River a Boer scout, Frederick Pohl, came across the badly decomposed body of another Boer scout. The name van der Walt was inscribed inside his hat but there were no other clues to identify the remains. Pohl gave him as decent a burial as circumstances permitted, but he never heard whether the man had been listed as missing or whether his relatives ever found out what had become of him.[153]

Next to the grave of an unknown soldier at Chrissiesmeer, is the grave of a Private J. Dow. Even more remarkable: Private Dow's grave is next to that of Lieutenant John Dow, whose memorial was erected by his mother, Grace Dow.

Gross negligence
The orders for the attack on Spion Kop instructed that only 20 picks and 20 shovels were to be carried to the top in regulation stretchers. Also, that pack mules would carry water in waterproof sheets – which are absolutely useless as water bags.[154]

Hand grenades
Schikkerling's commando made hand grenades by filling the hollow ornamental cast-iron tops of electric posts with dynamite, as well as ink pots and baking powder tins, which were also filled with metal nuts and scraps of iron.[155]

The Irish members of General Smuts's commando, with their love of explosives, made hand grenades from dynamite pillaged from the copper mines in the Northern Cape. They were used to good effect in capturing the forts defending the town of Springbok.[156]

Hand-shaking army
The Boer army was once dubbed the 'hand-shaking army' and Howard Hillegas explained why: "Whenever Presidents Kruger and Steyn went to the commandos, they held out their right hands to all the burghers who approached them, and one might have imagined that every Boer was personally acquainted with every other one in the republics. It was the same with strangers who visited the laagers, and many a sore wrist testified to the Boers' republicanism. Many of the burghers could not restrain from exercising their habit and shook hands with British prisoners, much to the astonishment of the captured."[157]

Hard of hearing
The British once shelled Doorie Hattingh's farmhouse near the Vaal River. Shells suddenly exploded all around the house, collapsing a wall. With that, Doorie's deaf mother-in-law stood up and shouted, "Doorie, go open the door! Someone's knocking!"[158]

Hats
After a fierce skirmish General de la Rey took off his cap and placed it on the face of a mortally wounded British officer to shield him from the sun. The dying officer requested his friend, Major Tudor-Trevor, to get de la Rey the "best hat that money can buy". At the end of the war the major carried out his last request and gave de la Rey a magnificent top hat.[159]

A British mounted infantryman, hotly chased, dropped his Baden-Powell-style hat, which his pursuer then stopped to pick up and thus saved his entire uniform, if not his life.[160]

The seer van Rensburg prophesied his friend General de la Rey's death. He saw the number 15 on a dark cloud from which blood issued, and then General de la Rey returning home without his hat. Immediately afterward he saw a carriage approaching covered with flowers. De la Rey died on 15 September 1914, having just lost his hat. Interestingly, the date 1914 adds up to 15.[161]

Generals de la Rey and Beyers were driving from Johannesburg to Potchefstroom to attend a meeting to discuss the forthcoming rebellion when they were instructed to pull over at a police roadblock near Langlaagte station. Although the roadblock had been set up to apprehend the members of the notorious Foster Gang who were terrorizing Johannesburg in a robbery and killing spree, the rebellious generals thought that the roadblock was meant for them and instructed their driver to speed on. One of the two policemen fired at a rear wheel and missed, hitting de la Rey in the back. The Daimler stopped and as the driver tried to lift him, the 'Lion of the Western Transvaal' whispered his last words to Beyers, "Krisjan, I've been hit …" Again the number 15 that Seer van Rensburg prophesied was significant: the car's registration number was TP 24, the numeric value 2 + 4 being 6, and the date of the 15th is the same, 1 + 5 = 6. De la Rey had spent the last night of his life at the Victoria Hotel in room number 15.[162]

Headless

The flight of the British into Ladysmith after the disaster at Nicholson's Nek was given fresh impetus when a horse of the 5th Lancers galloped through them. "The rider was firmly fixed in the deep cavalry saddle; the reins tossed loose with the horse's mane, and both hands were clenched against either side of his breast and his head was cut off clean at the shoulders."[163]

Hiding

After the disaster at Colenso the Boers sent a cheeky message across the Tugela: "How's Mr Buller? When is he coming for his next hiding?"[164]

Hijack

On 31 March 1900, General de Wet ambushed General Broadwood's convoy on the banks of the Koorn Spruit near Sanna's Post, 30 kilometres east of Bloemfontein. The general's brother, Piet de Wet, with about 300 men, hid in the drift on the main road to Bloemfontein. Broadwood had decided to withdraw his wagons and artillery to Bushman's Kop, and the column advanced without taking the precaution of sending out scouts. De Wet allowed the first few wagons to cross the spruit unhindered then quietly substituted his own drivers for

J. Bryant's cast-iron cross on the platform at Ogies railway station, Mpumalanga. This is the only military grave in the world situated on a railway platform.

J. Bryant's memorial on the platform at Ogies railway station on the left and the men's toilet on the right. When the men's toilet was built over his grave his remains were not moved; only his memorial.

The Prince of Wales does his duty as commander of the famous Hounds Brigade on the homecoming of his injured countrymen.

The Boer prophet *Siener* van Rensburg with his family. He is in the middle row, second from the left. This original photograph is badly damaged. *Source: Ockert Botha*

those of the British. Seeing the orderly progress of the column beyond the drift, the enemy was unaware that it had been hijacked. De Wet himself supervised the crossing of the drift, until matters became confused due to congestion and he was obliged to fire the first shot, the signal for the commencement of the fight. In the end de Wet captured 116 supply wagons, seven guns and 428 prisoners, leaving 159 British dead and wounded on the field.[165 & 166]

The war correspondent for the *New York World*, Howard Hillegas, witnessed the ambush from the Boer side when the first shot was fired. After the congestion had started at the drift, a solitary cavalry officer leisurely rode into the drift. The young captain was immediately captured and greeted by General de Wet. He offered his sword in surrender, but de Wet declined to accept it and told the officer to return to his men and ask them to surrender. "We have a large force of men surrounding you and you cannot escape. In order to save many lives, I ask you to surrender your men without fighting."

The officer remained silent for a moment, then looked squarely into the eyes of the Boer general and said, "I will return to my men and will order them to surrender." As he mounted his horse, the general told him, "I will rely upon your promise – if you break it I will shoot you."

General de Wet and several of his men followed the captain up the drift and de Wet levelled his rifle. "There was a momentary pause while the captain stood before his troops, then the horses were wheeled about and their hoofs sent showers of dust into the air as they carried their riders in retreat. General de Wet stepped forward several paces, raised his carbine to his shoulder, aimed steadily for a second, then fired. The bullet whistled menacingly over the heads of oxen and drivers – it struck the officer and he fell."[167]

Hillegas noted that, "Whether the officer was killed or only wounded by General de Wet's shot could not be ascertained." After reading many accounts of this battle, I was able to ascertain that the officer was Captain Dray, Roberts's Horse, and he was only wounded. His lieutenant, Percival Crowle was killed and is buried near the battlefield.

Holding hands

When setting explosives under the railway line, to avoid leaving giveaway footprints, the Boer sabotage party would walk some distance along the railway lines, one Boer on each line, holding hands for support.[168]

Hoodwinked

In preparation for the advance on Spion Kop the cunning sailors at Gun Hill near Chieveley, under great secrecy, constructed two dummy 4.7-inch naval guns. When they left Gun Hill on 10 January 1900, they unveiled the dummy guns and took the two real guns with them. They then received a heliograph message from the Boers above Colenso: "Do you take us to be such fools as not to know a dummy from a real gun?"[169]

Siener van Rensburg, the Boer prophet, is buried in this farm cemetery near Ottosdal.

Koornspruit drift where the Boer commandos hid and quietly took over the British wagons and guns from under the officers' noses. The ensuing battle became known as Sanna's Post after the name of the nearby railway station which the British subsequently defended. British losses were 159 against the Boers' 13, in this, the first successful Boer action of the guerrilla phase of the war.

Five hundred primary school children from Bloemfontein re-enact the Battle of Sanna's Post during the centenary commemorations in 1999. *Photo: Joan Abrahams*

On 31 March 1900 General de Wet ambushed General Broadwood's column as it was moving from Thaba Nchu (Lesotho) toward Bloemfontein. His commandos hid below the banks of the Koornspruit River (foreground) and quietly substituted their own drivers after capturing the British drivers. The unsuspecting British officers situated at Sanna's Post railway station (hidden in the trees at top right) watched the column enter and then leave the drift in orderly fashion. They only rode to the drift later to investigate congestion and then the battle started. General de Wet got away with 116 wagons loaded with supplies and ammunition, six guns belonging to 'U' Battery and one gun from 'Q' Battery, Royal Field Artillery. The two pillars mark the passage of the wagons. The small bridge was built over the drift long after the war.

Sanna's Post station in 2012. The wooden doors and window frames have been stolen and the small museum was closed years ago. Contractors are now in the process of bricking up all the gaps. At least the stack of bricks provided Joan Abrahams with a convenient table to serve our cake and coffee (with coloured sugar) on a freezing winter morning.

Horseracing

Riding on a borrowed horse with his colonel, Lieutenant Fuller touched Fat Belly's flanks and it took off like the wind, with the colonel and his horse in tow. "Stop that brute, you damned young fool, damn you! Can't you hold her?" shouted the colonel.

They passed the escort, they passed through the reserve, they shot through the supports and flew through the patrols of the advanced guard, arriving at Boschkoppies ahead of the whole column. Expecting a tirade from the colonel when he caught his breath, Fuller was surprised when he started screaming at Captain Williams, who eventually caught up with them.

"You damned idiots! Don't you know the difference between a rearguard and an advanced guard? Why the hell don't you carry out your orders? I have a good mind to put your under arrest!" He then turned to Fuller and exclaimed, "As for those cavalrymen, they aren't worth a damn!"[170]

When General Ian Hamilton took Heidelberg on 23 June 1900, he fell off his horse chasing the defenders and broke his collarbone.[171]

Horses

Much to their distress the British besieged in Ladysmith were forced to eat their horses or starve. The Boers heliographed Ladysmith, "How do you like horse meat?" The British replied: "Fine, when the horses are finished we're going to eat Boer."[172]

The Boers entrusted their lives to their horses: "In peaceful times there never can exist that same strong friendship between man and horse as in time of war, more especially in such a purely equine war as ours."[173]

On occasion a horse or mule had to be put out of its misery: "And when the beast, in the last stages of exhaustion, could no longer follow and after every device had been tried, rather than leave it to perish of thirst, or be killed by wild beasts, he would shoot it, and then sit weeping."[174]

And from the beast's point of view: "He put four bullets through the beast's head, two from either side, and, as he was coming away, the beast, still living, looked wistfully up at us."[175]

The War Office calculated that over 400,346 horses, mules and donkeys lost their lives during the war.[176] These losses on the British side excluded animals captured from the Boers, and those which had died in the service of the Boers.[177] It is therefore likely that the final casualty figure was in excess of 500,000. "Roberts's grand army swallowed horses as a modern army swallows petrol."[178]

Horse feed had to be imported from India and South America in great quantities. The legacy from this is both a curse and a delight in South Africa today. Khaki weed (*Tagetes minuta*) is a noxious weed, and cosmos (*Bidens formosa*), a beautiful autumn flower, both having arrived in the country in the imported hay.[179]

Ian Hamilton's revenge

On 27 February 1881, Ian Hamilton was a lieutenant at the Battle of Majuba during the First Anglo-Boer War. At the time it was the most humiliating defeat ever inflicted on Britain. Of the approximately 365 British soldiers engaged, there were 280 casualties, including General Colley. The Boers, similar in number and attacking a seemingly unassailable enemy position, lost one man killed and five wounded. This disaster influenced Hamilton's conduct during the Second Anglo-Boer War, not only because it left him with a permanently crippled arm, nor that his men, the Gordons, had been defeated, but he believed that the desperate situation could have been saved by a bayonet charge at a crucial point. As the Boers were storming the ridge he tried to organize a counter-attack and ordered his men to fix bayonets. This order was countermanded by his commanding officer, Colonel Hay, and Hamilton took the unusual step of running down to General Colley and appealing to him directly. He saluted and said, "I do hope, General, that you will let us have a charge, and that you will not think it presumption on my part to have come up and asked you." Sir George replied: "No presumption, Mr Hamilton, but we will wait until the Boers advance on us, and then give them a volley and charge."[180] Shortly after this the Boers overran the British line, and General Colley was killed.

On 6 January 1900, Colonel Ian Hamilton, directing the battle of Wagon Hill during the siege of Ladysmith, ordered a series of bayonet charges to be made against the Boers who had gained a small foothold there. Captain Codrington of the Imperial Light Horse was the first to charge and die. Major Mackworth was the next to fall in the King's Royal Rifles' charge. Lieutenant Raikes died leading the next charge, followed by Lieutenant Todd who covered three yards before he was killed and seven of his 12 men hit. Finally Major Bowen of the King's Royal Rifles and some of his men were killed in the next charge.[181]

Colonel Hamilton's obsession with bayonet charges next came to the fore at the Battle of Doornkop on 29 May 1900. In order to take Johannesburg, Hamilton and French with 20,000 men were ordered to outflank the Boer positions to the west. The Boers were entrenched on the ridge in and around the farmhouse where Jameson and his raiders had surrendered in 1896, an indirect humiliation for Britain, and a direct cause of the Second Anglo-Boer War. Here was the chance for revenge for Hamilton and the Gordons. He ordered the City Imperial Volunteers and the Gordon Highlanders to charge the position across open ground without supporting fire or adequate cover from the artillery. The CIV took proper cover and suffered few casualties; however, the Gordons reverted to tradition. "'Advance!' The

When there was congestion among the supply wagons at the Koornspruit drift near Sanna's Post, Captain Dray of Roberts' Horse rode up to investigate and was sent back by General de Wet to order his men to surrender. When Dray reached his men they wheeled around to retreat and the Boers opened fire. The young captain was wounded and Lieutenant Crowle was killed.

This statue by Danie de Jager at the Women's Memorial in Bloemfontein illustrates the desperate plight of the Boer burghers still in the field toward the end of the war. Exhausted and half-starved by Kitchener's scorched-earth policy, coupled with the uncertainty of the plight of the women and children who were dying in the concentration camps, the burghers had reached the 'bitter end'. In contrast to the statue of the departing burgher of 'The Farewell' statue, this burgher is now wearing clothing of hessian sacks and carries a captured Lee Enfield rifle but has only a few cartridges left in his bandolier.

A Boer burgher bidding farewell to his wife and child to report for commando duty after 5 p.m. on 11 October 1899. The statue at the Anglo-Boer War Museum, Bloemfontein, is by Danie de Jager. The farmer's wife is not wearing her apron which shows that she has already prepared the evening meal. A front foot of the horse is raised with hoof upturned to provide a hook for future generations on which to hang wreaths in memory of the half a million horses that perished during the war.

Tons of imported animal feed stored at the important railway junction at De Aar, Northern Cape.

Majuba Hill as seen from the Boer laager position during the First Anglo-Boer War, 1881. The British suffered a humiliating defeat on the summit of Majuba on 27 February 1881 which ended the war with the Transvaal Republic. General 'Fighting Mac' MacDonald was wounded and captured by the Boers at Majuba when he was a young lieutenant. He had his revenge on Majuba Day in 1900 when he urged Lord Roberts to make a final attack on Cronjé's laager at Paardeberg, the first decisive British victory of the war.

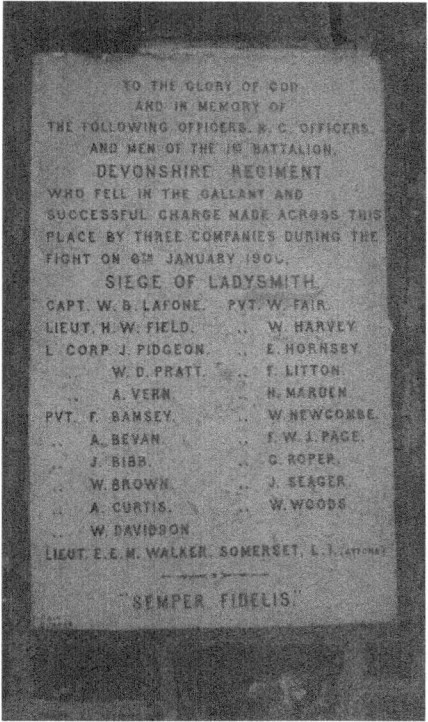

The memorial to the Devons at Wagon Hill, Ladysmith. The Devons finally swept the Boers off the hill by making a bayonet charge under cover of a fierce thunderstorm.

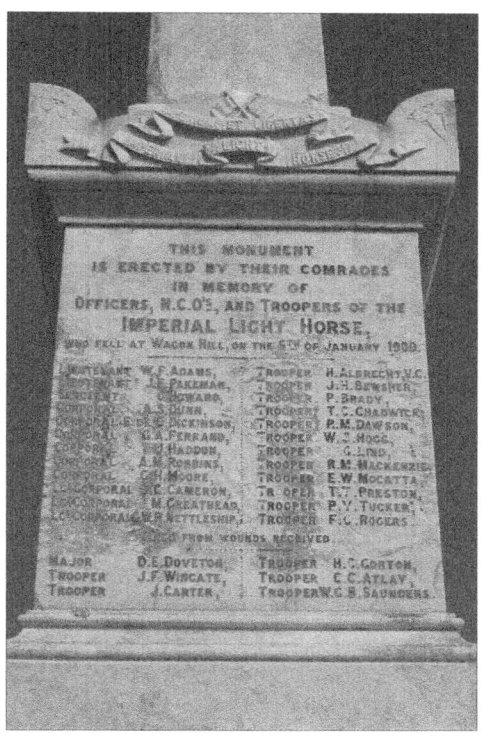

Memorial to the Imperial Light Horse on Wagon Hill, Ladysmith.

front line got up and walked slowly forwards down the slope. 'Advance!' and another kilted line rose and followed them, and then another. The lines were widely separated and there were gaps of about 15 yards between each man; otherwise, the advance was conducted with the same drill-book tactics that Hamilton had used at Elandslaagte (and, indeed, Raglan at Balaclava). Then, there was a gasp and murmur among the watchers. Against the backdrop of burned veld, sparkling in the sun, the ripple of steel. 'Fix bayonets!' The figures gained the skyline, a few at first, then more. There was a sharp, rapid exchange of shots, then the firing flickered and died away. The Gordons had the hill. They had lost a hundred men in ten minutes, but they had done the trick."[182] The loss of life from this unnecessary frontal attack was much criticized because General French and 7,000 mounted men had already outflanked the Boers farther to the west.

How did the men feel about the officers who carried out Hamilton's suicidal orders? In February 1989 I think I found the answer in the small military cemetery at Maraisburg, Roodepoort. The grave of Captain St John Meyrick, the only Gordon Highlander officer killed at Doornkop, has this inscription: "Well done good and faithful servant, enter thou into the joy of thy Lord. Matthew 26 v 23." However, this is a misquote as the text is actually taken from Matthew 25, verse 23. The text for Matthew 26, verse 23 quoted on the grave reads: "And He answered and said, he that dippeth his hand with Me in the dish, the same shall betray Me." I leave it for others to judge whether this was a deliberate misquote – the numbers on the headstone are clear and indisputable.

As Lord Roberts's protégé, Ian Hamilton continued with his successful military career into the First World War until Churchill shifted the blame for the failure of the Dardanelles campaign onto Hamilton. An echo of Colenso perhaps but with different players – sold by a politician? Like Hector MacDonald, one of his fellow officers whose career started at Majuba, Hamilton too ended his own life, on 12 October 1947, at his home, No. 1, Hyde Park Gardens, London. He was buried beside his wife at Doune in the very heart of Scotland.[183]

Ill-prepared

When General Buller was sent out as Commander-in-Chief to South Africa, he received no letter of general instructions from the government, neither prior to his departure, nor after his arrival. Furthermore, in the months leading up to the declaration of war, no council of war was held, and Buller was never summonsed before the Defence Committee, nor invited to attend the Army Board meetings at the War Office.[184] He had no instructions, and no plans of campaign had been discussed.

When Lord Roberts took over as Commander-in-Chief in South Africa, he pointed out to the Secretary of State for War that not a single commander in South Africa (including Buller) had ever had an independent command in the field.[185]

Despite the existence of a general outline of defence, which included the holding of Ladysmith, no attempt was ever made to do a reconnaissance of the Ladysmith area. General Hunter gave evidence to the commission of inquiry after the war, stating that only one officer had ever been to the top of Bulwana Hill – the most dominant geographical feature – that was later occupied by the besieging Boer forces.[186]

Immobilizing the horses

One of the Boer fighting tactics was to hamstring the enemy's mobility by stealing, stampeding or immobilizing his horses. During an attack on the Boers at the Klip River on 12 February 1902, the 28th Mounted Infantry approached the Boer position on foot. Veldkornet Kamffer led 20 men down a gully and found the British horses tethered in groups of ten, with a guard for each group. The guards ran away and the Boers shot one horse in each group, forcing the mounted infantry to abandon their attack, in case the Boers returned to claim their helpless horses.[187]

Impossible odds

At Paardeberg, entrenched in the banks of the Modder River, General Cronjé was surrounded by the British army. His force of nearly 4,000 men occupied a position less than a square mile in extent. Still, he determined to escape and on Sunday 25 February he commenced building a chain bridge across the swollen Modder River using the ropes and chains from his ox wagons. On Monday morning the British shelled the bridge unremittingly and no one was even able to approach it: "… hemmed in on all sides by an army almost as great as that which defeated Napoleon at Waterloo, surrounded by a chain of fire from carbines, rapid-fire guns and heavy cannon, the target of thousands of vaporous lyddite shells, his trenches enfiladed by a continuous shower of lead, his men half dead from lack of food, and stiff from the effect of their narrow quarters in the trenches, General Cronjé chose to fight and to risk complete disaster by leading his four thousand men against the forty thousand of the enemy." However, a council of war was held on the Monday night and it was decided that they would hoist the white flag in the morning. General Cronjé and Commandant Schutte were the only officers who voted against surrendering, and so on 27 February 1900, the anniversary of Majuba, Cronjé surrendered. "The bodies of ninety-seven burghers lay over the scene of the disaster, and two hundred and forty-five wounded men were left behind when General Cronjé and his three thousand six hundred and seventy-nine burghers and women limped out of the river bed and surrendered to Field Marshal Lord Roberts."[188]

Inaccessible treasure

The manifest of a train ambushed near Balfour showed that £60,000 was in a safe in the rear compartment. With no explosives left, the Boers tried firing into the lock, to no avail.[189]

At the outbreak of war Org Meyer of the Heidelberg district buried £16,000 worth of gold sovereigns on his farm Meyersplaas. Word must have spread somehow as when he returned after the war he found that local treasure hunters had dug many holes in the vicinity. To stop further digging, he made a treasure hunter watch him dig up the coins.[190]

Incomplete burial

When Lieutenant Fuller visited the Modder River battlefield sometime after the battle to find the grave of a brother subaltern, he found the bones of one of his feet sticking out and buried them as best he could.[191]

Irish courage

The Irish Brigade was organized by Colonel J.E. Blake, a graduate of West Point Military Academy and a former officer in the American army. It was not necessary to show an Irish birth certificate in order to become a member of the brigade; consequently there were Swedes, Russians, Germans and Italians marching under the green flag. When General Botha was forced to retreat after the relief of Ladysmith, Colonel Blake and his men positioned themselves on the road between Ladysmith and Colenso and awaited the arrival of Botha. They saw a force of British cavalry advancing out of Ladysmith, racing to cut Botha off from his retreating army. "Blake determined to make a bold bluff by scattering his small force over the hills and attacking the enemy from different directions. The men were ordered to fire as rapidly as possible in order to impress the British cavalry with a false idea of the size of the force. The seventy-five Irishmen and Americans made as much noise with their guns as a Boer commando of a thousand men usually did, and the result was that the cavalry wheeled about and returned to Ladysmith. Botha and his men, dropping out of their saddles from sheer exhaustion and hunger, came up from Colenso a short time after the cavalry had been driven back and made their memorable journey to Joubert's new headquarters at Glencoe. It was one of the few instances where the foreigners were of any substantial assistance to the Boers."[192]

Jewish courage

A Jew named Kaplan fought courageously for the Boers. On one occasion he crept up to a blockhouse with two bombs slung around his neck in a saddlebag. He was known for his astute business sense and during the Boer sporting contest at Pilgrim's Rest on 17 December 1901, he took on the role of bookmaker during the horseracing.[193]

Just desserts

Lieutenant Pohlman of the Johannesburg Police was one of the two officers under Veldkornet Emmett, who crossed the river at Colenso to capture Long's guns.[194] Badly wounded by shellfire, he was taken prisoner at Bergendal after the 100-gun bombardment.[195]

Captain Meyrick's headstone in Maraisburg cemetery, Roodepoort. The incorrect biblical reference is likely to have a sinister meaning.

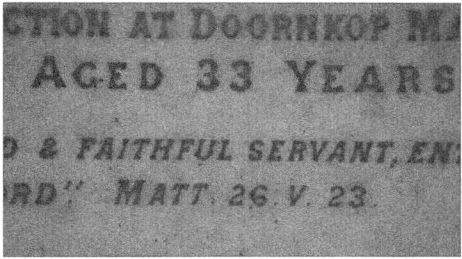

A close-up of the incorrect biblical reference on Captain Meyrick's headstone. A common quotation on soldier's headstones, this should read Matthew 25, verse 23.

This statue of 'The Exiles' by Danie de Jager recalls the thousands of Boer POWs who were shipped to camps overseas such as St Helena, Ceylon and India. Here a father and son stand at the prow of a ship wondering what new suffering awaits them.

General Cronjé's captured burghers rest on their way from the Paardeberg battlefield to Modder River. This was the first major victory for the British when Cronjé allowed himself to be surrounded and was relentlessly shelled in trenches dug into the banks of the Modder. He surrendered on 27 February 1900 after holding out for ten days. This victory was widely celebrated by the British as it took place on Majuba Day, the anniversary of the humiliating British defeat which ended the First Anglo-Boer War in 1881.

Keeping informed

It seems that the British made up for their lack of military intelligence by reading the newspapers. Opinion in the Boer lines at Colenso was that Hlangwane Hill was the key to their position, and the relief of Ladysmith. This was published in the French newspaper *Le Matin* early in February 1900. Later that month Buller attacked that position, and succeeded in his fourth attempt to relieve Ladysmith. This caused General Botha to write a letter to the Boer press, warning the newspapers to be more cautious in their reports.[196]

Kindness to the enemy

A British doctor was attending to a burgher who had received a bayonet wound at Monte Cristo, when his assailant walked past and recognized him.

"Is he bad, sir?" the soldier asked.

"Yes, pretty bad," came the reply.

"Well, I did it as gently as I could. Fact, it wasn't so much the shoving of it in as the drawing of it out that hurt him," said the Cockney. "Then I gave him a drink out of my canteen when I was done with him. I think it was a bit of luck for him to have met me, don't you?"[197]

Two commandos surprised and badly wounded an English officer near Heidelberg. They then dressed his wounds and took him into the nearest British camp. Their act of humanity was so appreciated that they were given supper and a bath before leaving the camp. After the war the officer's parents visited one of the commandos, Leonard Buys, to thank him for saving their son's life.[198]

Lord Metheun was the only British general to be captured by the Boers in reasonable shape. (The mortally wounded Major-General Penn Symons was a temporary Boer captive in Dundee, until he died). He was wounded in the thigh at Tweebosch and was captured by General de la Rey who, in spite of the protests from his commandos, sent him to the British hospital at Klerksdorp. After the war they became friends and when Metheun heard of de la Rey's death in 1915, he said, "I have lost a brave enemy in war, and a true friend in peace."[199]

During the guerrilla phase of the war, the Boers left their serious casualties behind for the British ambulances.

"Amid all the cruelty of farm burning and the hunting down of the civilian population, there was one redeeming feature, in that the English soldiers, both officers and men, were unfailingly humane. This was so well known that there was never any hesitation in abandoning a wounded man to the mercy of the troops, in the sure knowledge that he would be taken away and carefully nursed, a certainty which went so far to soften the asperities of the war."[200]

Knowledge

At a farm near Krugerspost in September 1901, Schikkerling admired the wide variety of fruit trees in the orchard but remarked, "Many surprises by the enemy were sprung upon our sentries in this garden before our arrival, so we concluded that the tree of knowledge grew not here."[201]

Kruger Millions

Shortly before Pretoria fell to the British in June 1900, the State Mint and the mines were stripped of all their gold and a fabulous fortune was loaded onto Boer trains and sent to safety of the Eastern Transvaal. This treasure became known as the 'Kruger Millions' and originally consisted of unstamped gold coins and associated gold waste as well as bar gold from the State Treasury and Mint, plus gold bars taken from the mines. Added to that were the gold hands from the clock tower of the Gereformeede Church opposite President Kruger's Pretoria residence. As a youth my father pointed out this clock on our frequent visits to the Pretoria museums. The hands were finally replaced in the 1970s … and they are not gold.

The unstamped gold coins and the gold waste from minting operations were sold to an overseas firm and left this country via Mozambique. However, most of the bar gold has never been accounted for. In 1930 the historian Hedley Chilvers put the total value of the bar gold at £2 million (approximately 480,769 ounces or 1,202 bars) which would have a value of US$826 million (R6.6 billion) today. 183,138 ounces of bar gold (457 bars) was taken from the Witwatersrand mines: Robinson Mine (198 bars), Ferreira Deep (104 bars), Ferreira Mine (96 bars) and other small mines (60 bars).[202] Books could be written about the number of quests to find the missing 'Kruger Millions' during the past 110 years but I guess that the most interesting and unpublicized stories will never be told.

Twelve years after the end of the Anglo-Boer War, the former State Mining Engineer of the South African Republic, Jan Munnik, publicly challenged Prime Minister Louis Botha to account for a portion of the missing 'Kruger Millions'. Louis Botha was the Commandant-General of the South African Republic at the time of the disappearance of the 'Kruger Millions' and was challenged to account for 134 gold bars (worth US$92 million today) by Munnik during an election meeting in Booysens, Johannesburg, on 29 September 1914. This is what he asked:

> I would ask General Botha what has been done with the 134 gold bars, worth roughly £750,000, which I had recovered from the mines, and which, at President Kruger's departure, were left in the hands of the Commandant-General, General Botha, and two others, by government resolution. Thus far the gold has never been accounted for, and if General Botha can give a satisfactory explanation, and if there is any gold left, I would say: 'Hand it over to help the Empire.'

A reporter from the *Rand Daily Mail*, L. van Gelder, who was present at the meeting, wrote the story which was published the next day. The prime minister read the story in a Cape newspaper and "his face grew black as thunder". The result was an action for criminal libel initiated by Louis Botha against Jan Munnik which was brought before Mr J.C. Juta in the old magistrate's court in Johannesburg on 27 October 1915. A huge crowd of spectators gathered to watch the legal battle between the prime minister of the Union of South Africa and a minor politician who was standing for election as the National Party candidate for a small slum suburb of Johannesburg. The trial lasted for three days, after which Munnik was convicted of criminal libel. On 17 December 1915 Munnik lost his appeal in Pretoria, which was heard before the Judge President of the Transvaal, Mr Justice J. de Villiers. The essence of Mr Juta's judgment of "Fight fair at election time, do not insinuate dishonourable actions to your opponents" was upheld.[203]

What was interesting about the trial was not so much the libel case, but the witnesses who appeared – all prominent Boer leaders during the war that had ended 12 years previously. Aside from Louis Botha himself there was General Schalk Burger, ex-vice-president of the South African Republic; ex-president of the Orange Free State, F.W. Reitz; and General Christiaan de Wet, then residing as a prisoner of the Crown in the Johannesburg Fort. He was one of the leaders of the 1914 rebellion who had been run to earth deep in the wilderness of Bechuanaland. A number of witnesses who had been involved with the removal of the gold from Johannesburg, Pretoria, Pilgrim's Rest and Barberton also gave testimony. This in fact supports the supposition that the 'Kruger Millions' vanished into thin air somewhere between Machadodorp and the Mozambican border, having been augmented by the addition of gold bars and amalgam taken from the Pilgrim's Rest and Barberton mines. Dr (later Mr Justice) F.E.T. Krause, who was responsible for the removal of the gold from the Johannesburg mines and its dispatch to Pretoria in 1900, gave specific evidence of the quantity of gold recovered from the Robinson Mine: 120,000 ounces. You will recall that the historian Chilvers estimated this quantity at only 78,958 ounces in 1930, so his estimation of the size of the original fortune is a possible underestimation!

Krugersdorp statue

Even though President Kruger died in exile in Europe after the end of the war, his memory is still held in the highest regard by many South Africans. In October 1962, there was much consternation in the town when Laurika Postma's statue of Kruger was unveiled. The congregation of Kruger's church, the Nederduitse Gereformeede Kerk ('Doppers') demanded to know why Kruger's statue was placed with its back to the church.

After some quick thinking, the town council explained that the orientation was deliberate as, "At least Kruger won't have to watch his back."

A mobile corrugated-iron field hospital which has been re-erected at the Anglo-Boer War Museum in Bloemfontein. These 'stationary' hospitals were actually mobile, being positioned along the lines of communication and could take 100 casualties on stretchers.

Patients being loaded onto a British hospital train near the Orange River early in 1900. Major Russell and Sister Rose are in attendance.

This is the church opposite President Paul Kruger's modest house in Church Street, Pretoria. He was a devout man who often preached in the church. After gold was discovered in the Transvaal, a gift of solid gold hands was made for the church clock. When the British advanced on Pretoria in early June 1900 the gold hands were taken off the clock and became part of the legendary missing 'Kruger Millions'. I remember my father pointing out the missing clock hands well into the late 1960s but they have since been replaced by an inexpensive set of hands.

An 1897 Kruger shilling, the tip of the iceberg as far as the missing 'Kruger Millions' are concerned. The unaccounted-for treasure amounts to 1,202 gold bars worth US$826 million today.

Ladies of the night

In March 1902, a black woman called at the Fordsburg Commando, alleging that a burgher owed her a blanket for services rendered. The burgher was picked out at an identification parade and the woman's husband, who was with her, remarked that she "often combined business with pleasure".[204]

In Cape Town, the ladies of the night promoted business by having their names and addresses stamped on a bright metal disc which looked like a sovereign. "They would walk about the streets smelling out their prey, and when they saw a likely catch would drop an address coin in front of him. I remember seeing a girl, perhaps unusually bold, walking through Green Point camp and throwing sovereigns' worth of trouble into the officers' tents."[205]

In Pilgrim's Rest, the chief's wife bartered her honour for safety matches which were very scarce. "As her honour waned from full moon, so the tariff of eleven matches diminished, but never below a number that would at least yield warmth, if not fire."[206]

Lady Airlie

On special religious days the tabernacle curtains made from Lady Airlie's wedding dress are hung at the altar in the Lady Chapel in the Anglican Cathedral of St Andrew and St Michael, Bloemfontein. Lady Mabell Airlie, daughter of the 5th Earl of Arran, joined her husband, Lieutenant-Colonel David Ogilvy, 11th Earl of Airlie, in May 1900 to nurse him during his convalescence at The Presidency, the official residence of the president of the Orange Free State Republic, in Bloemfontein. The earl had been wounded in the elbow on 2 May 1900 on the farm Isabellafontein near Brandfort while leading the 12th Lancers in General Ian Hamilton's march northward to Pretoria. Lord and Lady Airlie attended daily mass in the cathedral and were known to enjoy quality time together. Lady Airlie bought her husband a white horse during his convalescence and also asked that he would never ride the white steed into battle because it would make him an easy target. The earl recovered quickly and on 11 June he was at the head of the 12th Lancers charging to save the guns of 'Q' Battery at the Battle of Diamond Hill, north of Pretoria. His horse was shot from under him and he ordered a sergeant to fetch his white steed. Under heavy Boer fire, the sergeant was cursing profusely. As the earl mounted his white horse, he shouted at his sergeant, "Hold your tongue!" At that moment the earl was killed by a Boer bullet, but he had helped to save the guns that had almost been lost at Sanna's Post six weeks before. His widow returned to England and became Lady in Waiting to Queen Victoria. Lady Airlie sent part of her wedding dress to the cathedral in Bloemfontein to thank the city for the best two weeks of her life. Twice a lady, by birth and by marriage, she is always remembered in the 'Lady Chapel'.

'Krugerhof' at Waterval Onder: the last official residence of President Kruger as the Boer forces retreated toward the Mozambican border.

President Kruger's private railway coach which became his last 'residence' in the Transvaal before he crossed the border into Mozambique and exile in Europe. The missing 'Kruger Millions' disappeared from the train during his retreat from the advancing British troops somewhere between Machadodorp and Hectorspruit.

The statue of President Kruger in Krugersdorp caused much consternation when it was erected. His back is facing his own church, the spire of which is in the background to the left.

The title of this delightful example of Victorian pornography is 'Don't Tommy'. During the war there were few examples of infidelity; rather, the opposite occurred with many stories of wives and fiancées coming all the way out to South Africa after the war to pay their last respects.

Lady Roberts
One of the 4.7-inch naval guns was nicknamed 'The Lady Roberts' after the Commander-in-Chief's wife. It was captured by the Boers at Helvetia, and General Ben Viljoen wrote a letter to General Smith-Dorrien as follows: "I have been obliged to expel The Lady Roberts from Helvetia, this lady being an undesirable inhabitant of that place. I am glad to inform you that she seems quite at home in her new surroundings, and pleased with the change of company." General Smith-Dorrien replied: "As the lady referred to is not accustomed to sleep in the open air, I would recommend you to try flannel next to the skin."[207]

Last casualties
On 9 March 1953, more than 30 children and a schoolteacher were injured at the Crosby Afrikaans-medium school after a pupil, Jacobus Jordaan, accidentally dropped a three-pound British shell dated 1901, which he had found on a nearby koppie.[208] It is unlikely that this will end up being the last Anglo-Boer War casualty as there are still many unexploded shells waiting to be unearthed. In 1981 I took a live pom-pom shell, found in a vlei near Dullstroom, to the Military History Museum in Johannesburg for positive identification. The munitions expert refused to even come near it, and so I took it back to its discoverer in Dullstroom, where it is displayed with pride above the fireplace.

The last casualty at Spion Kop was Wynand Els of the Pretoria Commando, on the day after the battle. While looting from a dead British soldier, he grabbed his rifle by its barrel and it discharged, fatally wounding him in the stomach. The soldier died with his finger still on the trigger.[209]

The weekend before the centenary celebration of the Battle of Bakenlaagte, the author almost became the last casualty of the Anglo-Boer War. While I was hiking across the open veld from the Nooitgedacht farmhouse to Gun Hill, a large party of local farmers arrived at the farmhouse, formed up and commenced firing a series of volleys into the air. At first I thought that I was being attacked by a swarm of wild bees, but quickly hit the ground when I realized that they were bullets.

Last words
During the defence of Wagon Hill, Lord Ava put his head over a rock to fire at a Boer when he was hit. As he fell he exclaimed, "Done!"[210]

Although predating the Anglo-Boer War, I cannot resist including this reference to Matthew chapter 25, verse 23, which is a common inscription on many British war graves. The grave of Captain Butler in the military cemetery at Calcutta has the inscription: "In memory of

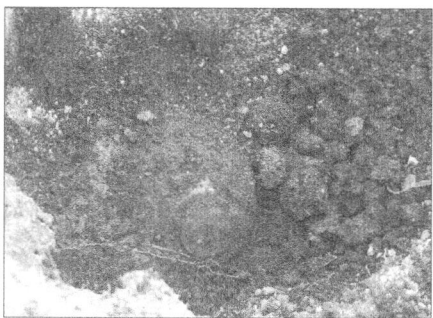

An unexploded shell found on Twin Peaks 110 years after the battle.

On special religious occasions the tabernacle curtains made from a section of Lady Airlie's wedding dress are hung at this altar in the Lady Chapel, Anglican Cathedral of St Andrew and St Michael in Bloemfontein.

The farmhouse at Nooitgedacht in the Kriel district of Mpumalanga where Colonel Benson died of his wounds after the Battle of Bakenlaagte on 30 October 1901. Commandant-General Louis Botha attacked the rearguard of Benson's column and the British lost 66 men killed and 165 men wounded as well as two guns. This was one of the last major actions of the war in which the Boers fearlessly charged their horses across open ground in the face of withering fire.

The memorial to the Earl of Ava on Wagon Hill with Ladysmith in the distance. He revived briefly from his head wound but died a few days later.

Captain James Butler, Royal Dublin Fusiliers, who was accidentally shot by his batman. Well done good and faithful servant."

In a voice trembling with emotion Sir George White addressed the people after the relief of Ladysmith: "I thank you men, one and all, from the bottom of my heart, for the help and support you have given to me, and I shall always acknowledge it to the end of my life. It grieved me to have to cut your rations, but I promise you that I will not do it again. I thank God we have kept the flag flying."[211]

Schikkerling, a Boer commando, observed that the three words most commonly uttered by dying men are mother, God and water.[212]

Just after 11 a.m. on 31 May 1902, the war ended with the signing of the Treaty of Vereeniging. Lord Kitchener then shook hands with each Boer present saying, "We are all good friends now."[213]

During the centenary of the war I visited towns and museums in all parts of this wonderful country and, in Afrikaans and English, this was the most frequent comment written in the visitors' books. In the exclusively British military cemetery at Sanna's Post, as a tribute to former enemies, the local Afrikaans schoolchildren had placed pebbles with their names and sometimes messages on the graves of British soldiers. Every grave had a flower on it. The capacity for forgiveness in South Africa never ceases to amaze me.

General de Wet faced his men on 10 June 1902 near Brandfort, after the peace of Vereeniging had been signed. Although he had voted against peace, he had to persuade his commandos to lay down their arms. His last words to them were: "Wherever I have led, you have followed unquestioning and uncomplaining, but in this hour I know that I can lead you only one way. Lay down your arms and let us enter the dark waters together."[214]

After the Heidelberg Commando had surrendered its arms on 5 June 1902, General Alberts ended his speech by quoting from Matthew chapter 25, verse 23: "His Lord said unto him, well done, good and faithful servant; thou hast been faithful over a few things, I will make thee ruler over many things: enter thou into the joy of thy Lord."[215]

On 2 June 1908 General Buller died. His last words were: "I am dying. Well, I think it is about time to go to bed now."[216]

Many versions of this posed contemporary photograph entitled 'The last drop of water' were taken for the British public. This is the final and most popular version where the soldier with the water bottle was instructed to turn his head so that the badge on the side of his sun helmet was visible.

On 9 October 1999, just before the centenary of the Anglo-Boer War, Bloemfontein schoolchildren laid wreaths and pebbles on the British graves at Sanna's Post.
Photo: Joan Abrahams

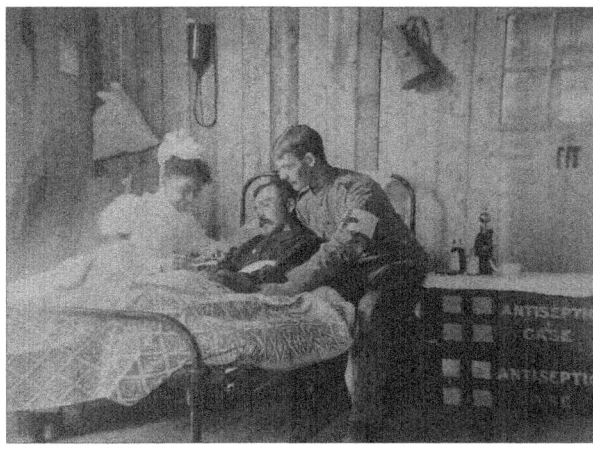

In this posed contemporary photograph a mortally wounded British soldier dictates his last letter home.

Lightning

Anyone who has been caught out in the open veld during a typical South African electric storm can testify to the fear and sense of helplessness experienced by the British soldiers. Many British war graves bear the inscription Killed by lightning'. It would be interesting to find out how many of the 798 'accidental' deaths were caused by this phenomenon. In a letter to my father in 1965, my great-uncle, a young gunner in the Royal Field Artillery during the Anglo-Boer War, wrote, "Christmas Eve 1901 all night march, at daybreak an artillery ambush. All the gunners and drivers were killed and, on the way to outspan, a flash of lightning killed seven of the Inniskilling Dragoons. Happened near Tafel Kop, between Standerton and Heilbron, not a great distance from Johannesburg." Uncle Archie's memory was commendably accurate 64 years after this incident. Creswicke reports that the ambush and lightning strike took place on the night of 19/20 December 1901, however he wrote that only three Dragoons were killed by lightning.[217]

Private Edmunds, the great-grandfather of my publisher and friend, Chris Cocks, had a series of miraculous escapes but lightning nearly got him in the end. A Mauser bullet hit him square in the chest and passed through his lungs. Another Mauser bullet had hit just below the first, raked his body, and came out in the thigh without breaking a bone. While lying almost pulseless for a number of days, he then contracted pleurisy. Almost recovered in the hospital tent and lying with his hand resting on the tent pole, the pole was struck by lightning and he was nearly killed by the shock.[218] Edmunds went on to serve as a major on the Western Front during the Great War.

On 11 January 1901, Kilmarnock House was struck by lightning. The sentry on guard at the court house in Krugersdorp was sent spinning, fortunately only receiving a severe shaking.[219]

Locust-screen

Captain Reynolds and his column of the South African Constabulary moved from the Lace Mines toward Bothaville to surprise the Boer laager. His initial success ended in failure when a group of Boers crossed the Valsch River and came up behind Reynolds, under cover of a dark cloud of locusts.[220]

Looking a gift-horse in the mouth

During the battle of Magersfontein, General Cronjé allowed 36 cannons, deserted by the British, to remain in several hilly positions for an entire night. The British removed them at ten o'clock the next morning. When he was asked why he did not send his men to secure the guns, General Cronjé replied, "God has been so good to us that I did not have the heart to send my overworked men to fetch them."[221]

The remains of one of the cast-iron crosses at the small cemetery next to the railway line near Randfontein. The Jameson raiders were buried close to the campsite where they had spent a miserable final night under continuous fire from the Boers. The words are from Lord Tennyson's poem, 'The Charge of the Light Brigade', and refer to the 600 raiders in Jameson's party.

The unveiling of the 'Whisky Train' memorial at the culvert where the British train was wrecked by the Boers near Val 112 years ago. Local historian Rita Britz is standing in front of the memorial plaque dressed in traditional clothes and carries the flag of the old Transvaal Republic. At the conclusion of the event, all the guests were treated to a tot of whisky.

Private Shaw's cast-iron cross in the old Ventersdorp cemetery in 1987. At the time of his execution and burial this was unconsecrated ground but the cemetery gradually expanded to include his grave in newly consecrated ground. Note the pepper tree on the left of the grave and the cypress tree on the right.

George Shaw's grave as it was in 1987. The lower branches and leaves of the pepper tree are on the left of his cast-iron cross and the stem of the cypress tree is on the right.

The *hartebeeshuis* where Martha Engelbrecht grew up and where she met Private George Shaw during a British farm-burning expedition. This photograph is taken from Martha's apple orchard where they fell in love. "Under the apple tree I woke you, in the place where you were born". The ancient pepper tree is on the left of the *hartebeeshuis* and the cypress tree is on the right which explains why Martha planted the same kind of trees on either side of George's grave after his execution.

John Martin Fleischer, the son of Martha Engelbrecht and Private George Shaw and the adopted son of John P.H. Fleischer, at the age of 98.

'Tannie Rensie' Kruger, the postmistress of Chrissiesmeer who took over from her predecessors, placing the heather on Lieutenant Swanston's grave every year between 1947 and 1957.

Joan Abrahams's doily of Grantham lace from the Barker family in Great Gonerby, Lincolnshire. The Afrikaans (Boer) owners of the farm Groot Kalliesfontein, near Philippolis, still tend to Lieutenant Barker's grave on their property 112 years after the war. In the photograph next to the doily the farmer's wife, Mrs van Rensburg, places flowers on the British officer's grave.

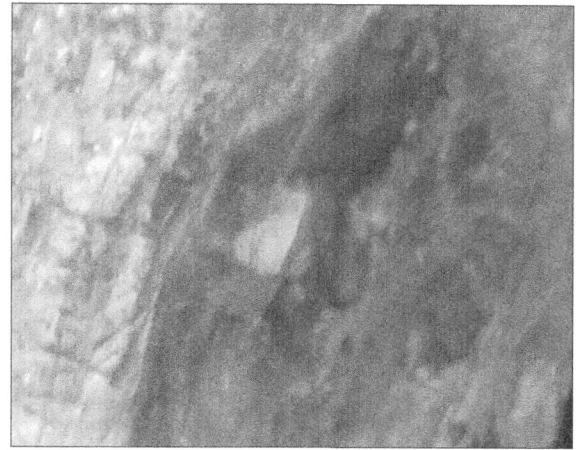

The ghost of the Boer woman in a long white dress of the Boer War era appears above the face of her British soldier lover on the two-metre-high cut stone at the entrance to the Bergendal cattle kraal. The ghosts appeared in broad daylight in a number of my photographs which I took during a visit to the battlefield on 27 December 2011.

When Louis-John Havemann and I visited Major Mac-Gregor's grave on 17 March 2012, a strange object above and to the right of the headstone was picked up by my camera. It looks almost like a ball of cotton-wool but did not appear in any of Louis-John's photographs. I said at the time that this had to be a message or warning from the late major. Three months later, his great-nephew suddenly passed away.

The Boers had a 'Long Tom' gun positioned on Groot Zuikerboskop above the town of Dullstroom during the Battle of Bergendal on 27 August 1900. This was the only battle where all four of the Boer Long Tom cannons were present. This photograph was taken in 1978, long before Dullstroom (in the background) developed into a fashionable trout fisherman's mecca. My history students are posing in the form of the barrel and wheels of the Long Tom.

I took this photograph in the Maraisburg cemetery, Roodepoort, in 2000. All the Anglo-Boer War cast-iron crosses have since been stolen as well as the metal posts and chains that used to enclose the area. The cast-iron crosses have now been replaced with small granite headstones; however, many of the details on the original headstones have been omitted—records now lost to us. The whole original atmosphere of the place has been lost; indeed, it is hard to even find the Anglo-Boer War section of the cemetery.

Sannaspos, or Sanna's Post, station near Bloemfontein in 1999. The British forces retreated to the station after the disaster at Koorn Spruit and managed to hold out with the assistance of the five remaining guns of 'Q' Battery Royal Horse Artillery under Major Phipps-Hornby who was awarded the Victoria Cross. Three of his men were also awarded VCs for trying to save their sixth gun as well as the six guns lost by 'U' Battery. This is the most highly decorated action in the history of the Royal Regiment of Artillery with three Distinguished Conduct Medals also being awarded. The station building has since deteriorated into a sad state of disrepair with all the wooden windows and doors missing and gaping holes in the wooden floorboards.

Here are some pebbles which the school children placed on the grave of Lieutenant Grover at Sannaspos (Sanna's Post) near Bloemfontein. Each pupil wrote their own message and the one at the top left reads, "Dankie vir die oorlog." (Thank you for the war.) I was quite amused as well as disturbed by this message but Joan Abrahams, the teacher who organized the tributes, explained it to me: had it not been for the second Anglo-Boer War we might all have been speaking German 15 years later. The Boers and English-speaking South Africans were united 12 years later in fighting the First World War for the British Empire. In very dark times for the Empire, South African troops conquered the Germans in South West Africa, giving the Allies their first victory of that war.

A double-storey British blockhouse high in the hills above Harrismith.

The Transvaal Republic coat of arms painted on President Paul Kruger's official railway carriage which is now at Kruger House in Pretoria. The official resolution of the *Committee Raad* in 1858 describes the coat of arms: "On a silver field there shall be a wagon and a golden anchor, and resting upon (the three) arms shall be an eagle. On the right side of the arms a man in local costume, armed with a rifle with appurtenances. On the left side a lion." The motto 'Unity is Strength' and the six national flags were added later. The motto on the present-day coat of arms of Gauteng Province is 'Unity in Diversity'.

Lone sniper

After the Battle of Bergendal, the Guards Brigade was ordered to advance and capture the towns of Waterval Boven (meaning 'above the waterfall') and Waterval Onder ('below the waterfall'). There is a steep mountain pass leading down to Waterval Onder and the Reverend Lowry explains what happened: "From even descending into that gorge the whole brigade of Guards was held back for four-and-twenty hours by a solitary invisible sniper, hidden, no one could find out where, in some secure crevice of the opposite cliff. One of our mounted officers riding down to take possession of the village was seriously wounded; and some of the scouts already there were compelled through the same course to keep under close shelter. So the naval guns, the field guns, and the pom-poms were each in turn called to the rescue, and gaily rained shot and shell for hours on every hump and hollow of that opposite cliff, but all in vain; for after each thunderous discharge on our side, there came a responsive 'ping' from the valiant Mauser-man on the other side. Then the whole battalion of Scots Guards was invited to fire volley after volley in the same delightfully vague fashion, till it seemed as though no pin point or pimple on the far side of the gorge could possibly have failed to receive its own particular bullet; but 'What gave rise to no little surprise, Nobody seemed one farthing the worse.' Just as the sun set the last sound we heard was the parting 'ping' of Brother Invisible. So no man might descend into the depths that night, hotel or no hotel! Even at midnight we were startled out of our sleep by the quite unexpected boom of our big guns, which had, of course during daylight, been trained on a farmhouse lying far back from the precipice opposite to us, and were thus fired in the dead of night under the impression that the sniper, and perhaps his friends, were peacefully slumbering there. If so, the chances are he sniped no more."[222]

The official records of the Guards Brigade record this incident less eloquently: "30/8/00. Brigade, with Henry's M.I., Field Co. R.E., naval 12-pounders, and one 5-inch gun marched for Waterval Onder at 9:30 a.m., preceded by French's cavalry. Boers made off as soon as the force appeared, except for a few snipers, who remained on the hillsides overlooking the town, and who, in spite of a heavy artillery and pom-pom fire and volleys from two companies of the Scots Guards, maintained their position till dusk."[223] It wasn't until 3 p.m. two days later that the British marched into Waterval Onder.

Perhaps it was the same sniper who, on 6 February 1901, held up a British column in the southeastern Transvaal. Major Crum of the 1st King's Royal Rifles tells the story: "I was still sitting talking to Wills of the 18th Hussars, who had a troop dismounted in advance of my Company, when from a ridge about 1,000 yards off 'ping-pong!' and my grey pony shied off as a bullet hit the ground at his feet. Back we all got ignominiously to where my Company was, and from the cover returned the fire at 1,800 yards, but with no effect on the sportsman, who kept up his firing with quiet regularity. The pom-pom opened, then the

Leicesters of the advance guard, and next two guns and two Maxims – all firing at this one Boer, who only occasionally showed his head. When there was a lull in our firing we heard the pick-pock of his Mauser, and a bullet close to someone was a signal like a wasp's sting for a renewed fusillade on our part. The climax was reached when the sportsman, standing boldly up, folded his arms and defied us while you could have counted twenty."[224]

Lost treasure

Two Boers are thought to have stolen the British paymaster's gold from the guard's van of the train wrecked near Greylingstad on 13 February 1901. One was killed, and the other hid the gold in an antbear hole. When he returned to fetch the gold he could not find it and, in spite of many treasure hunts for nearly a hundred years, it was always thought to be undisturbed.[225]

My good friend Ferdie Coetsee has owned a farm near Greylingstad for over 70 years, and tells the story of how his neighbour suddenly and unaccountably became fabulously wealthy. No names, of course, as this is a matter of etiquette for the old-fashioned Transvaal farmer. I shall call the neighbour 'the Welshman' for that he was. The Welshman immigrated to South Africa after the Second World War and, single and penniless, bought a state-owned farm near Greylingstad on terms and at the special price offered by the government of the day. His farmhouse was very old, having once served as a coach house for the coaches that travelled from Durban to Johannesburg before the railway was built. He obtained loans from the Department of Agriculture to buy a tractor and plough as well as seeds, fertilizer, and a few cows. The Welshman's income was low and his commitments high. Ferdie's late mother-in-law took pity on him and bought milk from her neighbour, as well as having him over for supper every night for over 20 years. In the late 1960s the poor struggling Welshman suddenly became unaccountably rich and bought a herd of Friesland cows, a milking machine, a refrigeration tank and a couple of tractors, as well as building a new stable and milking shed. Ferdie immediately became suspicious that the Welshman was getting the money from his mother-in-law but was able to verify that this was not the case as Ferdie used to complete her tax returns. Some years later the Welshman's staff found his tractor and hay baler running driverless through the veld. They managed to stop it and called Ferdie to help. He back-tracked along the mown path and found his neighbour lying dead in a ditch. It appears that the Welshman had suffered a heart attack and fallen forward under the mower blade. Ferdie subsequently bought the farm for his son John and was asked to check that everything was in order at the house just after John's wedding in the town. Ferdie found to his surprise that the house had been broken into and, in the one room he found a hole in the floorboards in a corner of the room. So how did the Welshman suddenly become wealthy, and why the hole in the floorboards? All that Ferdie will tell me on the subject is: "It seemed to me that someone else knew about the British paymaster's gold." Ferdie is, after all, a gentleman farmer and an ex-air force officer who will not welsh on a Welshman!

The grave of Private Pople in Machadodorp cemetery. Although he died during the British occupation after the war, he was one of many soldiers killed by lightning.

After the Battle of Bergendal a lone Boer sniper hidden on this cliff above Waterval Onder held up the entire Guards Brigade for more than a day.

The cupola of the magistrate's court in Krugersdorp where a British sentry was struck by lightning.

The wreck of the train looted of the paymaster's gold near Greylingstad on 13 February 1901.

Another view of the wreck of the train looted of the paymaster's gold near Greylingstad.

Love letters
Sorting through the English Christmas mail taken from a sabotaged train, a letter was found addressed by a titled lady to an army officer in which she wished her lawful husband "in hell". She mentioned that she had enclosed a cartridge belt embroidered with silk from her petticoat.[226]

During the early part of the war a Boer woman wrote an encouraging letter to her husband on commando: "Remain and do your duty. I do not wish to see you until the English have been driven thirty miles into the blue plains [the sea]. I can always find another husband, but not another Transvaal. P.S. Do not forget to bring a rifle for little Jan and a tame Englishman for the kitchen."[227]

Lucky escapes
When General Viljoen was ambushed by the British near Lydenburg on 25 January 1902, he and his companions were fired on by about 50 rifles. Three bullets killed his horse, and a bullet passed through his clothing and pocket book, leaving him unscathed.[228] Two years before, at the Battle of Vaalkrans, Viljoen had had a lucky escape when a shell burst overhead and four of his men were killed beside him, and his rifle was smashed.[229]

During the Battle of Bergendal the Grenadier Guards officers stationed at Monument Hill had just finished their breakfast and were strolling out of the mess when a Boer shell exploded precisely where they had been sitting.[230]

Another lucky escape happened when a shell struck the Ladysmith town hall. "The legs of the chair were cut from under him; the mess-tin from which he was breakfasting was punctured; the man himself had not a scratch, and lost nothing but his appetite."[231]

On 11 January 1901, three shots were fired at Private Venn, "... one going through his helmet and another through his greatcoat, jacket and shirt sleeve without harming him". He must have led a charmed life, for at the Battle of Paardeberg the previous year, two bullets had also passed through his clothing.[232]

During an abortive escape attempt by British prisoners of war from the cage outside Pretoria, the lights failed and shots were fired. "Kentish, who was playing chess, said that one of the bullets came in and took the head off his queen."[233]

Carbineer H. Watkins-Pitchford wrote to his wife from Ladysmith at the end of January 1900 and told her of a lucky escape. "The nearest shave I think I have seen is that of a dhooliebearer who has just come in with both his thighs scorched on the inside. He was stooping down cutting grass when a large shell passed between his legs and burst safely yards in front of him."[234]

Lucky shots

During the siege of Ladysmith an Indian, who was bent over his cooking pot, was hit squarely in the centre of his face by a 15-pound shell. "His head was not shattered – the forehead, chin, and ears were intact and perfect – but there was nothing but a clean-cut hole in between."[235]

Colonel Dick-Cunyngham V.C. was killed by an almost-spent bullet when crossing a bridge a mile and a half away from the fight at Caesar's Camp, Ladysmith.[236]

After a fight at Grootvlei (South Rand Mine) on 26 December 1900, Andries Beytel of the Heidelberg Commando knelt down to drink at Commandant Buys's Leeuspruit farm dam. With a high ridge between himself and the enemy, Andries was relaxed. As he stood up, he was hit by a stray bullet in the chest, which killed him.[237]

A Boer commando fired at Lieutenant Fuller and his black National Scouts near Doornkraal and, being outnumbered, Fuller retreated behind a hill. When they were a mile away from the Boers, a scout called Long Boy fired a single shot into the air. After the war, Fuller was chatting to some ex-commandos in the bar at the Grand Hotel in Kroonstad. It turned out that one of the Boers had taken part in the skirmish and he said, "We fired several shots and only one was returned, when the fugitives were out of sight, but would you believe it, it struck the heel of my left boot!"[238]

Masquerade

General Ben Viljoen, suspecting that some Boer refugees living in the ruined church at Dullstroom were passing information to the British, sent two of his men in British officers' uniforms to interview them. 'Roksak' Redelinghuis posed as Colonel Bullock and Bester, one of the general's staff, posed as Colonel Blood. The suspects handed over their cattle and valuables for safekeeping to the 'English officers' and promised to inform them of Boer commando movements the next day. However, they were surprised the next morning when a Boer commando arrived to arrest them. On 13 July 1901, three of them, including the two Steenkamps, were tried and sentenced to three months' hard labour, and their property confiscated. The prisoners later escaped during an attack on the Boer laager on 29 July.[239]

The Boers loved to stage concerts and plays, and in September 1901 at Pilgrim's Rest, produced a comedy around the incident of trapping the Steenkamps in the church at Dullstroom.

General Viljoen and Roland Schikkerling took part as the two condemned Steenkamps, together with some young ladies from the town.

"At the leave-taking scene between the condemned and their wives, prolonged kissing took place, longer than was set down in the part."[240]

Matters medical

The Boers were often accused of firing on medical personnel. In their defence the British surgeon, Blake-Knox, noted that since the Red Cross badge had a diameter of only an inch and a half, it could not reasonably be seen at a distance by the enemy.[241]

It is reported that the first skin graft took place in Ladysmith during the siege (although I have not been able to substantiate this). A young British soldier presented with a bad head wound and the surgeon had the local blacksmith fashion a metal plate to cover his shattered skull. The surgeon removed skin from his upper leg and sewed it into place over the plate. Apparently the soldier lived to a ripe old age and led a normal life; however, he could not stay out in the sun for long!

Shirley Stone's grandmother was a nurse at the small British military hospital at Burgersdorp in the Cape. One of her patients was a Scottish soldier, and when he was invalided home he said that he had nothing to give in thanks except a piece of his kilt. She had a doll made and dressed it with a scrap of tartan. Shirley still has the doll.

A volunteer for the Imperial Yeomanry was rejected for service on the grounds that he had bad teeth. He responded by protesting that he wanted to fight the Boers, not eat them.[242]

Being a volunteer army, the Boers had no medical screening and did not have to be certified as fit for military service. The ability to fight was the only requirement. This description of the Boer army was written in the early stages of the war: "… it is doubtful whether twenty per cent of the Boer burghers in the commandos would be accepted for service in any continental or American army. The rigid physical examinations of many of the armies would debar thousands from becoming regular soldiers. There were men in the Boer forces who had only one arm, some with only one leg, others with only one eye, some were almost totally blind, while others would have felt happy if they could have heard the reports of their rifles."[243]

During the night attack on the Long Tom at Ladysmith a guide called Godson was wounded by a shotgun loaded with steel ball bearings. Macdonald remarked, "Godson still has some of them in his leg, and is probably the only man in the British Empire going about on ball-bearings."[244]

The Welshman's farmhouse near Greylingstad. Once a coach house before the railway was built in the late 1890s, the recovered British paymaster's gold was hidden under the floorboards by the Welshman and the remaining gold was stolen again after the Welshman's accidental death. *Photo: Ferdie Coetsee*

The church in Dullstroom (restored after the war) where 'Roksak' Redelinghuis posed as Colonel Bullock to expose Boer traitors living in the ruins. I took this photograph in 1978 before the church was obscured by tall trees.

Wounded British soldiers took shelter from Boer shells in this old road cutting during the first battle of Silkaats Nek on 11 July 1900.

The small military cemetery at Ifafi near Hartebeespoort dam. The place was known as Rietfontein during the Anglo-Boer War and the British had a large camp here. There are graves and memorials to both battles at Silkaats Nek as well as other skirmishes in the area.

Shirley Stone's doll (sans head) made from a piece of kilt. This was a gift to her grandmother in return for nursing a Scottish soldier at Burgersdorp.

The lives of over 10,000 British soldiers may have been saved had the young personal staff surgeon to General Buller not volunteered for a very dangerous, if not suicidal, mission at the height of the Battle of Colenso on 15 December 1899. Captain Louis Hughes left Buller's headquarters to assist Lieutenant Inkson RAMC (later V.C.) to tend to the wounded gunners who were under heavy fire while trying to save their guns from the shame of enemy capture. He was fatally wounded almost immediately. At the time of his heroic death, Hughes was in the advanced stage of developing a vaccine against typhoid and, had he lived to continue this work, would have saved the lives of well over half the total number of British soldiers who died during the war. At the time of his death at the age of 32 this brilliant doctor had already published 20 scientific papers as well as a famous monograph in 1897, *Mediterranean, Malta or Udulant Fever* which continues to be quoted and praised by acknowledged experts today.[245] At the height of the typhoid epidemic in Bloemfontein nearly 1,000 troops had died by the end of April 1900.[246]

Military advice

His Hottentot servant Mooiroos ('Pretty Rose'), a dedicated *dagga* (marijuana) smoker, attended to Commandant (later General) Ben Viljoen during many of his battles. After the Battle of Donkerhoek, Mooiroos observed that "… defeat was due to disregard of his advice as to the manner of the defence, the neglect of opportunities that had presented themselves, and, lastly, to the cowardice of a few officers." Schikkerling noted that there was much truth in his observations, and that Mooiroos would not have made a bad commander.[247]

Mistaken identity

Lieutenant Fuller crept up on a Boer who was on sentry duty. At the "Hands up!" command, the Boer jumped up but still seemed no taller. He was a humpbacked dwarf, and Fuller burst out laughing. After disarming him, he demanded to know his name, which he gave as Christiaan de Wet. Thinking that he was pulling his leg, Fuller said, "Rot! What is your proper name?" "Christiaan de Wet," he replied, "but I'm not *the* Christiaan de Wet."[248]

At the Battle of Magersfontein an old Boer in the trenches had his first sighting of Scottish soldiers advancing in their kilts. At a distance the Boer took them to be a herd of ostriches from an ostrich farm that he knew to be in the district. He refused to fire on them and persuaded all the burghers in his trench and the neighbouring trenches not to fire at the Highlander 'ostriches'.[249]

The Boers knew nothing about Scottish customs and kilts and were amazed when they encountered "soldiers wearing skirts with cattle tails [sporrans] dangling in front". According to an old lady from Petrusburg, near Magersfontein, where her father had fought as a youngster, when the Boers first saw the Black Watch advancing they were hesitant to shoot. Their commanders thought that the soldiers were advancing behind their 'sisters' and using them as human shields. They quickly discovered that these 'sisters' were brawny, tough and very much male!

Mixed loyalties
A British captain told his group of black National Scouts that they could take their pleasure, if they wished with their female Boer captives. Botha, a National Scout fighting with them, intervened and protected the women every night until they were handed over to the authorities. There is a Trooper Botha – most likely the same man – of the 'Canadian Scouts' who is buried in the Kloof cemetery in Heidelberg.[250]

Money
On 12 May 1900, Veldkornet Eloff attacked the besieged Mafeking garrison before sunrise through a gap between two small forts, 'Hidden Hollow' and 'Limestone Fort'. After initial success, when they captured the old BSA barracks, less than 800 yards from Baden-Powell's headquarters, the British counter-attacked. A group of Eloff's men had taken refuge in a stone kraal, which was rushed by the British. One Boer hoisted a white flag, then threw it down and opened fire. A soldier saw him and flew at him with bayonet fixed. The Boer yelled, "*Moenie, moenie*!" (Don't, don't!) The Tommy paused, and then ran him through, shouting out: "It's not your damned money; it's your bloody life I want!"[251]

Monuments
During the retreat from Natal, the Boers prepared a defensive position at Laing's Nek, near Majuba. "In the succeeding days we dug trenches, scouted, mounted guard, blew in the tunnel, and generally augmented the historic interest of the place."[252] The Rifle Brigade later helped the Royal Engineers repair the Laing's Nek tunnel, which took them six days.[253]

The British systematically destroyed many of the Boer monuments as they occupied the towns. Examples are at Dullstroom, Belfast and the stones that were removed from the Paardekraal monument in Krugersdorp. The Dullstroom and Belfast monuments have since been repaired, but the cairn of stones removed from the Paardekraal monument was dumped into the Vaal River.

At a battle site such as Spion Kop there are seemingly endless lists of casualties on numerous monuments which may be meaningless to the modern-day visitor, but behind every name there is always a story. Here is an extract from a contemporary letter written to a grieving father whose son, Lieutenant Frederick Raphael, was killed at Spion Kop:

The captain of your son's company was shot during the first assault – your son then bravely took command and some two hours after his captain's death, was himself instantly killed by shell fire. He had been encouraging his men all morning by word and example, and is reported to have himself shot five of the enemy dead before his own noble death. Your son, all of him that is mortal, lies decently and reverently buried on that ill-fated ridge surrounded by comrades and friends.[254]

'Moses' stories

A Boer woman was forcibly removed from her farm and taken to a concentration camp. Despite her protests, which were probably not understood by the English-speaking troops, her seven-year-old son and her baby were left in the farmhouse. For over a week her young son cared for the baby, giving it goat's milk and mielie-meal porridge.[255]

When the Boers first entered Natal, Indians fled in panic. Sannie de Jager found an Indian baby on the banks of a river abandoned by its parents. She cared for and reared the child who later became her maid.[256]

Music

Lieutenant-Colonel Grant, who had a musical ear, made an interesting observation about the noise of battle: "I became aware that the note permeating a battle is one endless E flat ... dropping occasionally a third of a tone, but always re-ascending to its endless semibreve."[257]

Finding a smashed organ at a deserted farmhouse, a commando decided to use it as fuel. "I placed a kettle on the flaming flats and sharps of the organ, and it soon sang."[258]

Farm burning was sometimes an occasion for music. "We sat down and had a nice song round the piano. Then we just piled up the furniture and set fire to the farm."[259]

George Lynch, a war correspondent captured by the Boers, was much impressed by the Boers' hymn singing. "The chant rose and fell with a swinging solemnity. There was little of pleading or supplication in its tones; they were calling on the God of Battles; the God of the Old Testament rather than the Preacher of the Sermon on the Mount was He to whom they sang; and sometimes there was a strain of almost stern demand about it that gave it more the ring of a war-song than a prayer. Entering the door of that tent seemed like going into another century."[260]

The Rifle Brigade marched in short, jaunty steps to the tune of 'Ninety-five', while the King's Royal Rifles marched sedately to the 'Huntsman's Chorus'. If a soldier was dishonourably discharged and 'drummed out' of the army the band played the 'Rouge's March'.[261]

This posed photograph shows Colonel Porter's men at Naaupoort on 13 December 1899. Naaupoort was an important supply depot in the Cape Colony which was evacuated on 3 November 1899 when the Boers invaded the colony. It was re-occupied by Major-General Wauchope's Highland Brigade on 19 November 1899.

The headstone of Captain Hughes in the Clouston military cemetery near Colenso.

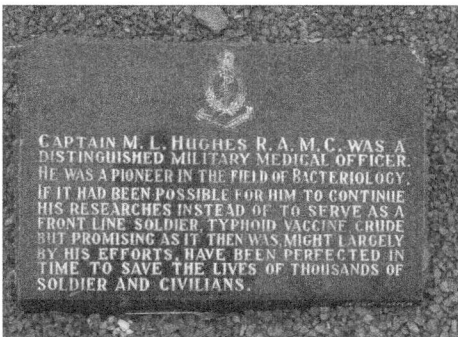

If Captain Hughes had not volunteered to attend to the wounded gunners at Colenso, it is possible that he would have perfected his work on a typhoid vaccine and saved thousands of lives during the war. At the time of his death Captain Hughes was serving as personal Staff Surgeon to General Buller.

The stone kraal attached to the old BSAP barracks in Mafeking where the Boer burgher was bayoneted after an ironic misunderstanding on his surrender.

Trooper Botha was a National Scout, a traitor, who died of wounds accidently received just before the end of the war. He is buried in the Kloof cemetery in Heidelberg. Possibly the only reason that his memorial remains in place today – unlike those of the traitors Beck and Nell – is that he protected the female Boer captives from being raped when they were being transported to a concentration camp.

During the Boers' retreat from Waterval Boven to Nelspruit, after the Battle of Bergendal, a ganger's lorry came racing past Schikkerling's commando. "A little while after, a ganger's lorry on which were a few of our companions with a piano which one was playing loudly, passed us running swift and free. We watched until the strains of the 'Blue Danube' could be heard no longer."[262]

The black sentries used by the British along the railway line were taught to whistle. "I was further instructed by some genius of a staff officer that countersigns were not to be used, as Blacks could not understand them, and that a bar of some popular melody was to be whistled instead, each Black of course receiving musical instruction before proceeding on duty."[263]

Natural interventions

The Devon Regiment arrived at about 3:30 p.m. on 6 January 1900, to reinforce the desperate garrison on Wagon Hill. The fate of Ladysmith hung in the balance as the Boers had a foothold on the hill and could not be dislodged, in spite of a number of suicidal bayonet charges ordered by Ian Hamilton. At this point, even Hamilton had had enough of blood-letting, but Sir George White overruled him and ordered the Devons, under Colonel Park, to storm the Boer positions. As they were preparing themselves, at 5 p.m., a terrific thunderstorm broke out. At the height of the storm, with hail pelting down, the Devons charged and swept the Boers off the hill. This was totally unexpected, and the Devons were among them with the bayonet before they could react effectively.[264] Thus it can be said that a thunderstorm helped save Ladysmith.

Naval warfare

Both of the republics were land-locked and had no need of their own navies. At the beginning of the war Dr Leyds, the Transvaal Republic's representative in Europe, contracted a ship in Las Palmas to serve as a commerce-raider. However, the republic failed to pay up, and the ship sailed on to other destinations in South America.[265]

An Italian ex-naval officer, a foreign volunteer, failed to convince the Boer presidents to adopt a visionary naval strategy. He proposed that three or four of the newly-invented submarines be acquired and based in German territory on the west coast to attack British troop transports and merchant ships.[266]

In January 1901, some burghers from General Hertzog's commando reached Lambert's Bay on the Northern Cape coast. They fired on a British warship anchored there, the HMS *Sybille*, but hastily retreated behind the sand dunes when fire was returned. So ended the shortest, and only, naval engagement of the war.[267]

The Transvaal Republic was forced to establish its own merchant navy in 1900 and acquired the steamship *Rousillon*. The *Gironde*, which was contracted to run contraband military supplies through the British blockade to Mozambique, had suffered a unique breakdown. However, the *Rousillon* never left the Mozambican port of Lourenço Marques as the crew was too frightened of the Royal Navy.[268]

When the sailors ran out of ammunition for their 4.7-inch naval guns, they were put on temporary latrine duty. They appropriately named the two latrine carts after their ships, 'The Powerful' and 'The Terrible'.

Near-fatal assumption
A young Boer reacted with terror during his first skirmish and, imagining that he was wounded, raced up to his veldkornet and asked him what blood smelt like. "Like dung!" screamed the exasperated officer. "Then, Veldkornet, I am mortally wounded!"[269]

Nicknames
General Buller, infamous for his vacillation and numerous defeats, was called 'Sir Reverse', 'The Ferry-man' (because he crossed the Tugela River so many times), 'General Debility' and 'General Paralysis'.[270]

'Roksak' Redelinghuis acquired his nickname ('pocket dress') because he always carried one of his wife's dresses with him. This served as a constant reminder of his wife, and on one occasion helped save his life. Badly wounded, and touching the dress he remarked, "If I die the general will take my fair-haired wife."[271]

Major-General W.G. Knox was known as 'Nasty Knox' because he had "a will of his own".[272] Reverend Kestell reports how nasty he was to the Boers. On 27 January 1902, he removed Commandant Koen's wife from her house and had one of his colonels cross-examine her like a criminal. "This officer told her that her husband had captured 18 of his Blacks the day before, and said that if her husband had those Blacks shot, he, the Colonel, would give the 1,000 Blacks under his command liberty to do with her as they chose."[273]

Fighting-General Sarel Oosthuizen was known as 'Rooi Sarel' (Red Sarel) because of the colour of his beard.

Colonel Baden-Powell was called 'Bathing-towel' by his men, as he often appeared dressed only in a towel after his baths in the field.[274]

The Boer Long Tom on Bulwana Hill was damaged by a British shell near the end of the barrel and sent to Pretoria for repairs. A section of the barrel was sawn off, and afterward the gun was known to the Boers as 'The Jew'.

Captain Reginald Stephens of the Rifle Brigade was called the 'Stiff 'un' by his fellow officers; it is perhaps prudent not to ask why.[275]

General Warren's nickname was 'Jerusalem' Warren due to his valuable contribution in the field of archaeology in Jerusalem between 1867 and 1870.[276]

Captain Congreve V.C. was called 'Squibby' after the Congreve rocket, which his great-grandfather had invented.[277]

The Boer gun on Lombard's Kop was given the nickname of 'The Franchise' by the Boers, because the difficult rules blocking foreigners from obtaining voting rights by the Transvaal government was a major cause of the war. Colonel Erasmus of the Staats Artillerie told a war correspondent that any foreigner who wanted The Franchise could get it for nothing.[278]

The South African Imperial Light Horse was known to the Zulus as the 'Sakkabulu Boys'.[279] This was because they usually wore the feathers of the long-tailed widowbird (*sakkabulu* bird) in their hats. They were also known as the 'Imperial Light Looters' due to their reputation for being long-fingered.

General Hart was known as 'No Bobs Hart' because he refused to duck or bob under fire.[280]

General Gatacre, often subjecting his men to long marches, was called 'Backacre'.[281]

One Tree Hill, across the Tugela from Spion Kop was renamed 'Maconochie Hill' because Maconochie army rations were so frequently issued there.[282]

For his ability to elude British columns on 'De Wet hunts', General de Wet was attributed with magical powers and was called 'De Wet o' de Wisp' by *Punch* magazine.[283]

General Kitchener was called 'Kitchener of Chaos' (from Kitchener of Khartoum) because he had centralized the once-efficient regimental transport system and turned it into chaos.

Major Pine Coffin of the Malta Mounted Infantry was actually his real name: would you serve under him?[284]

The ganger's lorry raced through this old ZASM tunnel near Waterval Boven accompanied by a pianist playing 'The Blue Danube'.

A wild horse stands on the patch of ground where the Devons made their final bayonet charge to drive the Boers off Wagon Hill under cover of a thunderstorm.

The Boers imported four 6-inch Creusot BL guns for their Pretoria forts before the war. They were never used in the forts but taken into the field instead where they were prominent in the sieges of Ladysmith, Kimberley and Mafeking. The guns fired 94-pound shells 11,000 yards (10,060m), outranging British guns at the beginning of the war. The four 'Long Toms' were destroyed after the conventional phase of the war to prevent them from falling into British hands.

Short of long-range guns to counter the Boer 'Long Tom' a total of 18 5-inch breech-loading guns were taken off British warships, mounted on adapted carriages and transferred to the field. Each gun weighed 40cwt (2,032kg) with the packed gun carriage weighing 74cwt (3,759kg), which had to be pulled by a team of 16 oxen. The guns fired 50-pound shells 5,400 yards (4,940m) on time fuse and 10,500 yards (9,600m) on percussion. This gun at the Union Buildings in Pretoria was used by the Royal Garrison Artillery, most likely at the Scottish Rifles campsite situated above Greylingstad.

Throughout the war the heavy guns were known as 'cow guns'. They acquired this nickname at the beginning of the war when each British 4.7-inch naval gun had to be drawn by a span of 30 oxen.[285]

Nicotine

By August 1901, the Boer smokers were desperate for tobacco. One Boer, Venter, had six inches of roll tobacco hidden in his saddlebag, and Dick Hunt, an American, caught him hiding behind his horse and biting off a quid. The angry American admonished him for not sharing, saying; "You are lower than a snake's backside and I would not spit on you if your guts caught fire."[286]

While a burgher was engaged in conversation, he casually pulled a small Bible from his pocket, out of which he tore a page from the Book of Revelation, and proceeded to roll a cigarette. He remarked that, "I do not know how to accept the Revelation."[287]

General Hendrik Schoeman was the Boer commander opposing the British at Colesberg. One day a 4.7-inch lyddite shell landed outside his tent but failed to explode. He kept the shell as a souvenir and, when the Boer forces retreated, he took it with him to his house in Pretoria and used it as an ashtray. Realizing the futility of carrying on the war when the British captured Pretoria, he took it upon himself to visit the commandos still in the field to try to persuade them to lay down their arms. He was imprisoned by the Boers, tried and sentenced to death.

While awaiting execution in Barberton gaol, the town was captured by the British and he was freed. Undeterred, he went on another mission and was re-arrested. Awaiting execution in Pietersburg gaol, he was again freed by the British and returned to his home in Pretoria. Every Sunday evening he held a piano concert for his friends at his town house in Pretoria, which included British officers.

On Sunday, 26 May 1901, he knocked his pipe out in the top of the lyddite shell, remarking to his companions about how safe the explosive was. Those were his last words for the shell exploded, killing him, a friend and his daughter.

His son erected a memorial to him on the top of a prominent hill at Saartjie's Nek near Hartebeespoort dam, site of the family farm. In his book about his father he described him as "... one of the great (perhaps the words 'highly principled' are more appropriate) sons of the South African Republic".[288]

Captain Naudé, on the other hand, had this to say about Schoeman: "In the whole Boer Army there was surely no less-capable officer. After Colesberg was besieged, he nestled with his commando in the hills as if he was glued there. He simply let the chance to advance farther south slip through his fingers."[289]

No escape
During the Battle of Belmont some of the Boers left their positions to escape on horseback. Commandant Greyling shot their horses, compelling them to re-occupy their places in the firing line.[290]

After the British had taken the Johannesburg Police positions at Bergendal, one of the Boers tried to escape from under the noses of the Rifle Brigade. "A solitary mounted Boer appeared from behind the farm and, making a dash for the gate, turned left and rode across our front. Everyone had a shot at him and everyone missed except Sergeant Ellis, who knelt down and took a steady aim and brought down the horse; it looked a wonderful shot and possibly it was a lucky one. The rider was knocked out with his sudden fall and was easily added to the bag of prisoners."[291]

General Viljoen was surprised to discover that the 2,000 British prisoners of war at Nooitgedacht were guarded by only 15 burghers armed with Martini-Henry rifles. There was also a great quantity of provisions, rifles and ammunition at the nearby railway station. Had the soldiers overpowered their guards, they would have found themselves fully armed and provisioned and able to cut off the retreat of half the Boer army from Bergendal. General Viljoen noted that, "… save for 'Tommy' being such a helpless individual when he has nobody to give him orders and to think for him, these 2,000 men might have become a great source of danger to us had they had the sense to disarm their 15 custodians (and what was there to prevent them doing so?) …"[292]

No quarter
The Boers were incensed by the British use of locally recruited black troops, as this was a 'white man's war'. During the action at Klip River on 23 November 1900, the Boers cornered a group of about 20 black soldiers who were fleeing the battlefield and wiped them out to a man.[293]

During the attack by General Smuts on Modderfontein Post, near Bank Station, on 31 January 1901, Commandant Breytenbach was killed while attacking the small forts to the east of the British positions. On discovering that these positions were manned by black troops, General Smuts attacked them, ruthlessly killing them all.[294]

The Boers raided a blockhouse near Heidelberg which was garrisoned by black National Scouts under the command of a white officer. The Boers lured 13 scouts out of the blockhouse and only one got away. A few weeks later the blockhouse was again attacked and the scouts, their women and officers were virtually wiped out. The survivors were later tried by the Boers and shot.[295]

No surrender

During the Battle of Spion Kop, a group of British troops in the main trench on the right threw down their arms and surrendered. As the Boers came forward to take their prisoners, Colonel Thorneycroft ran up to them and shouted, "I'm the commandant here; take your men back to hell, sir! I allow no surrenders." He then took some of the men to a line of rocks behind the main trench and opened fire on the Boers who managed to get away with only a few prisoners.[296]

O.K. Corral

During the battle for Wagon Point on 6 January 1900, a shoot-out reminiscent of the gunfight at the O. K. Corral took place between the opposing senior commanders. As Colonel Ian Hamilton and Major Miller-Wallnut of the Gordon Highlanders came up, the Boers renewed the attack and the British took flight. Six men, including Hamilton, stood their ground and stopped the flight. Then there was a desperate race between the Boers and British for the gun pit. "What a lethal race! First was Hamilton, who leaned on the sandbag parapet and fired at the nearest Boer with his revolver. Trooper Albrecht fired before Lieutenant Digby Jones with a Corporal Hockaday, Royal Engineers, appeared, each firing at a Boer. Suddenly, almost everybody was shot. De Villiers, de Jager and Gert Wessels lay dead. Miller-Wallnut got a bullet through the head and Trooper Albrecht fell a moment later. Lieutenant Digby-Jones ordered some of his nerve-shattered men back to their positions and was then shot through the throat, and died. Lieutenant Dennis, Royal Engineers, ran to his side to help and was also shot. Colonel Ian Hamilton, who had braved other such hair-raising events on other occasions, miraculously stood unscathed. It is said, and it was the opinion of Colonel Hamilton (later, of course, to become General Sir Ian Hamilton) that de Villiers shot Miller-Wallnut and Digby-Jones shot de Villiers. That courageous carnage seemed to settle Wagon Point and the charmed and charming Hamilton returned to the battle at Wagon Hill."[297]

Obedience

General Kitchener ordered a suicidal cavalry charge on the Boer camp at Paardeberg, a distance of 500 yards over open ground. Colonel Hannay, commanding the 1st Mounted Infantry Brigade and appreciating the absurdity of this tactic, sent his officers away on various pretexts before gathering 40 to 50 men together for the charge. Riding far in front of his men, his horse was shot from under him but he advanced on foot to within 200 yards of the laager where he fell, riddled with bullets. His adjutant, Captain Hankey, and a few of the men were killed, the others swerving to the left and to safety. Two officers and a handful of men actually reached the laager and were taken prisoner.[298] Hannay gave his life to demonstrate that a cavalry charge was inappropriate in the circumstances.

After the final British infantry charge at the Battle of Bergendal, Johannesburg Police mounted their horses in the cattle kraal on the right and galloped across open veld past the farmhouse in the distance. In spite of fierce fire from the victorious British soldiers, most of them made it to safety.

The grave of General Schoeman and his wife and daughter in Hero's Acre, Pretoria.

This is the original farmhouse at Bergendal built by H.J. Botha in 1874. It was used by the ZARPs as a base for their pom-pom gun during the battle. British shell damage can still be seen on the left of the front door.

The site of the British POW camp at Nooitgedacht, Elands River Valley.

A contemporary sketch of the British prisoners of war in the Nooitgedacht POW camp.

How is the Paardeberg battlefield connected to the sinking of the *Titanic* 12 years later? Colonel Hannay's headstone has this curious inscription, "Darkness comes over me, my rest a stone." These are words from the 19th-century hymn, 'Nearer, my God, to Thee'. It is also reputed to be the last song played by the string quartet as the *Titanic* sank. The ship's band leader, Wallace Hartley, who went down with the ship with all the other musicians, liked the hymn and wanted it played at his own funeral. The first few notes of the score are inscribed on his headstone in the town of Colne, England.

Opportunities lost

Just before Ladysmith was besieged, the British attacked the Boers at Nicholson's Nek. They were routed and 10,000 soldiers fled toward Ladysmith. The Boers had superior numbers and were mounted. While General Joubert hesitated, General Christiaan de Wet muttered to him, "*Los jou ruiters, los jou ruiters!*" (Release your horsemen).

Joubert held back and quoted a Dutch saying, "When God holds out a finger, don't take the whole hand."[299]

Veldkornet Isaac Malherbe remarked that, "It might be sound theology, but it was no good in making war."[300]

If Joubert had let his commandos pursue the fleeing soldiers, Ladysmith would most likely have fallen that day, changing the course of the war.

The British repeated this mistake after the relief of Ladysmith. Referring to the chaotic Boer retreat on 28 February 1900, General Lyttelton criticized Buller's inaction: "… dispirited by defeat, encumbered by a huge train of wagons, the Sundays River in flood behind them with only one bridge, they were at our mercy. Few commanders have so wantonly thrown away so great an opportunity."[301]

Surgeon Blake-Knox wrote: "Over Ladysmith floated a balloon. Had we known what its occupants saw, the Boer retreat might, by a combined advance of infantry, guns and mounted men, have been turned into a complete rout."[302]

When the Boers realized that General Yule and his column had left Dundee, they failed to follow them, being content to loot the British camp. They could have inflicted very heavy losses on the column during their four-day march; as it turned out, the 4,000 soldiers were an invaluable addition to the garrison of Ladysmith.[303]

It was impossible for General Botha to follow up his victory at Spion Kop by attacking the retreating enemy the next day. The commandos had fought continuously for eight days and built trenches every night. At about 9 o'clock on 24 January 1900, while firing still

The area in the foreground is in front of the British main trench on Spion Kop where Thorneycroft ran up to the Boers who were taking the surrender of British soldiers and told them, "I'm the commandant here; take your men back to hell, sir! I allow no surrenders." The Boer positions were on Aloe Knoll in the centre and Twin Peaks in the distance to the right.

The 'Lady Anne' gun pit at Wagon Point, Ladysmith, where the shootout took place.

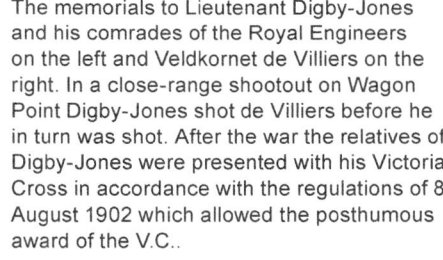

The memorials to Lieutenant Digby-Jones and his comrades of the Royal Engineers on the left and Veldkornet de Villiers on the right. In a close-range shootout on Wagon Point Digby-Jones shot de Villiers before he in turn was shot. After the war the relatives of Digby-Jones were presented with his Victoria Cross in accordance with the regulations of 8 August 1902 which allowed the posthumous award of the V.C..

Colonel Hannay's grave at Paardeberg. He gave his life for most of his men when ordered to lead a suicidal charge on the Boer trenches at the Battle of Paardeberg on 18 February 1900. There is an interesting connection between the inscription on his headstone and the sinking of the *Titanic* 12 years later.

continued on the Kop, an officer found General Botha and his staff around the table in Major Wolmarans's tent, asleep from exhaustion.[304] For the next two days the Boer army watched the British withdrawing across the Tugela without firing a shot at them. As the engineers dismantled the last of the pontoon bridges, Botha fired a single shell at them which splashed into the Tugela.[305]

Order of the Bath

Colonel Ignace Ferreira, a member of one of the oldest Boer families, who had fought under Lord Wolseley in the Anglo-Zulu War, received the Order of the Commander of the Bath from Queen Victoria for his herioc actions in defence of the Empire. However, during the siege of Mafeking he commanded one of the Boer commandos.[306]

Alfred Milner, the governor of the Cape and British high commissioner for South Africa, was awarded the Grand Cross of the Order of the Bath in the New Year's Honours List 1901. He had turned down the offer of a peerage saying, "My feeling is that for a man not rich, or well connected, and by nature a Bohemian, a title would be an encumbrance."[307] This was no doubt his reward for obeying Chamberlain's instruction to get the British into the war with the Boer republics. On 24 May 1901 Milner was in fact awarded a peerage by King Edward VII at Marlborough House: 'Baron Milner of St James's and Cape Town'.

Shortly after the signing of the Peace of Vereeniging, on 28 June 1902, Chamberlain informed Milner that the king had bestowed on him the title of viscount "... in recognition of the services he had rendered the Empire, especially those in connection with the close of hostilities".[308]

Owning up

Major Erasmus of the Staats Artillerie took the blame for the successful British attack on his Long Tom gun outside Ladysmith. He even went so far as to ask the State Attorney to place him under arrest.[309]

Colonel Bullock of the 2nd Devons took the blame for the loss of the ten guns at Colenso. He had been protecting the guns with two sections of his men and, being so far forward, had not received Buller's orders to retire. Although he refused to surrender when Veldkornet Emmett approached to capture the guns, some of his men, desperate for water, raised the white flag. When he reached for his revolver one of the Boers clubbed him over the head with a rifle butt, stunning him.

In the ambulance train he pinned a piece of paper to his breast reading, "I am the officer who lost ten guns at Colenso."[310]

The caption to this contemporary posed photograph is, 'Dordrecht 30 December 1899 after the Boer attack'. Closer examination shows that a couple of the wounded soldiers have their heads off the ground and are smiling.

The memorial to the gunners of the Royal Field Artillery (RFA) at Clouston cemetery. The number of gunners buried here is given as 29 whereas the total number of RFA killed at Colenso on 15 December 1899 was 16 according to the historian Darrell Hall. Seven Victoria Crosses were awarded in connection with the attempt to save the guns of the 14th and 66th batteries RFA. Of the 12 guns, two were saved.

The British pontoon bridge assembled over the Modder River by the Royal Engineers in a mere two hours. The Royal Engineers became very proficient in building these bridges, especially in Natal where General Buller repeatedly crossed the Tugela River at various places in order to lift the siege of Ladysmith. His nickname became 'The Ferryman'.

The Rifle Brigade advanced across open ground toward the Johannesburg Police positions in the foreground. The Rifle Brigade memorial is on the right at the point where they overran the Boer survivors.

A Red Cross ambulance wagon captured at Sanna's Post was found to be filled with rifles and ammunition. The Boers unloaded the wagon and told the physician in charge that he was free to take himself and the wagon back to British lines. The physician refused to go, saying that he had violated the rules of the International Red Cross and would therefore consider himself and his assistants prisoners of war. General Christiaan de Wet refused to accept them as prisoners and left them on the battlefield when he trekked southward with his booty.[311]

Peace
When an old Boer lady called Koekemoer was first told that peace had been made, she said to her informant, "May your mouth turn into gold."[312]

Pets
The Rifle Brigade had a pet liver-and-white springer spaniel which took part in their final charge during the Battle of Bergendal.

"He was well in front with his tail in the air and his nose on the ground. He seemed excited and puzzled; this kind of a shoot was new to him, the little puffs of dust the bullets kicked up as they struck the ground around interested him enormously, and he kept running up to first one and then another, but he could not make them out. When we paused for breath in our rushes he ran up and down our line while we lay close to the ground, and before long he stopped a bullet just behind his left shoulder. We thought the old dog was done for, but after the first shock he recovered a bit and managed to drag himself after us and finally rejoined the company after the position was won."[313]

General Kitchener rescued two baby starlings which had fallen down the chimney of his bedroom at GHQ in Pretoria; one died but he put the other one in a cage and made his senior staff responsible for its well-being, much to their disgust. While he was on a visit to Pietersburg the bird escaped and, on his return, he mobilized a small army made up of his staff and personally supervised a hunt for the bird. It was eventually found in a neighbour's chimney and the chief happily returned to headquarters covered in mud, "having repeatedly fallen prone in wet flower-beds".[314]

Picking up pebbles
In December 1880, the Transvaal burghers gathered at Krugersdorp and took a vow that they would fight for their freedom to the death, as a consequence of Britain annexing the Transvaal Republic in 1877. As a symbol of their vow each burgher placed a stone on a cairn. The Transvaalers subsequently won the First Anglo-Boer War, and built the Paardekraal monument over the cairn of stones. When the British captured Krugersdorp in 1900, they loaded all the stones from the cairn onto railway trucks and dumped them into the Vaal River.

Nearly half a century later, a package arrived from Lieutenant-Colonel H.F.M. Jourdain CMG, which contained one of the stones. He explained that he had been on guard at the Paardekraal monument when the stones were removed and that he had kept the stone as a souvenir, which he was now returning.[315]

Today the monument stands over the imaginary cairn of stones erected in 1880 and the single remaining stone is kept in a safe in Krugersdorp.

Porridge

After Eloff's unsuccessful attack on Mafeking, he and his men were held captive in the prison. One of his commandants was given a bowl of thin porridge for his dinner, a luxury during the final days of the siege. "He looked at it, then at his hands, and taking it for soap and water proceeded to wash in it."[316]

Pot plants

When raiding farms for supplies some items were useful and some were not. "There is a quantity of mealie cobs in the wagon house, which the women allow us to take; and also a few pot plants which we allow them to keep."[317]

Practical joke

The commandos camped outside the town of Pilgrim's Rest used the narrow-gauge miners' trolleys to race into town. Soon all the trolleys ended up in town, and so a few Boers laboriously pushed a trolley uphill to their camp to ensure an easy ride into town the next day. Even though they took the trolley off the rails as a precaution, while they were sleeping, some rascal, by way of a joke, rode it into town and wasted their hard labour.[318]

Premonitions

Major Childe, who led the South African Light Horse in the attack on Bastion Hill before the battle at Spion Kop, had a premonition of his death the night before the battle. He requested his brother officers to put an epitaph above his grave quoting 2 King's chapter 4, verse 26: "Is it well with the child? It is well."[319] Childe died from a head wound and his wish was granted. At his funeral service Lord Dundonald quoted from 2 Kings chapter 4, verse 19: "And he said unto his father, 'My head, my head,' and he said to a lad, 'Carry him to his mother.'"[320]

Chris Muller explains in great detail how, since the beginning of guerrilla warfare, whenever the British came close, a muscle just above his knee began to 'pull'. The nearer the enemy came the more it pulled. When fighting, if the muscle began pulling from behind, the British retreated or disengaged. He found this strange, but the enemy never once surprised him. After the war, it never recurred.[321]

Prophecy

General de la Rey was often accompanied by the famous Boer prophet *Siener* (seer) van Rensburg who had many visions, most of which were concerned with bulls or buck. Before the Battle of Tweebosch he had the following vision: "I see a red bull coming from the direction of Vryburg. His horns are pointing forwards. He is eager to fight. He is brave and strong but, when he arrives at Barberspan, his horns hang lower. His determination is failing and he begins to feel discouraged. But it will go even worse with him because, when he arrives at the Harts River, he will be completely dehorned. He will be unable to butt. He must be disarmed then."

The *siener* also saw the Boers walking about between the British guns and wagons. Inspired by this vision, on 7 March 1902, de la Rey smashed up Lord Methuen's column of 1,200 men and four field guns and captured Methuen.[322]

The day before the war ended with the Treaty of Vereeniging, General Hertzog said, "We are nearer the time when a Great War must break out. It is a known fact that the nations are arming themselves more and more, and building ships of war, which is all done in preparation for the day when war will break out in Europe."[323]

Queen's birthday

The British prisoners of war were determined that the Union Jack would fly over Pretoria on the Queen's birthday, 24 May 1900. "The Union Jack floated over Pretoria that day, for Haserick let loose a tame hawk with the Union Jack tied to its neck, and sent it hovering over the town."[324]

Queen's touch

Queen Victoria gave Lieutenant Roberts's posthumous Victoria Cross to his mother in a sealed packet, saying, "Do not open it until you get home, no other hands but mine have touched this."[325]

On 26 February 1900, the Queen's personal gift of chocolate arrived at the front lines of Buller's army which was about to relieve Ladysmith. With her own money she had bought a specially designed tin of chocolate for every British soldier serving in South Africa.[326] Many British soldiers sent the tins back home intact for safekeeping, as the gift was so highly prized. Private Tucker chose to eat his chocolate.

"The empty tin now became an object of interest, so I carefully wrapped it up and placed it in my haversack. I carried it during all the fighting my regiment was involved in until I had a chance to send it to England. I fear the box got a few knocks but it still remains the Queen's gift and much cherished."[327]

Two sparrows depicted on a half cent coin serve as a reminder of the women in the severe conditions of the Bethulie concentration camp. They had adopted the text from Matthew chapter 10, verses 29–31 as their survival motto: "Are not two sparrows sold for a farthing? And one of them shall not fall on the ground without your Father's consent. Fear ye not therefore, ye are of more value than many sparrows." Since 1923 the two sparrows have been depicted on South Africa's lowest-denomination coin in recognition of the women's wish to have their symbol of faith and hope remembered by all South Africans.

The Paardekraal monument, Krugersdorp, built over the cairn of stones which were solemnly placed there by the burgers before the First Anglo-Boer War. The stones were removed by the occupying British troops and thrown into the Vaal River, except one.

The koppie near Ottosdal where the Boer prophet *Siener* van Rensburg received many of his visions.

Ockert Botha, the grandson of the Boer prophet *Siener* van Rensburg, sits on his grandfather's favourite rock on a small hill near his farm in the Ottosdal district, Western Transvaal, where *Siener* van Rensburg received most of his post-Anglo-Boer War prophecies.

Shortly before her death, in January 1901, the 82-year-old Queen Victoria personally made four scarves for distribution to members of her colonial forces in South Africa. The scarves were made with thick brown wool, crocheted in a block pattern and were five inches wide, and long enough to be worn as a sash similar to a colour sergeant's sash of the period. The *London Gazette* No. 27443 of 17 June 1902 contains the last South African dispatch of Lord Roberts dated London, 1 March 1902, which ends:

> In conclusion, I desire to place on record that, in April 1900, Her late Majesty Queen Victoria was graciously pleased to send me four woollen scarves worked by Herself, for distribution to the four most distinguished Private soldiers in the Colonial Forces of Canada, Australia, New Zealand and South Africa then serving under my command. The selection for these gifts of honour were made by the officers commanding the contingents concerned, it being understood that gallant conduct in the field was to be considered the primary qualification. The names of those selected, to whom the scarves have already been presented, are as follows:

> Private R.R. Thompson, Royal Canadian Regt.
> Private A. Dufrayer, NSW Mounted Rifles
> Private H.D. Coutts, New Zealand Contingent
> Trooper I. Chadwick, Roberts' Horse

The *Sydney Bulletin* covered the presentation to the Australian recipient, Private (then Lieutenant) Dufrayer, making this remark, "It is a homely brown thing – such as any old lady might knit – but it has the merit of being entirely the late Queen's work." Later the newspaper remarked, "Until the scarf was unrolled we all thought it was a folded string bag." Although popular mythology has suggested that this award was the equivalent of the Victoria Cross, this is not supported by the evidence.

Quick answer

Late in December 1899, while besieged in Mafeking, Colonel Baden-Powell sent a letter to the Boer general Snyman. It was several thousand words in length and told the besieger that it was utter folly for the Boers to continue fighting the might of Great Britain and that the British army was invincible.

General Snyman sent Baden-Powell a four word reply, "Come out and fight."[328]

Railway warfare

Cornered by the British army at Hectorspruit, near the Portuguese border, the Boers destroyed the supplies and impedimenta that they were unable to carry north to the bushveld. Some men staged breakneck collisions between heavy goods trains, while others "dynamited the

Chamberlain: "Majesty, the last blank area down there must also become red!"

'Queen Victoria' presents a Victoria Cross to a schoolboy in October 1999 and says the following: "My subject, I honour your bravery with a Victoria Cross for getting the guns back to the station at Sanna's Post. "Thank you, your Majesty."
Photo: Joan Abrahams

British soldiers receiving Christmas presents and letters from home, Modder River, 1899.

After the schoolchildren had re-enacted the Battle of Koornspruit, Queen Victoria (actually Mrs Taylor, a very strict teacher) awards a Victoria Cross to one of the children. *Photo: Joan Abrahams*

The 'Lord Nelson', a 7-pounder muzzle-loading ship's cannon dated 1770, was pressed back into service for the defence of Mafeking after being relieved of its former duty of serving as a fence post and refurbished. Shell damage on the corrugated-iron sheet in the background is evidence of the effects of returning fire from the Boer 'Long Tom'.

bridges and then allowed locomotives at full speed to race to the river and throw themselves against the massive pillars in mid-stream and die down in the fizzling water and steam".[329]

When Commandant Buys blew up the goods train six kilometres east of Greylingstad on 13 February 1901, he found that it was closely followed by an armoured train, which started firing its cannon at his commando. The goods train had its carriages in front, so that if a charge blew up the tracks, the crew could uncouple the derailed trucks and steam off to safety. Buys's men raced to the train, uncoupled the engine, and engaged reverse gear, sending it racing at full steam toward the armoured train. "The armoured train was forced to steam backwards in order to avoid a collision. It was a race as far as we could see. I never discovered how far they travelled."[330]

Religious service

A Boer preacher and his congregation were fervently engaged in prayer when the preacher caught sight of approaching British horsemen from his superior vantage point. He leaped over his flock and onto his horse before his congregation knew what was happening.

A youth caught up to him in their wild flight and said, "Dominee, you forgot to say Amen!"[331]

Just before the relief of Ladysmith, on the night of Sunday, 25 February 1900, the Rifle Brigade was moved by the singing of the 100th Psalm from the Boer lines. They even stood up to listen but, just before the Amen had finished, they received a heavy volley from the Boer trenches which made them dive for cover.

"Only a minute before we had been giving them credit for their religious ways and were even praising their singing and this was the way they returned our kindness for letting them have their service in peace!"[332]

A padre approached the blockhouse line on his way from Vredefort, and asked whether he could hold a religious service there. This was to ease his conscience as he was hours late for a service at headquarters. He insisted on holding the service inside the blockhouse, which had a standard door measuring only four foot square. By the time the seven men and Lieutenant Fuller had crawled into the blockhouse, they had developed the giggles. A sudden noise outside startled one of the men who let off an 'explosion'. It drove the men out of the blockhouse in five seconds flat and, once in the fresh air, they all collapsed with laughter. Soon the padre joined in and on regaining his breath, exclaimed, "Well, well, well, with that man in your blockhouse you ought to be as safe as in the Tower of London!" He then produced a bottle of port and they had 'tea' together.[333]

Remains and controversies

The remains of an artillery emplacement can still be found on the top of Groot Zuikerboskop at Dullstroom, in original condition. Controversy still exists as to whether a Long Tom was positioned here during the Battle of Bergendal. Evidence from Schikkerling's diary indicates that it was. On 17 April 1901, Schikkerling's commando was in position above O'Grady's farm at Elandshoek, on the road from Dullstroom to Lydenburg,[334] watching the enemy advance toward them from Belfast.

"The enemy will probably place a gun in the same schantz on Suikerbosch Kop, in which Long Tom was placed during the Battle of Bergendal."[335]

Remembrance

On 7 November 1900, Commandant Hendrik Prinsloo was killed near Belfast while leading the Carolina Commando on an attack on General Smith-Dorrien's column. He was one of the Boer heroes of the Battle of Spion Kop, and was shot dead within sight of his wife and family. He was buried on the battlefield and every year on the anniversary of his death a few burghers gather together to stand in silence and pay tribute to "one of the few men who took away from Spion Kop a better reputation then he had brought to it."[336]

Reprisals

To discourage the sabotaging of railways, the British issued a proclamation that the farmhouse nearest to the damage would be razed. Thus Mr van Rensburg of the farm Houtpoort found himself standing with his wife and children in the veld after his farm had been destroyed as a result of the train destroyed just south of Heidelberg on 2 September 1900. (The high embankment where the train was wrecked can be seen next to the N3 freeway between Johannesburg and Durban at the Balfour off-ramp).[337]

During the guerrilla phase of the war, the Boers were compelled to wear captured British uniforms, as this was their only source of clothing. The British issued a proclamation stating that any Boer captured in British uniform would be shot. Reitz maintains that neither the commandos nor the local population were informed that the death penalty was attached to the wearing of British uniforms. In fact, many of Smut's' men who were taken prisoner were executed for wearing khaki, and his commando sincerely believed that the British had resorted to shooting prisoners.[338]

Frans Kruger of the Heidelberg Commando captured a British uniform after the action at Dam Plaats, near Frankfort, on 25 January 1902. Although the commando had strict instructions to cut all military insignia off captured uniforms, Frans was too tired to do so. Captured the next day, he was tried. found guilty of wearing a British uniform and executed.[339]

Research in reverse
I found some of the stories related by Fuller in his book *The Last of the Gentleman's Wars* so capricious that I decided to do some research in reverse. On pages 90 and 91 he describes the death of Private Appleby in a typical night skirmish, and relates that he was subsequently buried at Heilbron. Sure enough, I found private Appleby's grave in the military section of the cemetery at Heilbron and his date of death tallied with Fuller's diary.

Restraint
Although the British resorted to farm burning, the Boers showed restraint in not retaliating at the farmhouses of National Scouts. In November 1901, Schikkerling reported that the only house not burned down near Pilgrim's Rest was that of Harry Harber who led a band of National Scouts.[340]

Rock art
Bored soldiers on both sides spent many hours recording their presence on the rocks and boulders of lonely koppies. Petty Officer Franklin wrote in his diary on 28 November 1899: "I was cutting my name into a rock while the Fort was being shelled and one shell landed to the rear, striking the cookhouse ..." Brian Khaigan, a fellow historian, found Franklin's name engraved on a rock at Caesar's Camp, Ladysmith, nearly 100 years later. To cap this he also found the cookhouse in the shelter of some boulders, suitably engraved with a fork and spoon, scattered with rock fragments from the exploded shell.

Saluting the throne
Wherever he went a well-known officer (who must remain anonymous) carried with him a portable latrine, a seat and canvas folding screen. "During the battle [of Modder River] he had this pitched, and one morning as was his habit, he retired to it. Happily ensconced in his sanctum, a burial party consisting of a corporal and some half-dozen men of his unit marched by, whereupon a dust devil whirling over the veld neatly removed the canvas screen and carried it into the air. There was the great man enthroned. What could the corporal do? His duty of course; so he gave 'Eyes right!'"[341]

Schoolboy warriors
A wounded young Boer named Schultz was brought into Ladysmith after the Battle of Wagon Hill, having just seen his father killed at his side. His only uniform was his hat, which had his Grey College (Bloemfontein) badge on it.[342]

On 2 November 1901, President Steyn issued a proclamation lowering the age of compulsory military service to 14 years.[343]

Five Arch Bridge in the Elands River Valley near Waterval Onder. A railway bridge on the 'Eastern Line' from Pretoria to Mozambique, it was opened to traffic on 20 June 1894. The Transvaal Republic imported most of its arms and ammunition via Mozambique until the port of Lourenço Marques was blockaded by British warships.

The confined space of the basement in the three-storey blockhouse near Harrismith.

The grave of Private Appelby who was killed in a night skirmish near Heilbron.

Commandant Prinsloo's memorial near Belfast erected with funds raised after the war by his adversary, General Smith-Dorrien. My friends Huffy Pott and Alastair Moir pay their respects.

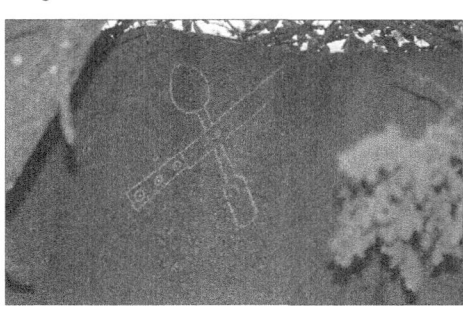

The site of the cookhouse at Caesar's Camp, Ladysmith, in which the shell exploded on 28 November 1899.

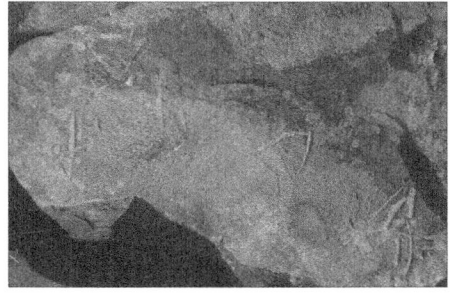

I found this rock on the walls of the canteen at the Scottish Rifles campsite at Greylingstad. The rock 'rings' with three distinct notes when struck by any hard object. The position of each note is indicated by three mysterious engravings. Is this an ancient stone accidently built into the wall or artwork created by a bored soldier versed in some ancient language?

During the fighting at Magersfontein a group of youthful Boers surprised about 100 Highlanders who had wandered too close to the Boer trench. On the cry of "Hands up!" the Highlanders promptly threw down their arms and advanced to the trench with their hands above their heads. After a brief consultation the youths decided to let them go. "When the young burghers arrived at the Boer laager with the captured rifles and bandoliers, General Cronjé asked them why they did not bring the men.

The youths looked at each other for a while; then one replied, rather sheepishly, 'We did not know they were wanted.'"[344]

Secret messages

The British prisoners of war held in the State Model School, Pretoria, were remarkably well informed about the progress of the war via secret daily messages from an unlikely friend. One of the prisoners, Captain Aylmer Haldane of the Gordon Highlanders, noticed a man walking past the prison with his St Bernard dog making odd tapping noises with his walking stick. He realized that the tapping of the walking stick was actually Morse code and that it conveyed brief news of recent action. At least the POWs received short messages such as 'British Victory' or 'British Defeat'. On one occasion he whispered a message to Winston Churchill, who was hanging over the rails: "The British have given the Boers hell at Belmont". However the dog-walker was under suspicion by the guards and warned not to walk near the school. He then visited the family of the house across the road from the school, the Cullingworths, and taught their two young daughters to signal the latest news to the POWs. After the British occupation of Pretoria, it turned out that the POWs' friend was Mr Patterson, a telegraphist in the service of the South African Republic. He received letters of congratulation for his efforts from many quarters, including a letter from the British Supreme Commander, Lord Roberts. After the war Patterson received a letter and a silver salver from some of the officers in recognition of his services to the POWs during their confinement. Patterson became an assistant superintendent in the Transvaal Post Office in 1904 and by 1911 was postmaster of Pretoria. The matter should have rested there but it did not, in fact it resulted in an unusual libel case.

In 1917, 15 years after the war ended, the details of Patterson's secret communications with the POWs became common knowledge with the publication of a book by T. Hopkins entitled *The Romance of Escapes*. The book review pointed out that Patterson had taken the oath of allegiance to the republic and this point was taken up by the Afrikaans newspaper *De Volksstem* under the heading 'The Value of an Oath'. This newspaper went as far as saying that Patterson had taken an active part in Captain Haldane's escape from the State Model School, after Churchill's famous escape on 12 December 1900. The postmaster of Pretoria, Patterson, heard about the article and sued *De Volksstem* for £1,000 in damages, declaring that the article was false and defamatory. The case came before three judges including the Judge-President of the Transvaal, and proceedings began on 7 June 1917. Patterson stated that he had been born in England and had joined the Republican Post Office as a telegraphist in 1890, taking the oath of allegiance after the Malboch War in 1894. He admitted that he had frequently passed the State Model School while the prisoners were confined there and communicated with them from time to time. "As a rule," he said, "I did not do more than signal by means of the Morse Code, that the British had gained a victory, or had suffered a defeat." Patterson stated that he only kept the prisoners informed on the progress of the war to the extent that it was in the public domain – he never revealed secret information from the telegrams that he was responsible for auditing. The plea by *De Volksstem* of justification and the right to fair comment was dismissed by Mr Justice de Villiers, who found that there was no evidence of any kind to prove that Patterson had helped prisoners of war to escape, and even the training of the two young ladies to signal to them did not cover this. The Judge-President took into account the fact that Patterson had broken his oath of allegiance to the republic, "… and that cannot be excused in a Court of Law".

At the end of his judgement he said, "Patterson has received commendations from many quarters and it is unnecessary for me to say anything about that, except that the impression his bringing an action of this nature makes upon one, is that, as long as his conduct was approved of, he was satisfied, but when his conduct was blamed, he resented it. I have therefore come to the conclusion that an amount of £1 with costs, against both Defendants, will satisfy the justice of this case."

Mr Justice Bristowe remarked that, "Patterson's acts at the time were regarded in many quarters, not as blameworthy, but as rather meritorious, and that he had received his reward for them. Up to the present moment he has been rather proud of them than otherwise."[345]

Sense of humour

President Kruger had a wonderful, but wicked, sense of humour; hard to imagine from his dour appearance and demeanour. He granted the Jewish community four stands in Johannesburg (free of charge) to establish a second synagogue and a Jewish school. This was known as the Park Synagogue, situated on the corner of Joubert and De Villiers streets. When Kruger arrived from Pretoria in September 1892 for the opening ceremony, he told his hosts that he had come to convert the Jews. Legend has it that he then declared the synagogue open "… in the name of our Lord Jesus Christ".

However, it is more likely that this was the conclusion to his Christian grace, which he said at the banquet in his honour after the opening ceremony, much to the embarrassment of his hosts.[346]

General Botha had a great sense of humour which prevented him from seeing the worst of the situation. "It kept his sympathies bright, and helped him to realize the other man's point of view. He lit the torch of racial toleration."³⁴⁷ On one occasion, while travelling with General Smuts and Sir Thomas Cullinan near Tzaneen, an old farmer engaged them in conversation. He told them that now that the English were running the country: "We can't punish the natives. It's a pity. But I've found a way out. I just tie them up by the feet and tickle them very gently that way."

Years after this, on an occasion when Botha was attacked in parliament, he suddenly turned to Cullinan and said, "These fellows deserve to be tied up by the feet and tickled a bit, don't they?"³⁴⁸ Botha maintained that his most humorous experience occurred near Heidelberg when the Boers were looting a British convoy. A serious old greybeard who had never seen seafood came up to Botha with an open tin of oysters and asked, "Who will give me a tin of jam for this little tin of birds' stomachs?"³⁴⁹

Shaving

A Natal policeman was shaving on Christmas Day 1899, when a 90-pound shell fired at Ladysmith passed between the mirror and his face, stunning him. For the next hour he sat with his face in his hands mumbling, "Not hurt, not hurt."³⁵⁰

Preparing for a visit to a farm one evening, Schikkerling managed to shave one side of his face with a borrowed razor before it became hopelessly blunt. "I posed side-faced all evening and, like the moon, showed always the same side of my face to the inhabitants of the earth."³⁵¹

The State Model School in central Pretoria. Captured British officers, including Winston Churchill, were incarcerated here during the early months of the war. Mr Patterson, an Englishman in the employ of the Transvaal Republic, walked his dog past the school every afternoon and tapped out the war news in Morse code with his walking stick.

A portrait of Paul Kruger, president of the Transvaal Republic.

Signs in the sky

On the anniversary of the Transvaal's independence day, 16 December 1900, there was a total eclipse of the moon, which the besieged in Ladysmith interpreted as a sign for the eclipse of Boer independence.[352] Outside Ladysmith the relieving force was paraded at midnight but did not move out of Frere camp until 3.30 a.m., only to return to camp. While waiting for orders, they amused themselves by watching the eclipse of the moon.[353]

Toward the end of April 1901, a comet with a long tail appeared in the east. By early May, during the full moon, the comet appeared in the west with two tails. Later in May the comet appeared faintly in the north.[354] A Boer commando, Deneys Reitz, observed that the comet was shaped like the letter 'V'. Seer van Rensburg interpreted this as a sign of peace: the first letter in the word *vrede*, which means peace, but the commandos jokingly said that it signified *vlug*, or retreat.[355]

On the British side, Fuller noted: "On May 2nd I first noticed a comet in the East; the next night, as I watched it, it seemed to me to have two tails. Then, on the 6th, there was no doubt as to this; it had a short bright tail fanning out toward a bright star below Orion's Belt, and a long dim tail fanning out toward four stars which may have been the Southern Cross, though the sketch in my diary does not say so."[356] It is interesting that Fuller did not try to attach any meaning to the appearance of the comet.

Shortly before peace was concluded, on the night of 22 April 1902, there was another striking eclipse of the moon.[357]

Silence

In numerous defensive battles the Boers held their fire as long as they could, and this had a profound psychological effect on their opponents. It was used to great effect at the battles of Modder River, Colenso and the Tugela Heights. "One can imagine nothing more gloomy and terrible than this deathly silence of crowded trenches and frowning gun-pits. Even on the imperturbable British private it is not altogether without its effect, and one may notice a corresponding silence – a bad sign with our soldiers in action – and uneasy glances at the hill-tops and ridges."[358]

On 25 February 1900, after vicious fighting just before the relief of Ladysmith, a truce was concluded to enable the British to collect their wounded and bury their dead. Both sides were so moved by the scenes of suffering and slaughter they had just witnessed, that they were unwilling to commence hostilities, and they reluctantly resumed four hours after the end of the armistice.[359]

Smokescreens

The Boers lit veld fires to conceal an attack or to cover a retreat. On 25 May 1901, General Ben Viljoen attacked one of Plumer's convoys near the farm Mooifontein, between Bethal and Standerton, using a veld fire to cover their approach. However, after a running fight of some 14 kilometres, they were beaten off.[360]

After the relief of Ladysmith the retreating Boers eluded their pursuers by means of smokescreens. "The foremost of our men had set fire in hundreds of places to the grass on either side of the road, and the smoke obscured many of us from the enemy. Had it not been for the smoke and the dust raised, we of the tail-end would have fared badly indeed."[361]

The Earl of Dundonald, commanding officer of the Mounted Brigade, remembered his unusual inheritance while lying awake on the night after the Battle of Spion Kop, the area still shrouded in the smoke of that day's exploding shells. His grandfather, Admiral Lord Dundonald, had conceived the idea of using smokescreens to cover naval attacks. He decided that the secret would be passed on to succeeding generations and would only be revealed in the event of a national emergency. Colonel Dundonald disclosed his secret to the War Office during the First World War, and smokescreens were successfully used for the first time on the Western Front.[362]

Snakebite

Looking for supplies in a dark barn, a commando called 'Swart Lawaai' (Black Blusterer) received a stinging bite. He was carried outside to die, because he had convinced himself that a poisonous snake had bitten him. While one of his comrades read the Bible to the dying man, others went to the barn to see if they could catch the snake. Three men levelled their rifles while the fourth investigated a pile of straw with a long pole. Much to the embarrassment of the dying man, they discovered a broody hen, which had defended her eggs with a sharp peck. Swart Lawaai, after a remarkably short convalescence, recovered his strength but never his reputation.[363]

Socialism

A new Colt automatic machine gun was brought to Ladysmith for evaluation, and it did sterling service during the battles for Wagon Hill and Caesar's Camp. Macdonald commented that, "One of the men connected with it is said to be a well-known socialist leader, whose projects for levelling the masses have evidently taken a new turn."[364]

Sporting chance

During the attack on Red Fort near Bell's Kop, Ladysmith, Robert Reinecke was under severe fire from the British while trying to carry a wounded comrade to safety. The Tommies, realizing his predicament, ceased firing and allowed him to return to the firing line unmolested.[365]

Stampeding cattle

The Boers well knew that cattle are not always docile. In order to force a way through the line of British posts at Steynskraal, 19 kilometres south of Heidelberg, a party of 150 Boers charged the wire defences behind a herd of stampeding cattle.[366]

General de Wet and President Steyn escaped from a British trap on 23 February 1902, near Kalkkrans in the Orange Free State, by rounding up cattle and stampeding them through a guarded pass. "Without mercy, the crazed beasts trampled on those English who could not scatter fast enough. Everybody and everything in their path, including the cannon and machine-guns, were bowled over. Utter confusion reigned. Injured English soldiers tried to crawl away from the flying hooves, whereas others were trampled to death. Those who could escape did so without firing a shot at us."[367]

State of undress

A commando was trapped by the enemy on the brink of a precipice near Waterval Onder. "In order to escape, they had been obliged to slide down the monkey-ropes and trees, and nearly all their clothing had been torn from their bodies. We met Leipoldt without any trousers, carrying on his back a small Maxim, also many others, more or less naked, and we had many jokes at their expense."[368]

During the second Battle of Colenso a number of Boers swam across the river and surprised a platoon of British soldiers who had lost their way. An old Boer had discarded most of his clothes before entering the river and stood in front of the prisoners in his shirt and bandolier, carrying his rifle. "One of the soldiers went up to the *takhaar*, looked at him from head to foot, and, after saluting most servilely, inquired, 'To what regiment do you belong, sir?' The Boer returned the salute, and, without smiling, replied, 'I am one of Rhodes's uncivilized Boers, sir.'"[369]

Staying cool

Deneys Reitz accompanied his uncle on picket duty to a point just 400 yards away from the English defences outside Ladysmith. They drove out on a buckboard, to which they tethered the horses, and then slept on their feather bed, complete with pillows and blankets.[370]

During the attack on Wagon Hill, Ladysmith, Reitz was pinned down by British fire in front of Bell's Kop. Bored, he spent the day sleeping and reading a newspaper. His commando, watching from the rear, thought that he was showing a white flag as he turned the pages of the newspaper, and news spread throughout the laager that his force had surrendered.[371]

With Hussar Hill under heavy shelling by the Boers, General Warren had to devise a way of impressing on his troops that they were there to stay. He ordered his batman to warm some water and put it in a small shell hole, and then proceeded to take a bath. General Buller was not impressed when he sent a messenger to Warren requesting him to fetch his orders. Warren responded by asking the messenger to request Buller in turn to deliver the orders himself. Buller arrived with his large staff on horseback as Warren got out of his bath and covered himself with a towel. "General Buller gave me his instructions and then rode off, and I felt I had done what I could for the day to amuse the men – for there was a great crowd of men peeping on, at a respectful distance, and the incident got into the English and Continental papers."[372]

Storming a blockhouse

The Boers developed an effective tactic to force the surrender of blockhouses. Some men would direct a heavy fire on the loopholes at a distance from the fort, making it impossible for the defenders to fire. The rest of the men then rushed up to the walls, the covering fire stopped, and the commandos were able to stand and shoot through the loopholes.[373] With the bullets ricocheting about to devastating effect, the defenders would soon surrender. The British learned to defend the approaches to the blockhouses with wire entanglements, although the Boers sometimes managed to crawl under the barbed wire and gain the walls.[374]

The double-storey masonry blockhouse which still stands in Krugersdorp was originally a square structure. When it was found that the Boers actually had the audacity to attack blockhouses, two bastions were added on the diagonal so that the defenders could enfilade the enemy in case they gained the walls.

Straight-shooting

On a visit under a flag of truce to Commandant David Schoeman's camp in the Steenkampsberg, a British officer, Alexander, asked the Boers what had become of all their good shots. "Their reply was that they often asked themselves the same question without arriving at a satisfactory conclusion, admitting readily that they were not the marksmen of twenty years ago, though there were still some crack shots among them. Game was not so plentiful as formerly; also many of the population, owing to the mining industry, had been absorbed, so had not handled a rifle for years. With sly humour they pointed out that the English soldiers no longer fought in a red coat and white helmet; in khaki he presented a very inconspicuous target."[375]

Many of the major set-piece battles of the war had taken place by mid-December 1899 – Talana, Elandslaagte, Rietfontein, Nicholson's Nek, Belmont, Graspan, Modder River, Stormberg, Magersfontein, and Colenso – before the British discovered that their new Lee Enfield rifles were shooting 18 inches to the right at 500 yards. No wonder the unfortunate soldiers couldn't shoot straight. This was discovered by recruits of the Imperial Yeomanry during musketry practice, and was due to a problem with the rifle's sighting. Twenty-five thousand rifles had to be re-sighted.[376]

General Warren observed that the Boers, being used to the outdoors, had better long-range vision than his troops. "As our men have no knowledge of distances beyond the barrack square, the cricket field or the end of the street, I prefer situations where our moderate-ranged vision can be of more service, such as those of mountain warfare and bush fighting." Many of the British commanders testified at the commission of inquiry after the war that distances were often misread because of the clear and clean air, which affected the range of bullets and artillery shells.[377]

British soldiers attacking Modder River on 28 November 1899, in one of many posed stereoscopic combat photographs produced during the war. In this photo rifles are lying on the ground, the men are looking down or around, the photographer is obviously shooting from a standing position and there are clearly no Boer snipers in the vicinity. Although there were very few actual combat photographs taken during the war, these stereoscopic photos show fine details of the uniforms and equipment of the time and surviving examples are a delight to see in full 3D, besides being highly collectible.

The British blockhouse in Krugersdorp known as 'Fort Harlech'. Note the addition of two bastions on the diagonal to protect the walls in case they were rushed by burghers.

Problems with gun-sights were not confined to the army; the navy also had its problems. Captain Percy Scott of the HMS *Terrible* found that the sights of his 9.2-inch guns were wrongly constructed and unserviceable. His 12-pounder guns were mounted so that the gunners were unable to see their targets at all; furthermore the guns could not be loaded as there was not enough room to open the breech.[378]

Strategic withdrawal
During the guerrilla phase of the war, the Boers wisely gave way when the ground was unsuitable. On 26 December 1900, while resting after the Battle of Nooitgedacht, a British column approached the Boers from the direction of Potchefstroom. "... as there was no object in fighting except on ground of our own choosing, General Beyers gave them the satisfaction of thinking that we were running away, and at dark we drew off to spend the night near the village of Ventersdorp."[379]

Tactical changes
By early 1901, the British had learned to emulate some of the Boer fighting tactics and started making night raids. The Boers responded by camping before nightfall and then, under cover of darkness, moving their camp some distance away.[380]

The Boers perhaps learned this tactic after an unusual night attack on 20 October 1900, when de Wet's famous commando was thoroughly beaten. Heavy rain followed by a strong wind saw the commando preparing themselves for a wet night beside the dam on Mr Singleton's farm. Without warning thousands of frogs emerged from the dam and leaped into the camp, probably as a result of the water being stirred up by the wind. "Here one tumbled on the blanket of a sleeper, then another placed his wet feet on the face of another, and you heard screams in the darkness, as of persons shrinking back from cold baths. It was thought that the attack could be repulsed by blows from hats and boots. But the amphibious enemy had not the least inclination to sound the retreat. They unceasingly renewed the attack, and were continually being supported by fresh reinforcements from the dam. The human beings retreated. Here one man snatched up his bedding and fled – and there another. I must record it. Our warriors lost the battle, and were forced to evacuate their positions before an attack of – frogs!"[381]

Tainted reputation
General Hector MacDonald was wounded and taken prisoner during the First Anglo-Boer War at the Battle of Majuba after his heroic defence of 'Macdonald's Kopje', having ended up fighting with his bare fists.[382] His courage at Majuba so impressed the Boers that Commandant-General Joubert personally handed back his captured sword, saying, "A brave

man and his sword should not be separated."[383] Although he had a distinguished career during the Second Anglo-Boer War, being affectionately known as 'Fighting Mac', he ended up shooting himself in the Hotel Regina in Paris. He had fallen victim to a love affair with a Ceylonese boy and died like a gentleman to save the reputation of the army and his wife.[384] This was a few days after an audience with King Edward "… who was rumoured to have suggested that only suicide would avert the public scandal of a court-martial."[385] MacDonald was one of the few general officers to have been promoted from the ranks, as a result of his brilliant service in India with Lord Roberts, from Kabul to Kandahar.[386]

Tears
At the end of the war the Boer leaders and representatives debated whether to accept the British peace terms. General Wynand Viljoen of the Lydenburg district reported back to the burghers in the field on progress and "he saw stern and rugged men rise to speak. Yet, before they could utter many words, they were choked with emotion and had to wipe away their tears."[387]

The generals
Fighting-General Oosthuizen of the Krugersdorp Commando fought at Majuba, took part in the surrender of Jameson at Doornkop, and distinguished himself during the Second Anglo-Boer War until he died of wounds received at the Battle of Dwarsvlei. As a veldkornet in Natal, he captured Winston Churchill after the train ambush at Chieveley.[388]

Lord Roberts died at the age of 82 as a result of a chill he caught at Bailleul in France. This was at the beginning of the First World War as he made his way to the front to encourage his beloved Indian troops.[389] In 1904 Lord Roberts was sacked, and it is ironic that one of Long's guns – which his only son had died trying to save – was used as the gun carriage at his funeral in 1914.[390]

After the Anglo-Boer War, on 4 March 1907, General Louis Botha became the first prime minister of the Union of South Africa. He personally led the South African forces to the first Allied victory of the First World War by conquering German South West Africa. Sir Winston Churchill's tribute to him was, "The three most famous generals I have known in my life won no great battles over a foreign foe. Yet their names, which all begin with a 'B', are household words. They are General Booth, General Botha and General Baden-Powell." Louis Botha died at his home on 27 August 1919 and was laid to rest in Hero's Acre, Pretoria.

Captain Congreve, who won a Victoria Cross at Colenso trying to save Long's guns, became a lieutenant-general during the First World War and commanded the XIII Corps at the Battle of the Somme. It was he who ordered the South Africans to "hold Delville Wood at any cost".[391] I mention this because the Anglo-Boer War had many unforeseen consequences. Who would have thought that a few years after this war, Boer and Brit would be fighting side by side for the Empire? W.A. Beattie's poem about the Battle of Delville Wood expresses this sentiment:

> Of Boer and British stock were they, and lean and lithe and tanned,
> Yet mingling there as brothers fighting for one Motherland;
> For kith and kindred o'er the sea, for King and Country now
> Their hands they join in fellowship, and took the filial vow.

On the subject of Delville Wood, it is interesting to note that a memorial cross in Pietermaritzburg, made in 1918 of timber salvaged from the splintered trees of Delville Wood, 'weeps' resin on the anniversary of the battle, 14 July, and continues for a week or two.[392] "On 14 July, 121 officers and 3,052 other ranks comprised the 1st South African Infantry Brigade. Six days later Colonel Edward Thackeray marched out with two wounded officers and 140 other ranks. Of the survivors, one officer and 59 men of the light trench mortar battery had joined as reinforcements two days earlier."[393]

During the Battle of Rietfontein General Lukas Meyer, one of the Boer patriarchs suffered a nervous breakdown. This opened the door of opportunity for young Veldkornet Louis Botha, who went on to make a name for himself at the battles of Colenso, Spion Kop, Vaalkrans and others, eventually becoming Commandant-General of the Transvaal.[394]

General French and Major Douglas Haig escaped on the last train out of Ladysmith and were forced to hide under the seats, like ticket dodgers, when their train came under Boer rifle fire. Major Douglas Haig later commanded the British army in France during the First World War.[395]

Lord Metheun and Lord Loch rode ahead of their infantry to a place called Bloedzuikerspan where there was a well, served by a Bakkies pump. When the infantry arrived they found the general and Lord Loch operating the pump for the benefit of the parched and travel-worn soldiers.[396]

After the war, General Colvile, sacked by Roberts, was knocked down and killed by a car while cycling near Bagshot. Ironically, the car was driven by Colonel Rawlinson, who had served on Lord Roberts's staff in South Africa.[397]

Fighting-General Oosthuizen's grave in Krugersdorp cemetery. As a veldkornet in Natal he captured Winston Churchill after the armoured train disaster on 15 November 1899. He was mortally wounded during the action at Dwarsvlei on 11 July 1900. One of his adversaries, Captain Younger V.C., was killed in this action and is buried nearby.

The 'weeping cross' in the Garden of Remembrance, Pietermaritzburg. It is made from wood collected at Delville Wood in 1918, two years after the battle. Every year the cross weeps a mysterious substance on the anniversary of the first day of the battle, 14 July 1916, and this continues for about two weeks. I have seen this myself as late as 26 July.

Winston Churchill, then a war correspondent for the *Morning Post*, was captured near this spot when the scouting train on which he was travelling was ambushed by the Boers.

Captain Younger's headstone in the old Burgersdorp cemetery, Krugersdorp. He was killed at the Battle of Dwarsvlei on 11 July 1900, the same battle where Fighting-General Oosthuizen received his fatal wound. He would have been recommended for a Victoria Cross had the rules allowed a posthumous award. After the accession of King Edward VII the rules were changed and Captain Younger's family received his Victoria Cross.

The headstone of Private Bishop in the West End cemetery, Kimberley. He died of enteric fever (typhoid) on 18 March 1902, possibly caused by drinking contaminated water. His parents had a sense of humour in spite of their tragedy, his epitaph being 'Early Promotion'.

General Smith-Dorrien also died as a result of a car accident at Chippenham, Wiltshire. During the Anglo-Zulu War, serving with the 95th Regiment, he was the only man who escaped from the Battle of Isandlwana on foot.[398] After his distinguished service during the Anglo-Boer War, he commanded the 2nd Army during 1914–15 in France. During the retreat from Mons he saved the British Expeditionary Force in defiance of orders from General French by making a stand at Le Cateau. In the deadly silence of a small room in the village of Bertry he said to generals Allenby and Hamilton, "Very well, gentlemen, we will fight …" At the time French told him that he was risking a second Sudan. Smith-Dorrien later replied to French, saying, "I have more to fear from the rear than from the front." French never sent a reply but relieved him of his command and recalled him to England in April 1915.[399]

The legend of the flowers

During the early days of farm burning, in the latter part of 1900, women and children were given ten minutes to gather their personal belongings and forced to watch their homes being burned to the ground by British troops. The defenceless victims were then chased away to fend for themselves on the open veld which had been denuded by British scorched-earth operations. The scattered family remnants would gather together and try to live off the land, sometimes under the protection of roving Boer commandos, to which they attached themselves and followed as best they could.

At this time an emotional incident occurred outside a small *hartebeeshuis* close to the town of Ventersdorp in the Western Transvaal.

A farm-burning contingent of the 1st Loyal North Lancs marched up to the *hartebeeshuis* and ordered the occupants to remove what personal belongings they could in ten minutes, then assemble in the orchard to witness their home being razed to the ground. One of the young women, 23-year-old Martha Engelbrecht, wept bitterly as she waited for the commanding officer's order to torch her home. A young soldier, Private George Shaw, took pity on Martha and felt so strongly about her plight that he took the unusual step of approaching his commanding officer directly (this should have been done through his non-commissioned officer). He remonstrated with the officer about the cruel and destructive farm-burning policy and demanded that this home be spared. The exasperated officer said, "Well, Shaw, if you don't like it, why don't you go and fight for the Boers?"

I don't know what happened to change the officer's mind but the *hartebeeshuis* was spared and still stands today in a dilapidated condition. However, Shaw did indeed desert and joined the Boers as an unarmed transport rider. He fell in love with Martha, the instigator of his desertion, and spent many happy hours with her, helping her with household chores and in the orchard. Today most of the orchard survives: there are ancient pear trees in a neat row. Sadly, the apple trees have long since died.

It was under their favourite apple tree that Martha and George became lovers. From their spot underneath this tree they had a good view of the *hartebeeshuis* that was flanked on the one side by a pepper tree and on the other by a cypress tree:, or *arbor vitae*, the tree of life.

While carrying out his duties as a transport rider for the Boers, George Shaw was captured by the British. By this time he had grown a beard and was dressed in rough Boer farm clothing so he was not recognized and managed to escape. He was captured a second time. There are two stories about how he came to be recognized: the first is that he was taken to Ventersdorp station with other Boer prisoners to await a train which would transport them to a prisoner of war camp. Rations were issued and George gave away his British military training by standing to attention when his meal was handed to him. The second story involves a suspicious NCO who unexpectedly barked at George to stand to attention. George instinctively did so and was led away. That night he was court-martialled, found guilty of treason and sentenced to death, to be shot the following day.

Private Shaw was executed in a very inhumane way. Instead of being shot blindfolded and standing up, he was seated and tied to a *riempie* chair. To increase his agony, the firing party deliberately missed with their first volley. He died in the second volley and his body was untied and buried in unconsecrated ground about 50 metres away from the British military section of the old Ventersdorp cemetery. Martha watched his cruel execution from her nearby hiding place in some bushes and her heart must have broken when his corpse was placed in his grave. She no doubt wished she were dead too, and buried with her lover. However, Martha had a very special reason to carry on: she was pregnant with George Shaw's child. She also had some precious verses from the Bible that they had shared and adopted together. 'Song of Songs' chapter 8 verses 6 and 7 would comfort her all her life, and would be read at her own funeral 57 years later.

After George was laid to rest, Martha planted a pepper tree (for bitterness) on the left of his grave and the *arbor vitae* (for life) on the right, to remind them both of the view from the apple orchard and the Bible verses that George had quoted to her from 'Song of Songs':

> Under the apple tree I woke you,
> In the place where you were born.
> Close your heart to every love but mine;
> Hold no one in your arms but me.
> Love is as powerful as death;
> Passion is as strong as death itself.
> It bursts into flame and burns like a raging fire.
> Water cannot put it out;
> No flood can drown it.

Although Martha later married, she remained faithful to George's memory. Early every

Friday morning for over 50 years, before the cemetery opened, she placed flowers on his grave. When she was nearly 80 years old, frail and suffering from cancer, she made a final visit to the grave and placed a casket of everlasting flowers on it. At Martha's funeral very few people knew the significance of the words quoted at her graveside by the minister: "Many waters cannot quench the fires of love, neither can the floods drown them." This is the first love story within the unfolding 'legend of the flowers'.

Going back in time to the year 1901, Martha gave birth to her son and married a friend of George's, John Fleischer. John gave his name to Martha and George's son and brought him up as his own. John Fleischer senior died on 12 May 1950 at the ripe age of 78, seven years before his wife, Martha. When I met his son in 2000, John junior told me about his happy childhood and wonderful relationship with his father. He was very touched when I promised to place flowers on his mother's and father's graves. This is the second love story in 'the legend': John Fleischer senior loved his adopted son as his own and saved him the humiliation of growing up fatherless in the unforgiving Edwardian age.

I met John Fleisher junior on his farm outside Ventersdorp when he was nearly 100 years old, in April 2000. He refused to discuss his mother and 'the legend', but his daughter-in-law privately confirmed the story to me in the kitchen. We had tea together and John gave me directions to his mother's and father's graves, as well as to the *hartebeeshuis* where Martha grew up. We said goodbye and when I promised to place flowers on his mother's and *both* fathers' graves, John broke down. He knew that I knew the story and that it was true. The third love story is that John never spoke about 'the legend' to protect his mother's reputation, and to honour his adoptive father.

The fourth part of the love story took place after I met John and was finalizing my manuscript for the first edition of *Anecdotes of the Anglo-Boer War*. Showing respect for John while he was still alive, I decided to omit the truth about his role as the 'love child' in my version of 'the legend of the flowers'. Instead, I merely mentioned that I had met Martha's son and I submitted a photograph of John for inclusion in the book. This is where a divine hand took over: by some mix-up every one of my photographs was published except this one! I now became part of a love story that had started during the Anglo-Boer War over a hundred years previously. I was protecting John Fleischer and his mother and divine intervention ensured that I did so properly.

I gave a talk to the Military History Society in August 2000 that concluded with 'The legend of the flowers' and I was asked to write a postscript to the original story which had already been posted on their website. Late on the night of 17 August I had just finished writing the postscript late that night when Martha Engelbrecht first 'spoke' to me. She said, "I have chosen you to tell my love story." I was absolutely shaken, disturbed by this silent and yet very emphatic message from beyond the grave.

I then added a comment to the postscript which still stands on that website today and

The back of the humble *hartebeeshuis* where Martha Engelbrecht grew up.

John and Martha Fleisher's grave in the old cemetery, Ventersdorp.

My wife, Bronislava, beside John Martin Fleischer's grave in the new Ventersdorp cemetery. According to my research, his date of birth should be 1901 not 1899.

Private George Shaw's cast-iron cross in 2000. The pepper tree planted on the left-hand side of his grave after his execution was removed in the early 1990s to make way for a storm-water drain. The cypress tree, *arbor vitae* or the tree of life, planted on the right of his grave remains. "The bitterness has gone [the pepper tree], and only life remains [the *arbor vitae*]."

Private George Shaw's cast-iron cross in 1987 framed by leaves of the pepper tree planted shortly after his execution, a symbol of bitterness.

John Martin Fleischer, the son of Martha Engelbrecht and Private George Shaw.

reminds me of the deep emotions I experienced that night: "Still deeply moved, I feel that Martha has shown us the special love that is in her heart, and is passing on that inspiration to enhance our own love relationships."

The next time that Martha spoke to me – in what I learned was her typically forceful way! – was on 16 February 2001 when I was mentally revising 'The legend' and other stories for a talk I was going to give in Walkerville, south of Johannesburg. She said, "You got it wrong in my story in your book. The words from 'Song of Songs' were George's words to me, not my words to him!" I quickly turned up page 138 and realized that she was right. The words in 'Song of Songs' say, "Under the apple tree I woke you, in the place where *you* were born." Yes, she was right: they fell in love under the apple tree at *Martha's* childhood home!

At this time, Bronislava and I were courting – she lived in Durban – and one day, early in October 2001, I was sitting by myself at the dining-room table when Martha spoke to me again: "My son is dying," she said. "I want Slava to meet him because I know that your love story will turn out the way that I wished for George Shaw and me." Bronislava and I decided that she should come to Hennops River the next weekend and we would go to Ventersdorp to visit John Fleischer. A week later a friend phoned to say that he had just heard that John had died.

As soon as we could, we went together to Ventersdorp and visited John's grave at the new Ventersdorp cemetery. Appropriately his epitaph reads, 'His life was peaceful, and he left it peacefully'. This is a direct follow-on to his mother's epitaph, "My peace I give you …' On 13 January 2004, while comparing the photo of George Shaw's grave taken in 1987 with that taken in 2000 (the pepper tree had been removed), Martha spoke to me again: "The bitterness has gone [the pepper tree] and only life remains [the *arbor vitae*]."

Theft

General Ben Viljoen had occasion to reprimand some commandos who had taken absence without leave. While he was reprimanding them, one of his two shirts, which he had hung out to dry, was stolen.[400]

Being short of firewood for cooking and heating, on 11 February 1901, the Boers uprooted all the wooden telegraph poles between Belfast and Dullstroom.[401]

As the Boers were preparing to leave Hectorspruit to escape the victorious British army, through what is today the Kruger National Park, they became adept at stealing from one another. "Cattle, wagons, saddles, harness and boxes of tinned dainties were stolen and re-stolen back and forth, countless times a day. Meeting Manie Mentz, I obtained from him for our journey, one case of cocoa, one of jam, and one of condensed milk. Then, while I went round the corner for further supplies, these were irrecoverably stolen."[402]

Too many chiefs

Confusion reigned as to which British officer was in charge on the summit of Spion Kop. General Warren, at the suggestion of General Buller, had appointed Colonel Thorneycroft in command after General Woodgate was mortally wounded but neglected to tell anyone except Thorneycroft. General Coke arrived later on the summit with reinforcements, thinking that he was now in command. When the Scottish Rifles under Colonel Cook arrived, being senior to Colonel Thorneycroft, Cook thought he was in command, and had an argument with Thorneycroft before going to General Coke for adjudication. Coke added to the confusion by declaring that he was in overall command but that another new arrival, Colonel Hill of the Middlesex Regiment, was the senior soldier on the summit.[403]

Later, General Warren completely forgot about his earlier appointment of Thorneycroft and asked General Coke to temporarily give command to Thorneycroft when he recalled Coke from the summit for consultations.[404]

Torture

During an attack on armed black men on 17 February 1902, a Boer called Venter went missing. His badly mutilated body was found five days later, having been tortured to death. While he was alive, his ears were cut off and both his legs chopped off above the knee. He lived until the morning when he was found by the lover of one of the blacks killed during the attack. "She sat alongside of the mutilated man and slowly thrust a spear into different parts of his body until he died."[405]

A black National Scout called Simon disappeared after a skirmish in the Orange Free State. A notice was found written in pencil on the whitewashed walls of a farmhouse: "Pray to God you're not caught for we will shoot every one of you as we did Simon and the English officer too who leads you, John Straightman." Simon's body was later found near a place called Doornbult. He had been shot in many places: through the knee, heart, breast, head and elbow. It was clear by signs on the ground that after his capture he had been tied to a horse's tail and dragged for about 400 yards with Boers shooting at him from a distance.[406]

Trafalgar

In the same spirit that Lord Nelson ignored orders at Trafalgar, Colonel Buchanan-Riddell of the 60th Rifles ignored General Lyttelton's lunatic order to abandon Twin Peaks during the Battle of Spion Kop. The capture of Twin Peaks was the only sensible move the British had made during the battle and would have led to their victory. At 6 p.m. Colonel Buchanan-Riddell was killed and, on being advised by Lyttelton that they would get no support from the thousands of idle soldiers in the camp, Major Bewicke-Copley, his second-in-command, withdrew his troops.[407]

Traitor's Nek

In the Lydenburg district there is a gap in the mountains (a saddle, or *nek* in Afrikaans) near Kruger's Post called Verraaiers (Traitor's) Nek. On 13 March 1901 Colonel Park was told about a Boer laager on a ridge to the north of Kruger's Post. His informant was Gert Vosloo, a Boer who had surrendered to the British and worked for them as an intelligence scout. Park's plan was to march at night and attack at dawn. He set out with a considerable force made up of three companies each of the Devons, the 2nd Rifle Brigade, the Royal Irish, Mounted Infantry and a company of the 19th Hussars, together with four guns and a pom-pom. His dawn attack was partially successful, killing two Boers, wounding three and capturing 36, for the loss of two men killed and four wounded, all from the Royal Irish Regiment. However, the Boer commandant, Piet Schwartz, and about 20 Boers managed to escape. Gert Vosloo's brother, Johannes Vosloo, had not been feeling well and had stayed overnight on his mother's farm. Early in the morning of 14 March he set out for the laager but was killed by the British en route. Gert was ostracized by his people after the war for betraying his people and his brother and this incident caused a major rift between the two brothers' families. Only 100 years later has there been some reconciliation between them. Both brothers are buried in the same family cemetery. The epitaph on Gert Vosloo's grave – the traitor – is Psalm 83, verse 3: "They are making secret plans against your people; they are plotting against those you protect." The epitaph on his brother Johannes's grave is 2 Samuel, chapter 1, verse 27: "The brave soldiers have fallen, their weapons abandoned and useless." Gert had an older brother who survived the war. When the older brother was on his deathbed Gert went to him, crawling up the steps into the house and begged his forgiveness. The answer was, "No. Only God can forgive you."

Treasure found

Camped at a farmhouse, a Boer set out a trail of mielies attached to fishhooks to capture a few chickens, which he succeeded in doing. Later he found a diamond in one chicken's stomach, which he sold for £9. After the war, he secured the right to prospect in the area and to purchase the farm at a nominal price. He successfully mined the diamonds and became a wealthy man.[408]

Trenches

Trenches were first used successfully at the Battle of Cerignola in 1503 when the Spanish defeated the French. However, de la Rey's use of trenches at Magersfontein caught the British by surprise. In spite of their observation balloons, the British did not detect a 20-kilometre defence line that consisted of carefully camouflaged trenches, stone sangars, and earthworks.[409]

Despite the system of blockhouses built along the railway lines, the Boer commandos persisted in crossing at night with their wagons, cattle and horses. In order to prevent their

The cross marks the spot where General Woodgate, in command at Spion Kop, was fatally wounded by a shell splinter at 8:30 a.m. He died a month after the battle and is buried in the Anglican Church cemetery in Mooi River.

The British main trench on Spion Kop extends northeast toward Aloe Knoll in the centre distance. Many of the soldiers in this section of the trench suffered fatal wounds in the right side of their heads as the trench was enfiladed by Boer snipers on Aloe Knoll. Twin Peaks are in the middle distance just above the twin crosses on the top of the trench.

A surviving example of the trenches dug parallel to the railway lines to prevent the Boers crossing them at night with their supply wagons. My son Simon stands in this one which is near the Belfast station and runs between the remains of two rice-pattern blockhouses.

The grave of the Boer traitor Gert Vosloo at Verraaiers Nek near Lydenburg. *Photo: Marion Moir*

wagons from crossing, the British dug trenches hundreds of kilometres parallel to the railway line. A good example, which has survived the years, can be seen between Wonderfontein and Belfast in Mpumalanga.

Tribute

After the war, General Botha realized that the only hope for South Africa lay in reconciling the differences between English and Dutch, and that some grand gesture should be made. Accordingly, in August 1907, he proposed to the Transvaal government that they acquire the recently discovered Cullinan diamond and present it to King Edward. The gift was to be a token of the loyalty of the people of the Transvaal and in commemoration of the grant of responsible government. The king was advised to refuse the gift because the Transvaal was "too poor to make such a kingly gift". He finally accepted it as "The token of the loyalty and attachment of the people of the Transvaal to my throne and person". When the diamond was cut the largest portion, 516.5 ct, went into the king's crown and another gem of 309 ct was set aside for the queen's crown.[410]

During the conference of Versailles at the end of the First World War, Lord Milner (the man regarded by the Boers as having instigated the Anglo-Boer War) and General (now Prime Minister) Botha met again. For once, they were in agreement, both being in favour of offering moderate terms to Germany. Botha addressed the Empire delegation to the conference as follows: "Seventeen years ago my friend [Milner] and I made peace at Vereeniging – it was a bitter peace for us, bitter hard, but we turned our thoughts and efforts then to saving our people; and they, the victors, helped us. It was a hard peace for us to accept, but as I know it now, when time has shown us the truth, it was not unjust – it was a generous peace that the British made with us, and that is why we stand with them today, side by side in the cause which has brought us all together."[411] If Botha's and Milner's views on moderate peace terms had prevailed, the stage for Hitler's ascent to power may never have been set.

Underwear

The British captured the personal female belongings of the Russian–Dutch ambulance, which was assisting the Boers, shortly before Pretoria surrendered. In gentlemanly fashion they were returned to the nurses in St Petersburg some time later.[412]

Commandant Schoeman had his laager at Die Berg, a prominent position east of Lydenburg. The Rifle Brigade drove him from his laager after an attack and a few days later, a cape-cart approached the British camp at Lydenburg under a white flag. When the elderly Boer driver was asked why he had come in a cart and not on a horse, he replied that he had a letter from his commandant for the British general and that he knew the contents. The British had taken the trunk containing the commandant's underwear when they looted the camp. "Now, if your general agrees," Schoeman wrote, "that robbing a man of his spare vests and pants is not playing the game in civilized warfare, the necessary articles may be restored, and I cannot carry a portmanteau on horseback."

The general returned the underwear and the old burgher remarked to his escort as he left, "You English fight fair."[413]

Unfortunate decision

At nightfall on the day of the Battle of Spion Kop, the British were in a favourable position in spite of the terrible slaughter that had occurred Artillery was on its way up, as were reinforcements, sandbags and communication equipment. The Boers had largely abandoned the Kop and Thorneycroft's men were tired but determined to stick it out. Suddenly rifle fire flared up on the British right flank. This was just enough to break Thorneycroft's resolve and he gave orders to abandon Spion Kop. Unbeknown to him, the fire came from just a handful of burghers led by Commandant Prinsloo trying to recover his brother's body before abandoning the Kop. Although Thorneycroft was exhausted and sickened by the slaughter, he made three tactical mistakes after nightfall which turned the British victory into a humiliating defeat: he made no attempt to reconnoitre the Boer positions after dark; with 5,000 men at his disposal on the Kop, he made no attempt to probe the Boers with a night attack; when abandoning the Kop he gave no consideration to leaving a small holding force, and there was no determined attempt to remove all the wounded.[414]

Unidentified flying objects

On 24 October 1899, soon after the commencement of the war, two mysterious disks were observed moving in the night sky over the Transvaal, from Irene in the Pretoria area toward Springs near Johannesburg. They were accompanied by "searchlights moving about the sky" and were reported to General Joubert as being possible British observation balloons. If the balloons had already arrived in South Africa, they were many hundreds of miles away and no explanation was ever forthcoming. Today, this event would have been classified as a UFO sighting.[415]

Uniforms

By July 1901, Boer uniforms were getting really interesting. "He wore knickerbockers, his bulging calves were enclosed in a pair of lady's stockings, and in his hat he sported a white feather. The assemblage looked very much like a cannibal fancy dress meeting. One officer wore a jacket of monkey skin, hair to the outside; another officer a jacket of leopard skin. One looked a cross between Attila the Hun, and Sancho Panza. Others wore odd garments of sheep, goat and deerskin, and of green baize and gaudily coloured blankets. Quite evidently the apparel does not here proclaim the man. Only last week, a man who bore the remains of one of his friends to the grave was decked out in green baize trousers and a dress suit jacket."[416]

"Kokkie addressed the court, emphasizing with his right hand, while with his left he held up his trousers, and in some fashion kept together also his coat which was split open the whole length of his back."[417]

During the final, successful attempt to relieve Ladysmith, a Prussian officer, Colonel von Braun, was taken prisoner. The Tommies were fascinated by the fact that he wore an oilskin coat reinforced with steel netting.[418]

In September 1901, Schikkerling's commando passed through a village in the northeastern Transvaal and was greeted enthusiastically by the local women and children. "We who were gaily dressed rode up to them and accepted flowers and milk; others had no trousers, or were clothed in grain bags and bits of blanket or carpet, kilt-fashion, rode on the far side. Fortunately I was able to put my best foot forward, and the boot showing my sunburned toes remained on the starboard side. I was dressed for a left-hand view."[419]

Unique souvenir
During the fighting at Pont Drift near Ladysmith a bullet struck General Meyer's field-glasses, flattened itself and dropped into one of his coat pockets. He made a brooch out of it and gave it to his wife.[420]

Unwanted gratitude
After the successful night attack by General Muller on Monument Hill, also known as Fosberry's Post, near Belfast, piercing cries for help were heard from a deep and open latrine. "Someone risked going forward, and by holding down his gun, with much difficulty, rescued the half-drowned man, who said his leg had been shot off. The soldier in his misery kept hopping after his saviour, who, holding his nostrils, shouted, 'Don't come so close!'"[421] Manned by 83 men of the 1st The Royal Irish Regiment under Captain Fosberry, the garrison was overwhelmed after a desperate fight in which Fosberry was one of the 40 men killed or wounded. Private J. Barry was posthumously awarded the Victoria Cross for gallantry in rendering the post's Maxim gun useless.[422]

Useless booty
The morning after the Heidelbergers' looting of the wrecked goods train near Greylingstad, they opened a large chest labelled 'Handle with Care'. There was much amusement when they found that it contained wax dolls and dolls' prams.[423]

Die Berg near Dullstroom, the site of Commandant Schoeman's laager.

A 'four in hand', an example of Victorian pornography.

The main British trench on the eastern side of Spion Kop. Owing to the rocky ground the trenches were only 40 centimetres (16 inches) deep, affording the soldiers little cover. After the battle the British dead were buried in the trenches, hence the rocks that had to be piled on top of the shallow graves.

A contemporary stereoscope photograph entitled 'Kit inspection Cape Town docks'.

The monument at Monument Hill erected on 15 December 1886 at the place that was renamed Fosberry's Post during the British occupation of Belfast. There are numerous bullet marks on the monument as a result of General Muller's night attack on the Royal Irish Regiment under the command of Captain Fosberry.

With soldiers hot on their heels, two burghers raided some Indian stores near Vereeniging and quickly grabbed anything they could. When they reached their camp they were disappointed to find that much of the booty consisted of women's underwear and baby clothes.[424]

Vegetables

Veldkornet van As and his commando ambushed two carts and a mule cart laden with fresh vegetables, destined for the National Scouts in Heidelberg. The three drivers, two of whom they knew well from pre-war days, were made to strip. The Boers then placed pumpkins on their heads and made them walk back to Heidelberg.[425]

Mielies were the most important source of food for the Boer commandos. "It is our meat and drink and all that sustains our animals. It is eaten green and ripe, boiled and roasted, in porridge and in cakes. It is also toasted and treated as 'coffee'. Take it away and we could not remain in the field ten days longer. Without it we would have had to abandon the war more than a year ago. A mielie cob should be on our coat of arms, to which it has more claim than all the fond images thereon."[426] Schikkerling's wish was granted nearly 100 years later when a mielie cob was incorporated into the coat of arms of the North West Province.

Before the war General Christian de Wet attempted to buy the entire supply of potatoes in South Africa with the intention of becoming the sole supplier of potatoes to the Johannesburg market. However, in attempting to push up the price, he held onto his potatoes for too long. The new crop was harvested and as a consequence he had to file for bankruptcy. Later, he appeared as a potato farmer near Kroonstad and, still later, at Nicholson's Nek in Natal where he captured 1,200 British prisoners and, incidentally, a large stock of British potatoes which seemed to please him almost as greatly as the human captives.

War graves

During the war British soldiers were buried close to where they fell which has proved to be of great value to military historians searching for skirmish and battle sites. However, this has been an obstacle to farmers, dam- and road-builders, and urban developers. In the 1960s the War Graves Commission supervised the exhumation and relocation of scattered graves and small cemeteries into the bigger towns. In Krugersdorp, for example, there is a memorial to the hundreds of soldiers who have been reburied there, and the lists of names by regiment – and sometimes date of death – do not have any additional details and hardly attract notice. Nevertheless, there are often interesting stories attached to these names. The second name listed under 'Kitchener's Horse' on the memorial in Krugersdorp cemetery is that of Lieutenant Borghys (spelt elsewhere as Borghuys). On Thursday, 29 November 1900, Sergeant-Major Carpenter demanded a weekend pass from his lieutenant. When this was refused he shot Lieutenant Borghys. Needless to say, Carpenter was court-martialled and executed on 18 December 1900. Carpenter's grave is unrecorded but is probably located outside of consecrated ground as was the practice at the time.

Lists of new graves were made by the Guild of Loyal Women, which later became the Victoria League and then became defunct. Cast-iron crosses in various designs were procured from different factories in Cape Town, and the Guild was subsidized to the tune of half a crown per cross by the government. The ladies' spelling and writing were not the best, hence a lot of discrepancies between the information on the crosses and the burial records. Only one name register has survived; the other registers must be in safekeeping somewhere but they have never been found.

Close to the grave of Captain Meyrick in the Maraisburg cemetery, Roodepoort, is a cast-iron cross dated 12 January 1906 to the memory of Nurse Lydia Gluyas who died at the age of forty-eight. In 1989, as I commenced research on this grave with the National Monuments Council, a great-nephew of Lydia's wrote to the Council from New Zealand to inquire about her last resting place. Mr Carruthers, her great-nephew, wrote to say that Lydia had been a nurse at various hospitals around London and had joined up as an army nurse during the war, when there was a call for 'Young ladies of good character and address' to go to South Africa. She put her age back by six years and was accepted for service. She fell in love with South Africa and after the war decided to live here, but only enjoyed peace for four years. According to Mr Carruthers, "She was quite an accomplished artist and used to send my mother several paintings and drawings she made around South Africa. Sadly, few if any have survived over the years, and I think it may be due to a poor war-time grade of paper which just crumbled away to powder."

On exhumation and relocation of war graves to make way for 'progress', a South African archaeologist, Elizabeth Voight of the Transvaal Museum, commented in her 1984 report, 'Report on Military Burials on the Farm Elandspruit, District Lydenburg': "I believe that more honour would have been given to the dead if the gravestones alone had been moved and a simple monument erected above the future water level of the dam, indicating that the original place of rest lay beneath the waters."

Her account of the exhumation of the Strathcona Horse mass grave is interesting: "The length of the grave and the extended position of the leg bones suggest that the men may have been buried in a sitting position with their legs extended straight in front of them." We sometimes find mass graves which are aligned north–south instead of east–west (e.g. Chievely) and this would be a logical explanation. Also of interest from this report (and for the information of would-be grave robbers), very few artefacts remain in anything like recognizable condition due to the generally acidic nature of the soil in South Africa.

General Andy Wauchope, killed at Magersfontein, was buried at Matjiesfontein, hundreds of kilometres away. This is reputed to be as a result of a misunderstanding.[427]

Baden-Powell's simple grave in Nyeri, Kenya, shows his name, title, dates of birth and death and the Boy Scout trail sign for 'I have gone home': a dot within a circle.[428]

Warrior women

During the fighting at Pieter's Hill on 28 February 1900, which resulted in the relief of Ladysmith, a Boer woman aged 19 was captured by the British forces. She had been fatally wounded and before she died she told her captors that she had been fighting in the same trench with her husband and that he had been killed only a few minutes before she received her fatal wound.[429]

Mrs Otto Krantz, the wife of a professional hunter, fought beside her husband throughout the Natal campaign. "In the Battle of Elandslaagte, where some of the hardest hand-to-hand fighting of the war occurred, this Amazon was by the side of her husband in the thick of the engagement, but escaped unscathed.[430]

Helena Herbst Wagner of Zeerust was a spunky Boer woman who spent five months in the laagers and trenches without her identity being revealed. Under Commandant Viljoen she faced the bullets, shells and lyddite at Spion Kop, Pont Drift and Pieter's Hill.[431]

Water

Springs were found halfway up Spion Kop which gave the troops some relief.[432] During their retreat the troops slaked their thirst there until they were told that the medics had been using the water to wash out wounds.[433]

A man was having a relaxing bath on his veranda in Ladysmith when a shell bounced off a tree and hit the house without exploding. It then rolled along the veranda and upset the bathtub and its fortunate occupant.[434]

Toward the end of the siege of Ladysmith, a German engineer arrived to supervise the construction of a dam on the Klip River intended to flood the town. On Sunday, 25 February 1900 the Anglican vicar appropriately preached a sermon on Noah and the great flood.[435] The Boer attempt was unsuccessful.

With the Highveld winter setting in, the colonel of the 1st Rifle Brigade issued orders forbidding any man to wash himself before 11.00 a.m. "He does not like cold water himself!"

Consolidated war grave in Krugersdorp cemetery, including Lieutenant Borghuys, Kitchener's Horse.

The grave of Nurse Gluyas in Maraisburg cemetery, Roodepoort. Her cast-iron cross has since been stolen and replaced with a small granite memorial.

Lord Baden-Powell's grave in Kenya. His epitaph, a dot within a circle, is the Boy Scouts' trail symbol for 'I have gone home'. He was the British hero in the defence of Mafeking and formed the Boy Scouts to assist in the siege. *Reproduced by the kind permission of The Scout Association Trustees*

This is how the military section of the Maraisburg cemetery now appears. Small granite headstones have replaced the stolen cast-iron crosses and smashed stone headstones. Nurse Gluyas died in 1906 and Corporal Andrews died of wounds received at the Battle of Doornkop, 29 May 1900.

was Private Tucker's comment. On 6 June 1900 nine men were caught bathing a few minutes before 11.00 a.m. and sentenced to eight days' defaulters. "Another typical indication of the sort of man we have in charge of us."[436]

What if?
What if Winston Churchill had been wounded at the Battle of Spion Kop? Mahatma Ghandi, who was a stretcher-bearer there, might have taken him to the field hospital. Instead, they became bitter adversaries in later life, with Churchill referring to him as, "That half-naked fakir."[437]

White flag
Captain R.C.H. Miers of the South African Constabulary, based in Heidelberg, visited the Boer commandos under a white flag to persuade them to give up the struggle. On 25 September 1901, he approached Veldkornet van As and two burghers in their observation post. Van As sent one of the burghers, Louis Slabbert, to meet Miers to ensure that he did not get too close to the observation post. After refusing to stop, Miers, who was armed with a revolver, rode up to van As and du Toit. A shot was fired and Miers fell off his horse, dead, his revolver rolling away. Van As claimed that Miers drew his revolver and aimed at him before he shot him. After the war, in spite of General Louis Botha's assurances that he would not be harmed, van As was tried by the British and sentenced to death. On 23 June 1902 van As was executed by a ten-man firing squad of the Somersets at the back of the old Heidelberg gaol. His body was dumped in a pan 600 metres away but he was later reburied in the Kloof cemetery (near Miers). The British government later admitted to van As's father that he had not been given a fair trial and that the conviction and sentence were unjust.[438]

Wild animals
Leading up to the Battle of Bergendal, during the engagement between the Liverpool Regiment and the Heidelberg Commando at Geluk, a steenbok burst through the British lines heading toward the Boers. Both sides fired at him and at times it was completely covered in dust from the near-misses. However, it disappeared into the ridges unscathed and the soldiers resumed their fight.[439]

Near Fourteen Streams a lyddite shell exploded at the entrance to a jackal's lair. The animal bounded out of another entrance and ran off, tail between its legs.[440]

In 1962 gunner Archie Wilson recalled an incident in the Eastern Transvaal: "There was no reserve [i.e. the Kruger National Park] when I was in South Africa; in fact, we had an outpost killed by lions one night. That happened in the bushvelde away near Amsterdam in the very far Eastern Transvaal."

When camped near Moordenaar's Poort in the Northern Cape, and hard-pressed by the British, Smut's commando was rendered helpless for a number of hours by a porcupine. It had wandered through the camp at night and stampeded the horses.[441]

At the height of the Battle of Three Tree Hill on 20 January 1900, a hare dashed through the British infantry. About a hundred men leaped up from their firing positions and chased the hare, regardless of danger, but it got away safely.[442]

General de Wet, when challenged by General Joubert on his decision to give the burghers two weeks' leave after the fall of Bloemfontein, responded: "I cannot catch a hare, general, with unwilling dogs."[443]

A painted rectangle highlights the bullet marks from Veldkornet van As's execution by a ten-man firing squad of the Somersets on 23 June 1902. One of the conditions of the peace treaty was that van As would be handed over to the British for trial as a result of a 'white flag' incident in which Captain Miers of the Somersets was killed on 25 September 1901.

Lieutenant Miers of the Somersetshire Light Infantry, serving as a captain with the South African Constabulary, was killed in a 'white flag' incident by Veldkornet van As. Van As was tried and (wrongfully) executed for this crime after the war and is now buried near his victim.

Appendices

Appendix 1
The Jameson Raid: military conflict and aftermath

After reading the 'women and children' letter purportedly from the reformers in Johannesburg, Jameson left Pitsani, Bechuanaland for the Transvaal on Sunday, 29 December 1895 with 356 men and 16 officers of the Rhodesian Mashonaland Mounted Police (MMP). He crossed the border at 5 o'clock the next morning where he united with the Bechuanaland Border Police (BBP) at Malmani (now Ottoshoop) which had assembled at Mafeking under Major Coventry. The latter force was far more experienced than the MMP but, after numerous desertions, consisted only of 113 men and nine officers. With the 17 staff officers, Jameson's total force totalled 511 officers and men, 150 native drivers, 640 horses, 158 mules, and eleven carts. His armaments consisted of eight Maxims (with 45,000 rounds), Lee-Metford rifles (with 50,000 rounds), two 7-pounders and one 12-pound cannon. A number of food stores had been positioned along the 174-mile route, although due in part to harassment from the Boers, these proved to be inadequate and, by the third day of their ride, the men were exhausted from hunger and lack of sleep. The remounts provided at Malan's farm turned out to be useless as most of them were coach horses and this inconvenience necessitated a halt every seven hours to rest the tired beasts.

The telegraph wires to Pretoria and Cape Town had been cut before the border was crossed, but a small branch line connecting Zeerust indirectly with Pretoria was overlooked. President Kruger was thus continuously informed of the raiders' progress by the Boer horsemen who shadowed the column after it had crossed into the Transvaal. On Tuesday evening, 31 December 1895, Jameson ran into Lieutenant Sarel Johannes Eloff (a grandson of President Kruger's) at Boon's store, where he promptly disarmed and arrested him. Jameson then released Lieutenant Eloff after making him promise to remain at the store for two hours after the raiders' departure. Jameson's light-hearted remark that he could fetch his rifle in Pretoria was later used to prove that the object of the raid was to enslave Pretoria rather than free Johannesburg.

Growing numbers of Boer commandos followed the column closely until the afternoon of New Year's Day. During this time Jameson had received, and ignored, various urgent messages from both the Boers and the British urging him to return to Bechuanaland. At about half past one, Jameson's force left Hind's store, about seven miles from Krugersdorp, and soon came upon a Boer force occupying a 400-foot-high ridge. Jameson brought his guns to bear and the Boers retreated.

The raiders now faced the Boers under General Cronjé at the ruined Queen's Mine just to the west of Krugersdorp. The Boers occupied the old mine workings, farm buildings and the stamp-battery building on the westward-facing slope, with a stream and vlei in front of them. Willoughby, the military commander, ordered the shelling of the Boer positions but this appeared to have no effect. He then led a charge in an attempt to storm the ridge but was beaten off with heavy losses.

The raiders then turned south toward Randfontein under the directions of a guide who was later thought to have been a Boer agent. Gunfire was heard from the direction of Krugersdorp and Willoughby, dumping his baggage in the road, turned back to effect a junction with the supposed relief force of Reformers from Johannesburg. However, this turned out to be the Boers celebrating the arrival of their artillery from Pretoria. As it was almost dark, Jameson and his raiders established a campsite on the edge of a large vlei near the Krugersdorp–Randfontein–Potchefstroom railway line. Here they spent a miserable night subjected to incessant fire from the Boers sheltering behind the railway line.

"It was then decided to form laager and a camp was eventually pitched in a suitable position on the brink of a large vlei with precipitous sides affording excellent cover. Hardly were the squares formed, when the Boers again opened fire, killing one man and wounding several. Orders were immediately given that no lights were to be lit in the camp, the only light allowed being in the tent of one of the wagons temporarily used as a hospital for the wounded. This light afforded a good mark for the Boers, who kept up an incessant fire, the rattle of the guns being deafening. Most of their bullets, however, went overhead on account of the well-chosen position occupied by the column. The Boers were also very advantageously placed behind the Potchefstroom railway earthworks. A lot of the troopers' horses stampeded and were lost. Some of the troop took advantage of their position to snatch a few hours sleep, notwithstanding the din caused by the firing of the Boers, who evidently intended to harass the now worn-out men."[444]

Two troopers were killed that night and were buried on the spot in shallow graves: "… they were buried with less pomp than the dead at Corunna. Next day a visitor to the battlefield was shocked to see the feet of one of these poor fellows sticking out from the heap of earth which his comrades had shovelled over him."[445] A headstone was later erected over the graves of troopers Beatty-Powell and Davies – presumably after they were properly buried. In the early 1980s the graves were exhumed and the headstone was moved to the small cemetery next to the Krugersdorp–Randfontein railway line because of the encroachment of recycling activities from the adjacent mine dump.

At 5 a.m. on Thursday, 2 January 1896, the raiders set off in a southerly direction before turning east toward the farm Doornkop. Surrounded on all sides and faced by the Staats Artillerie, they occupied an area around the farmhouse and a stone kraal. After a period of intense firing from both sides, Jameson surrendered. The raiders' casualties totalled 16 other ranks killed in action, one officer and 14 other ranks severely wounded, with three officers and 38 other ranks slightly wounded: a total of 72 casualties. The badly wounded officer and five troopers subsequently died of their wounds. Captain Barry of the BBP died on 31

January 1896 and is buried in the old Krugersdorp cemetery, next to troopers Wiid and Fraser who also died of their wounds.

Roodepoort residents say that their relatives watched the action at Doornkop from the headgear on Durban Deep Mine and Krugersdorp residents claim that their relatives brought baskets of food to the hungry and exhausted troopers who were kept under guard in the market square in front of the magistrate's court. "On they went to the market square and there dismounted. Some of them at once fell asleep at their horses' feet. Jameson, Willoughby, and the rest of the officers were ushered into the courthouse on the edge of the square, where the defeated doctor made his way into a corner, and sat down in a veritable stupor of despair. Baskets of food were brought in (but Jameson would not eat) and provisions were given to the troops in the square. Cronjé meanwhile was holding a general inquiry in the courthouse, and when this was over the move to Pretoria began!"[446]

According to the *Standard and Diggers News* at the time, "On 2nd January 1896 Jameson had surrendered at Doornkop (near Krugersdorp) and as far as can be ascertained the Johannesburg Vrijwilliger [Volunteer] Corps took no part in the actual action; but from information gleaned from one Leon Kooyker, I learned that Commandant van Diggelen and members of his mounted troops escorted Jameson and some of his followers, through the night, from Krugersdorp to Pretoria." *The Star* newspaper reported on Friday 3 January, "The Volunteer Cavalry with 20 prisoners arrived in town late last night. Jameson, Willoughby and Col. White, the latter two in uniform, were brought in by Commandant Erasmus and party shortly after nine o'clock and located at the goal. They look very haggard. The balance of Jameson's force, some six hundred men, are close to town in charge of a strong escort. They will be camped on the commonage for the present."[447]

The six hundred men referred to in *The Star* is significant. Five hundred and eleven officers and men and 150 drivers crossed the Transvaal border as the raiding party: a total of 661 men. The epitaph of the raid is inscribed on three metal crosses over the graves of three of the troopers (Hennessey, Foster and Bletsoe) next to the Krugersdorp–Randfontein railway line: "Theirs was not to reason why, Theirs was but to do or die." This is a quotation from Alfred, Lord Tennyson's poem 'The Charge of the Light Brigade'. Perhaps the next line should also have been added: "Into the Valley of Death rode the six hundred."

Jameson and his raid inspired the poem *If-* by Rudyard Kipling which is still Great Britain's favourite poem according to a poll conducted by the BBC programme *The Bookworm* in 1995 (much to the BBC's chagrin).[448] The result of the abortive raid is summed up in the third verse:

> If you can make one heap of all your winnings,
> And risk it on one turn of pitch-and-toss,
> And lose, and start again at your beginnings,
> And never breathe a word about your loss.

In later life Jameson refused to discuss the raid and would even leave the room if the subject was raised.

A stone memorial marks the surrender site at Doornkop, where the names of 20 of the raiders are recorded, together with four of the Boers who fell. Two of the troopers' names have been omitted from this monument (Beatty-Powell and Davies), as well as one of the Boers (van Tonder). Captain Barry's name is recorded as 'Captain Barr'. Thus the final tally of those who fell is 22 raiders and five Boers. Twelve of the raiders were buried in a prospector's trench on Doornkop farm, five next to the Krugersdorp–Randfontein railway line and five in the old Krugersdorp cemetery close to the elaborate memorial to the five Boers who fell. This memorial records that Boer George Jacobs was shot while trying to give water to a wounded enemy.

Lieutenant Sarel Eloff is also buried in the old Krugersdorp cemetery. According to some authorities, Eloff took the first news of Jameson's surrender to Pretoria. Three months after the raid he was involved in a drunken brawl at the Krugersdorp races and is reported to have said, "All Englishmen are bastards and the Queen of England is a xxxx!" He was tried for this offence and acquitted, then promoted to the position of senior lieutenant of police in Pretoria. He died in Middleburg on 10 May 1926.

After being held for some months under appalling conditions in goal in Pretoria, Dr Jameson, Sir John Willoughby, Major Coventry and the two Colonel Whites were handed over to the British for trial and the prisoners were returned to England. They were tried in London and sentenced to various prison terms of between five and 15 months; however, Jameson and Coventry were soon released due to ill health. The junior officers and men were sent off to the town of Volksrust on the Natal border where they were incarcerated in wool sheds before being handed over to a British escort and taken to Natal. Later, Jameson became prime minister of the Cape Colony (1904–08) and one of the founders of the Union of South Africa.

The four Jameson raiders' graves next to the Randfontein–Krugersdorp railway line.

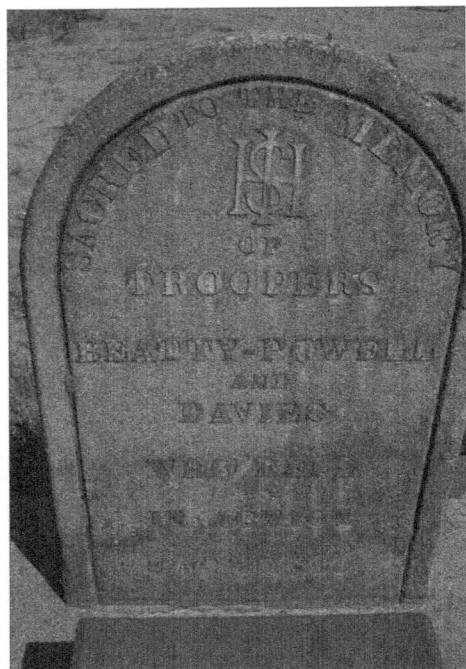

The Jameson raiders' graves of troopers Beatty-Powell and Davis next to the railway line at Randfontein.

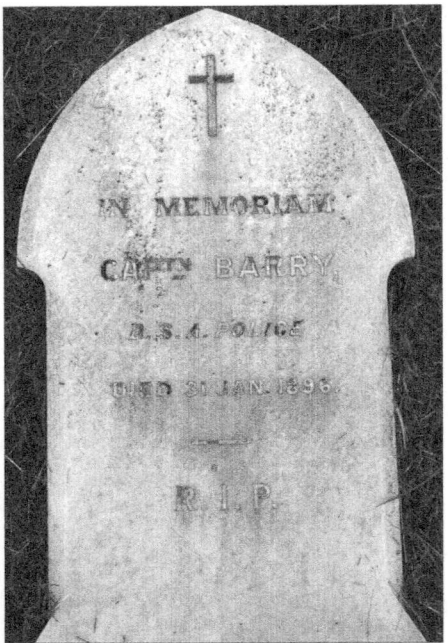

The headstone of Captain Barry, BSA Police, who was killed during the Jameson Raid.

The graves of four of the BSA Police in Krugersdorp cemetery. Captain Barry's headstone on the left has been pushed over and the elaborate cast-iron railing around the grave on the extreme right has been stolen and no doubt sold to a scrapyard. The Boer memorial is in the far distance.

The memorial in Krugersdorp cemetery to the five Boers killed during the Jameson Raid.

The four intact Jameson raiders' headstones in Krugersdorp cemetery 15 years ago. The elaborate cast-iron railings and inscriptions on the right-hand grave of Trooper Lamb have since disappeared.

The old magistrate's court in Krugersdorp which was built in 1890. The captured officers who took part in the Jameson Raid spent a few hours in the holding gaol behind the courthouse while the captured men were being fed in the town square in front of the magistrate's court.

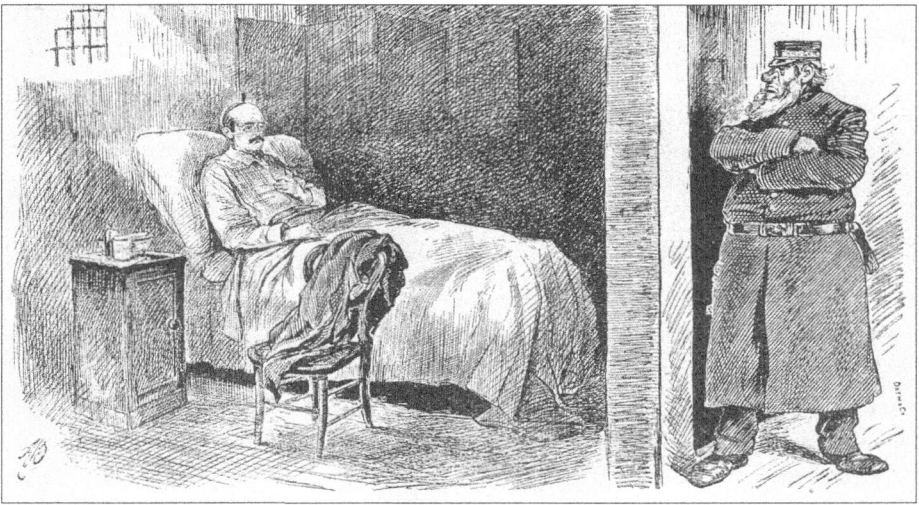

Dr Jameson and his warder (President Kruger).

Appendix 2
The development of the British blockhouse system during the Anglo-Boer War

February and March 1900 marked a turning point in the war for British forces. After the victory at Paardeberg and the relief of Ladysmith, they advanced rapidly on Bloemfontein and Pretoria, largely alongside the railway lines which were vital for bringing up fresh troops and massive quantities of supplies. By 22 September 1900, the British had occupied Hectorspruit on the Mozambican border and found themselves in control of a vast territory which could not be adequately administered. The Boers began attacking their lines of communication and the British were forced to safeguard the railway stations and bridges. The erection of permanent masonry blockhouses thus commenced. Eventually 441 were built, designed and supervised by the Royal Engineers. Many of these single-, double- and three-storey blockhouses still survive in various states of disssrepair.

The single-storey blockhouses did not have machicouli galleries to cover the blockhouse walls themselves. An early Boer tactic was to rush the walls and fire rifles through the loopholes where the bullets would ricochet around the inside of the blockhouse, causing the occupants to surrender. Consequently, the British had to add new walls on the corners of these blockhouses in order to cover the main walls.

The troops occupying the smaller towns designed and built their own makeshift stone and mortar forts without the supervision of the Royal Engineers. The 2nd Battalion Royal Dublin Fusiliers built their own fort, Fort Craig, above the Kenmare dam just outside Krugersdorp. This fort was rediscovered in 1986 and a meticulous site recording was undertaken by members of the South African Archaeology Society under the leadership of my late friend and mentor, David Panagos. An unusual feature of Fort Craig was the carefully designed crenallations, or loopholes, which provided the defenders with maximum arc of fire and protection from bullets angled into the firing loops.

The Krugersdorp town council erected a protective razor-wire fence around the fort; however, a couple of years later both the fence and the fort were flattened by a bulldozer to make room for a golf-driving range. No legal action was taken against the new lessee of this town council property but the fragility of our heritage sites was brought to the attention of the council and local residents. Soon after Fort Craig was destroyed, a proposal to demolish the old magistrate's court in the centre of Krugersdorp (where the Jameson raiders were briefly detained) was declined. The proposed new 5-star hotel would not have been a fitting replacement for one of the oldest official buildings still standing in the province.

Masonry blockhouses became too expensive and slow to build and experiments were made using various plans based on the principle of using a double wall of corrugated-iron sheets, with the gap in between filled with gravel and small stones. The advantages of this kind of structure were that it was cheap and quick to erect and could be erected by 'unskilled labour', i.e. ordinary soldiers instead of Royal Engineers. A few square and rectangular blockhouses were erected before the later rice-pattern circular blockhouse became the standard and was widely rolled-out throughout the country. As far as I am aware, the only surviving example of an experimental rectangular blockhouse is in Barberton.

Early in 2012, I was shocked at the condition of the Barberton blockhouse, compared to 12 years ago. The heavy steel door, with its brass National Monument plaque, has been stolen, as has the barbed wire around the base of the blockhouse. The roof and corrugated-iron walls are rusting and in a state of disrepair, and squatters have moved in. The immediate area is strewn with rubbish, making for an unpleasant visit to a potentially interesting tourist attraction. I am told, however, that plans are afoot by the Friends of the Museum, Barberton, to restore the structure.

There is an interesting twist to the location of the Barberton blockhouse: luckily it was never attacked by the Boers, as it can easily be enfiladed from three sides. It is therefore up in the ratings with two masonry blockhouses that were built with a similar lack of foresight: 'Fort Mistake' near Volksrust and 'Barton's Folly' near Hekpoort.

In March 1901, Major Spring R. Rice of the Royal Engineers designed a circular corrugated-iron blockhouse which was then widely manufactured and erected in blockhouse 'lines' across the country. The Boers had very few guns by this time and the rice-pattern blockhouse was only designed to protect its eight-man garrison from rifle fire. The components were manufactured in kit form in various railway workshops and transported for erection on site. A 1.3-metre-deep trench was first dug around the area and the blockhouse was assembled on a rock platform. Fifteen-centimetre wooden wedges were placed between the two corrugated-iron circles to keep them the correct distance apart and then the space in between was filled with sand and pebbles. These blockhouses were situated within rifle range of each other and connected with barbed-wire fences to hinder the free movement of Boer commandos. Eventually 6,883 corrugated-iron blockhouses were built to cover a total distance of 6,000 kilometres. After the war the corrugated iron was sold on auction or given to burghers returning home.

This is a three-storey British blockhouse built to guard the railway line, bridge and river crossing. It is one of 441 masonry blockhouses designed by Major-General Elliot Wood. They had steel portholes and machicouli galleries (battlements with openings in the floor and walls) to cover the blockhouse itself in case the Boers reached the walls. This blockhouse housed about 25 men and has a retractable steel access ladder.

This double-storey British blockhouse is situated high on a mountain in the Magaliesberg overlooking Hartebeespoort dam. The design is distinctive to the area where mountain passes had to be defended and has become known as a Magaliesberg-pattern blockhouse. These examples have crenellated parapet walls on the top floor which protect the flat roof. This photograph was taken in 1969 by my late father with me on the parapet.

An unusual British single-storey square masonry blockhouse at Jacobsdal, Free State. There is no protection in the event of the Boers rushing the walls and the water tank is totally exposed to gunfire.

This is a double-storey rectangular British masonry blockhouse in Krugersdorp which guarded the main road to Johannesburg. Two bastions were added on to opposite corners as an afterthought: see the single-storey extension on the left-hand side. These were subsequently added to enfilade the walls after the Boers developed the tactic of storming right up to the walls and firing their rifles through the loopholes. The devastating effect of Boer bullets ricocheting around the inside of the confined space of the blockhouse resulted in a few surrenders. The reason that this blockhouse has survived 112 years in such good condition is that soon after the end of the war it was recycled as an electrical sub-station.

In 1986 an unusual masonry structure was found on a hill above the Kenmare dam in Monument township, Krugersdorp. David Panagos and a team from the South African Archaeological Society cleared the site and conducted detailed site recordings. We concluded that this was the long-lost Fort Craig, built by the British as part of the defences of Krugersdorp in late 1900.

Fort Craig, Krugersdorp: detail of one of the crenallations. A crenallation is a rampart built around a fort with regular gaps for firing guns. The crenallations on this fort provide adequate room for the defender's head and shoulders combined with allowance for a good field of fire for the muzzle of the rifle.

Soon after the discovery of Fort Craig, the Krugersdorp town council erected a protective razor-wire fence around it; however, the whole site was illegally flattened by a bulldozer a couple of years later to make way for a golf driving range.

Almost in the centre of Barberton, this unusual rectangular blockhouse is situated at the corner of Judge and Lee roads. It was manned by local volunteers of the Barberton Town Guard under the command of J.W. Winter. Luckily, it was never attacked as it can be enfiladed easily from all but one side. I took this photograph in 2000 before the blockhouse was vandalized.

The condition of the Barberton blockhouse in 2012. The iron door and brass National Monument badge have been stolen and tramps now live inside.

The front of the blockhouse in Barberton which faces high ground a short distance away.

A rice-pattern blockhouse re-erected at the Anglo-Boer War museum in Bloemfontein. Note the protective wall which provides cover for the entrance. The stone wall built around the blockhouse is not historically correct as additional protective dry walling was usually built one or two feet away from the corrugated-iron walls. The reason was that the gravel and pebbles used to fill the gap between the two corrugated-iron walls settled with time and Boer bullets could then easily penetrate the twin corrugated-iron walls. These blockhouses were erected by the thousands in lines to prevent and hinder the free movement of Boer commandos. They were erected within rifle range of each other and joined together with barbed-wire fences. Late in the war the British would assemble large armies to sweep across the veld to trap the Boer commandos against the blockhouse lines. One hundred and twelve years later, it is easy to follow these rice-pattern blockhouse lines. Although the corrugated iron was auctioned off after the war, it is simple to find the circular blockhouse foundations (interior diameter of 19 feet) and their associated dry walling and trench defences.

Appendix 3
Battlefield guide: chronology of major battles (date sequence)

Battles and Skirmishes of the Anglo-Boer War

Name	Date From	Date To	Nearest town	Casualties British	Casualties Boer	Boer to British loss Ratio
Kraaipan	12 October 1899		Kimberley	26	-	0.0%
Siege of Mafeking	13 October 1899	17 May 1900	Mafeking			
Siege of Kimberley	14 October 1899	15 February 1900	Kimberley			
Talana Hill	20 October 1899		Dundee	261	109	41.8%
Elandslaagte	21 October 1899		Ladysmith	263	363	138.0%
Nicholson's Nek (Battle of Ladysmith)	30 October 1899	31 October 1899	Ladysmith	1,272	200	15.7%
Siege of Ladysmith	2 November 1899	28 February 1900	Ladysmith			
Capture of Churchill at Chieveley	15 November 1899		Colenso	134	7	5.2%
Willow Grange	21 November 1899	22 November 1899	Escourt	83	5	6.0%
Belmont	23 November 1899		Hopetown	297	150	50.5%
Graspan/Enslin	25 November 1899		Van Wyksvlei	397	100	25.2%
Modder River	28 November 1899	29 November 1899	Kimberley	483	60	12.4%
Stormberg (1st defeat Black Week)	10 December 1899		Molteno	713	34	4.8%
Magersfontein (2nd defeat Black Week)	11 December 1899	12 December 1899	Kimberley	895	255	28.5%
Colenso (3rd defeat Black Week)	15 December 1899	1899	Colenso	1,138	50	4.4%
Wagon Hill	6 January 1900		Ladysmith	424	190	44.8%
Wagon Point	6 January 1900		Ladysmith			
Spionkop	24 January 1900		Ladysmith	1,185	198	16.7%
Vaalkrans	5 February 1900	7 February 1900	Ladysmith	333	80	24.0%
Klipdrift (Relief of Kimberley)	15 February 1900		Kimberley	21	6	28.6%
Paardeberg	18 February 1900	27 February 1900	Kimberley	1,620	4,850	299.4%
Pieters Hill/Thukela Heights	12 February 1900	27 February 1900	Ladysmith	2,300	200	8.7%
Relief of Ladysmith	28 February 1900		Ladysmith			
Poplar Grove	7 March 1900		Kimberley	1,100	5,000	454.5%
Driefontein	10 March 1900		Bloemfontein	424	124	29.2%
Bloemfontein captured	13 March 1900		Bloemfontein			
Sanna's Post (Koorn Spruit)	31 March 1900		Bloemfontein	159	13	8.2%
Mostertshoek (Reddersburg)	3 April 1900	4 April 1900	Reddersburg	585	7	1.2%
Wepener (Jammerberg Bridge)	4 April 1900	21 April 1900	Wepener	178	36	20.2%
Warren's Fort (Mafeking)	12 May 1900		Mafeking	9	139	1544.4%

Battles and Skirmishes of the Anglo-Boer War

Name	Date From	Date To	Nearest town	Casualties (including killed, captured, wounded & missing) British	Casualties (including killed, captured, wounded & missing) Boer	Boer to British loss Ratio
Relief of Mafeking	17 May 1900		Mafeking	118	101	85.6%
Doornkop (Battle for Johannesburg)	29 May 1900		Krugersdorp	8	5	62.5%
Ses Myl Spruit (Six Mile Spruit)	4 June 1900		Pretoria	227	5	2.2%
Roodeval (Rhenoster River & Bridge)	7 June 1900		Koppies	162	50	30.9%
Diamond Hill	11 June 1900	12 June 1900	Cullinan	178	10	5.6%
Silkaat's Nek	11 July 1900		Brits	41	80	195.1%
Dwarsvlei (Onrust)	11 July 1900		Krugersdorp	65	1,544	2375.4%
Brandwater Basin	30 July 1900		Fouriesburg	7	3	42.9%
Silkaat's Nek 2	2 August 1900		Brits	57	26	45.6%
Elands River Siege (Brakfontein)	4 August 1900	16 August 1900	Swartruggens	120	74	61.7%
Bergendal	27 August 1900		Belfast	58	26	44.8%
Frederikstad	20 October 1900	25 October 1900	Frederikstad	19	103	542.1%
Bothaville (Doornkraal)	6 November 1900		Bothaville	568	90	15.8%
Nooitgedacht	13 December 1900		Krugersdorp	293	8	2.7%
Helvetia	29 December 1900		Machadodorp	40	13	32.5%
Monument Hill (Fosberry's Post)	7 January 1901		Belfast	7	2	28.6%
Modderfontein (Modderfonteinrante)	31 January 1901		Potchefstroom	75	80	106.7%
Lake Chrissie (Chrissiesmeer)	6 February 1901		Lake Chrissie	57	5	8.8%
Wilmansrust	12 June 1901		Bethal	285	14	4.9%
Blood River Poort	17 September 1901		Vryheid	81	56	69.1%
Itala	26 September 1901		Nkandla	214	56	26.2%
Moedwil	30 September 1901		Rustenburg	231	145	62.8%
Bakenlaagte	30 October 1901		Kriel	385	44	11.4%
Tweefontein (Groenkop, Krismiskop)	25 December 1901		Kestell	187	51	27.3%
Ysterspruit	24 February 1902		Klerksdorp	394	51	12.9%
Tweebosch	7 March 1902		Barberspan	87	127	146.0%
Rooiwal	11 April 1902		Delareyville	18,264	14,945	81.8%

Appendix 4
Battlefield guide: chronology of major battles (name sequence)

Battles and Skirmishes of the Anglo-Boer War

Name	Date From	To	Nearest town	Casualties (including killed, captured, wounded & missing) British	Casualties Boer	Boer to British loss Ratio
Bakenlaagte	30 October 1901		Kriel	231	145	62.8%
Belmont	23 November 1899		Hopetown	297	150	50.5%
Bergendal	27 August 1900		Belfast	120	74	61.7%
Bloemfontein captured	13 March 1900		Bloemfontein			
Blood River Poort	17 September 1901		Vryheid	285	14	4.9%
Bothaville (Doornkraal)	6 November 1900		Bothaville	19	103	542.1%
Brandwater Basin	30 July 1900		Fouriesburg	65	1,544	2375.4%
Capture of Churchill at Chieveley	15 November 1899		Colenso	134	7	5.2%
Colenso (3rd defeat Black Week)	15 December 1899	1899	Colenso	1,138	50	4.4%
Diamond Hill	11 June 1900	12 June 1900	Cullinan	162	50	30.9%
Doornkop (Battle for Johannesburg)	29 May 1900		Krugersdorp	118	101	85.6%
Driefontein	10 March 1900		Bloemfontein	424	124	29.2%
Dwarsvlei (Onrust)	11 July 1900		Krugersdorp	41	80	195.1%
Elands River Siege (Brakfontein)	4 August 1900	16 August 1900	Swartruggens	57	26	45.6%
Elandslaagte	21 October 1899		Ladysmith	263	363	138.0%
Frederikstad	20 October 1900	25 October 1900	Frederikstad	58	26	44.8%
Graspan/Enslin	25 November 1899		Van Wyksvlei	397	100	25.2%
Helvetia	29 December 1900		Machadodorp	293	8	2.7%
Itala	26 September 1901		Nkandla	81	56	69.1%
Klipdrift (Relief of Kimberley)	15 February 1900		Kimberley	21	6	28.6%
Kraaipan	12 October 1899		Kimberley	26	-	0.0%
Lake Chrissie (Chrissiesmeer)	6 February 1901		Lake Chrissie	75	80	106.7%
Magersfontein (2nd defeat Black Week)	11 December 1899	12 December 1899	Kimberley	895	255	28.5%
Modder River	28 November 1899	29 November 1899	Kimberley	483	60	12.4%
Modderfontein (Modderfonteinrante)	31 January 1901		Potchefstroom	7	2	28.6%
Moedwil	30 September 1901		Rustenburg	214	56	26.2%
Monument Hill (Fosberry's Post)	7 January 1901		Belfast	40	13	32.5%
Mostertshoek (Reddersburg)	3 April 1900	4 April 1900	Reddersburg	585	7	1.2%
Nicholson's Nek (Battle of Ladysmith)	30 October 1899	31 October 1899	Ladysmith	1,272	200	15.7%
Nooitgedacht	13 December 1900		Krugersdorp	568	90	15.8%
Paardeberg	18 February 1900	27 February 1900	Kimberley	1,620	4,850	299.4%
Pieters Hill/Thukela Heights	12 February 1900	27 February 1900	Ladysmith	2,300	200	8.7%

Battles and Skirmishes of the Anglo-Boer War

Name	Date From	Date To	Nearest town	Casualties (including killed, captured, wounded & missing) British	Casualties Boer	Boer to British loss Ratio
Poplar Grove	7 March 1900		Kimberley	1,100	5,000	454.5%
Relief of Ladysmith	28 February 1900		Ladysmith			
Relief of Mafeking	17 May 1900		Mafeking			
Roodeval (Rhenoster River & Bridge)	7 June 1900		Koppies	227	5	2.2%
Rooiwal	11 April 1902		Delareyville	87	127	146.0%
Sanna's Post (Koorn Spruit)	31 March 1900		Bloemfontein	159	13	8.2%
Ses Myl Spruit (Six Mile Spruit)	4 June 1900		Pretoria	8	5	62.5%
Siege of Kimberley	14 October 1899	15 February 1900	Kimberley			
Siege of Ladysmith	2 November 1899	28 February 1900	Ladysmith			
Siege of Mafeking	13 October 1899	17 May 1900	Mafeking			
Silkaat's Nek	11 July 1900		Brits	178	10	5.6%
Silkaat's Nek 2	2 August 1900		Brits	7	3	42.9%
Spionkop	24 January 1900		Ladysmith	1,185	198	16.7%
Stormberg (1st defeat Black Week)	10 December 1899		Molteno	713	34	4.8%
Talana Hill	20 October 1899		Dundee	261	109	41.8%
Tweebosch	7 March 1902		Barberspan	394	51	12.9%
Tweefontein (Groenkop, Krismiskop)	25 December 1901		Kestell	385	44	11.4%
Vaalkrans	5 February 1900	7 February 1900	Ladysmith	333	80	24.0%
Wagon Hill	6 January 1900		Ladysmith	424	190	44.8%
Wagon Point	6 January 1900		Ladysmith			
Warren's Fort (Mafeking)	12 May 1900		Mafeking	9	139	1544.4%
Wepener (Jammerberg Bridge)	4 April 1900	21 April 1900	Wepener	178	36	20.2%
Willow Grange	21 November 1899	22 November 1899	Escourt	83	5	6.0%
Wilmansrust	12 June 1901		Bethal	57	5	8.8%
Ysterspruit	24 February 1902		Klerksdorp	187	51	27.3%
				18,264	14,945	81.8%

Appendix 5
GPS locations of battles and important skirmishes (alphabetical order)

Battles and Skirmishes of the Anglo-Boer War					
	GPS co-ordinates (degrees, decimal minutes)				
Name	Latitude			Longitude		
	Degrees	Minutes	Seconds	Degrees	Minutes	Seconds
Bakenlaagte	26	20	851	29	8	017
Belmont	29	25	590	24	22	321
Bergendal	25	43	803	30	04	714
Bloemfontein captured	29	06	914	26	13	111
Blood River Poort	27	46	941	30	32	176
Bothaville (Doornkraal)	27	27	558	26	34	688
Brandwater Basin	28	33	810	28	23	143
Capture of Churchill at Chieveley	28	52	407	29	46	088
Colenso (3rd defeat Black Week)	28	44	127	29	49	620
Diamond Hill	25	47	103	28	29	306
Doornkop (Battle for Johannesburg)	26	15	051	27	47	253
Driefontein	28	59	718	25	40	066
Dwarsvlei (Onrust)	25	54	971	27	42	718
Elands River Siege (Brakfontein)	25	38	956	26	42	456
Elandslaagte	28	24	0	29	57	0
Frederikstad	26	31	230	27	09	891
Graspan/Enslin	29	23	058	24	23	712
Helvetia	25	34	843	30	18	199
Itala	28	33	549	31	09	726
Klipdrift (Relief of Kimberley)	29	01	556	24	44	953
Kraaipan	26	17	661	25	18	850
Lake Chrissie (Chrissiesmeer)	26	14	862	30	10	848
Magersfontein (2nd defeat Black Week)	28	58	320	24	41	911
Modder River	29	05	013	24	40	385
Modderfontein (Modderfonteinrante)	26	39	277	26	59	106
Moedwil	25	37	792	27	01	651
Monument Hill (Fosberry's Post)	25	40	455	30	04	152
Mostertshoek (Reddersburg)	29	39	590	26	15	574
Nicholson's Nek (Battle of Ladysmith)	28	29	254	29	45	566
Nooitgedacht	25	50	923	27	33	884
Paardeberg	28	59	274	25	04	931
Pieters Hill/Thukela Heights	28	40	081	29	51	274
Poplar Grove	28	54	533	25	21	950
Relief of Ladysmith	28	33	476	29	46	927
Relief of Mafeking	25	51	438	25	38	804
Roodeval (Rhenoster River & Bridge)	27	15	657	27	32	818
Rooiwal	26	49	256	25	38	111
Sanna's Post (Koorn Spruit)	29	09	358	26	32	092
Ses Myl Spruit (Six Mile Spruit)	25	48	512	28	02	402
Siege of Kimberley	28	44	147	24	46	192
Siege of Ladysmith	28	33	476	29	46	927
Siege of Mafeking	25	51	438	25	38	804
Silkaat's Nek	25	42	097	27	53	950
Silkaat's Nek 2	25	42	097	27	53	950
Spionkop	28	38	954	29	31	096
Stormberg (1st defeat Black Week)	31	16	983	26	17	336
Talana Hill	28	09	086	30	15	916

Battles and Skirmishes of the Anglo-Boer War						
Name	GPS co-ordinates (degrees, decimal minutes)					
	Latitude			Longitude		
	Degrees	Minutes	Seconds	Degrees	Minutes	Seconds
Tweebosch	26	39	328	25	44	038
Tweefontein (Groenkop, Krismiskop)	28	14	197	28	39	459
Vaalkrans	28	40	569	29	37	195
Wagon Hill	28	35	452	29	45	549
Wagon Point	28	35	428	29	45	311
Warren's Fort (Mafeking)	25	52	128	25	37	819
Wepener (Jammerberg Bridge)	29	41	533	26	59	409
Willow Grange	29	05	958	29	54	081
Wilmansrust	26	09	794	29	28	544
Ysterspruit	26	58	280	26	38	837

Note for appendices 3, 4 and 5:

1. These are the most important battle and skirmish sites referred to in the text.
2. This is not a complete database but a work in progress, being built up as the author locates and visits the lesser-known skirmish sites.
3. The casualty figures on each side vary materially according to the different contemporary accounts.
4. The Boers rarely kept accurate records of their casualties, these figures being good estimates.
5. During the guerrilla phase of the war the Boers captured and then released prisoners of war within days or even hours, and have generally not been included in the British casualty figures.
6. The author has visited most of the sites and taken accurate GPS co-ordinates. Sites not visited have been carefully plotted using Google Earth, taking into account contemporary maps and accounts.

Bibliography

Ash, Chris, *The If Man*, 30° South, Pinetown, 2012
Baker, D.C., *Military History Journal*, Vol 11, No 2, 1998
Bateman, Philip, *Generals of the Anglo-Boer War*, Purnell & Sons, Cape Town, 1977
Birdwood, Field Marshal Lord, *Khaki and Gown: An Autobiography*, Ward, Lock & Co, London, 1941
Blackburn, Douglas, *Secret Service in South Africa*, Cassell & Co, London, 1911
Bleszynski, Nick, *Shoot Straight, You Bastards!* Random House, Milson's Point, 2002
Bosman, Herman Charles, *Mafeking Road*, Central News Agency, Cape Town, 1964
Bryant, Arthur, *Jackets of Green*, William Collins Sons & Co, London, 1972
Chilvers, Hedley A., *Out of the Crucible*. Juta & Co, Johannesburg, 1948
Chilvers, Hedley A., *The Seven Lost Trails of Africa*, Cassell & Co, London, 1932
Coetzer, Owen, *The Road to Infamy*, Waterman, Johannesburg, 1996
Creswicke, Louis, *South Africa and the Transvaal War*, Caxton, Edinburgh, *c* 1902
Crow, Bella, unpublished diary, Ladysmith Museum
Crow, George, *The Commission of* HMS *Terrible 1898–1902*, George Newness, 1903
Crum, Maj F.M., *With the Mounted Infantry in South Africa, Being Side-lights on the Boer Campaign 1899–1902*, MacMillan & Bowes, Cambridge, 1903
Danes, Richard, *Cassell's History of the Boer War 1899–1902*, Cassell & Co, London, 1903
Danzeiger, C., *The Jameson Raid*, MacDonald, Cape Town, 1978
de Klerk, Dr Willem (ed), *Krugersdorp 100 Years*, Town Council of Krugersdorp, Krugersdorp 1987
de Waal, D.C., *With Rhodes in Mashonaland*, Books of Rhodesia, Bulawayo, 1974
de Wet, C.R., *Three Years' War*, Archibald Constable & Co, Westminster, 1902
Dictionary of South African Biography Vol 2 (DSAB), Human Sciences Research Council, Pretoria, 1972
Eliot, T.S. (ed), *A Choice of Kipling's Verse*, Faber & Faber, London, 1963
Flower-Smith, M. and Yorke, E., *Mafeking! The Story of a Siege*, Covos Day, Weltevreden Park, 2000
Forsyth, D.R., *Africana Notes and News*, Vol 13, No 7, Africana Society, Johannesburg, 1959
Fuller, Maj-Gen J.F.C., *The Last of the Gentleman's Wars: A Subaltern's Journal of the War in South Africa*, Faber & Faber, London, 1937
Goldstuck, Arthur, *The Ghost That Closed Down The* Town, Penguin, Johannesburg, 2006
Good News Bible, Bible Society of South Africa, 1976
Grabandt, Kees (compiler), *Weeds of Crops and Gardens in Southern Africa*, Ciba-Geigy, Johannesburg, 1985
Great Britain, Army, Brigade of Guards, *The Official Records of the Guards Brigade in South Africa,* Keliher, J.J., London, 1904
Great Britain: Parliament Command Paper Cd 893, 1902
Griffith, Kenneth, *Thank God We Kept the Flag Flying*, Hutchinson & Co, London, 1974
Guest, H.M., *With Lord Methuen and The 1st Division*, H.M. Guest, Klerksdorp, 1902
Hall, Darrell. *Halt! Action Front!: With Colonel Long at Colenso*, Covos Day, Weltevreden Park, 1999
Hall, Darrell, *The Hall Handbook of the Anglo-Boer War 1899–1902*, University of Natal Press, Scottsville, 1999
Halpérin, Vladimir, *Lord Milner and the Empire, the Evolution of British Imperialism*, Oldhams Press, London, 1952
Hamilton, I.B.M., *The Happy Warrior: A Life of General Sir Ian Hamilton GCB, GCMG, DSO*, Cassell & Co, London, 1966

Harfield, Maj A.G., 'Early Signalling Equipment': Pamphlet No 1, 'The Heliograph', Royal Signals Museum, Blandford, 1981

Hensman, H., *Cecil Rhodes: A Study of a Career*, Struik, Cape Town, 1974

Hillegas, Howard C., *With the Boer Forces*, Scripta Africana/Hans Strydom, Johannesburg, 1987

http://www.awm.gov.au/encyclopedia/scarf/doc.asp (Aus)

http://www.ramcjournal.com/1969/4/hughes.pdf (RAMC)

Izedinova, Sophia, *A Few Months with the Boers*, Perskor, Johannesburg, 1977

Jameson, L.S., *From Manifesto to Trial* (reprint), State Library, Pretoria, 1970

Jones, H.M. & M.G.M., *A Gazetteer of the Second Anglo-Boer War 1899–1902*, Military Press, Milton Keynes, 1999

Kandyba-Foxcroft, Elisaveta, *Russia and the Anglo-Boer War 1899–1902*, Cum Books, Roodepoort, 1981

Kaplan, Mendel & Roberts, Marian (eds), *Founders and Followers: Johannesburg Jewry 1887–1915*, Vlaeberg, Cape Town, 1991

Kestell, J.D., *Through Shot and Flame*, Africana Book Society, Johannesburg, 1976

Kruger D.W. & de Kock W.J., *Dictionary of South African Biography* Vol 2, Tafelberg for the Human Sciences Research Council, Cape Town, 1972

Lee, Emanoel, *To the Bitter End*, Viking Penguin New York, 1985

Lee, Emanoel, *To the Bitter End: A Photographic History of the Boer War 1899–1902*, Penguin, Harmondsworth, 1985

Longford, E., *Jameson's Raid*, Weidenfeld & Nicholson. London 1982

Lowry, E.P., *With the Guards Brigade from Bloemfontein to Koomati Poort and Back*, Horace Marshall & Son, London, 1902

Macdonald, D., *How We Kept the Flag Flying* (2nd ed), Covos Day, Weltevreden Park, 1999

Maurice, Maj-Gen Sir Frederick & Grant, Capt M.H., *History of the War in South Africa, 1899–1902*, Hurst & Blackett, London, 1906–10

McFadden, Pam, *The Battle of Elandslaagte*, Ravan, Randburg, 1999

Muller, C.H., *Oorlogsherinneringe*, Nasionale Pers, Cape Town, 1936

Orford, J.G., *Military History Journal* Vol 2, No 2. Johannesburg, 1971

Orford, J.G., *Military History Journal* Vol 4, No 2, Johannesburg, 1977

Pakenham, Thomas, *The Boer War*, Jonathan Ball, Johannesburg, 1997

Pohl, Victor, *Adventures of a Boer Family*, Faber & Faber, London, 1944

Pretorius, Fransjohan (ed), *Scorched Earth*.: Human & Rousseau, Cape Town, 2001

Pretorius, P.J., *Volksverraad*, Libanon, Mossel Bay, 1996

Ransford, Oliver, *The Battle of Majuba Hill: The First Boer War*, John Murray, London, 1967

Ransford, Oliver, *The Battle of Spion Kop*, Camelot Press, London, 1969

Reitz, Deneys, *Commando: A Boer Journal of the Boer War*, Faber & Faber, London, 1929

Romer, Maj C.F. & Mainwaring, Maj A.E., *The Second Battalion Royal Dublin Fusiliers in the South African War*, A.L. Humphreys, London, 1908

Rosenthal, Eric, *Apology Refused*, Howard Timmins, Cape Town, 1959

Rosenthal, Eric, *The Best of Eric Rosenthal*, Howard Timmins, Cape Town, 1975

Rosslyn, The Earl of, *Twice Captured: A Record of Adventure During the Boer War*, William Blackwood & Sons, Edinburgh, 1900

Rotberg, R.I. & Shore, M.F., *The Founder: Cecil Rhodes and the Pursuit of Power*, Southern, Johannesburg, 1988

Schikkerling, R.W., *Commando Courageous*, Hugh Keartland, Johannesburg, 1964

Schoeman, J., *Generaal Hendrik Schoeman: Was Hy 'n Veraaier?*, J. Schoeman, Broederstroom, 1950

Schoeman, Karel (ed), *Witnesses to War*, Human & Rousseau, Cape Town, 1998

Scholtz, G.D., *In Doodsgevaar: Die Oorlogservarings van Kapt. J.J. Naudé*, Voortrekker Pers, Johannesburg, 1940

Smith-Dorrien, Gen Sir Horace, *Memories of Forty-eight Years' Service*, John Murray, London, 1925

Snyman, Adriaan, *Voice of a Prophet*, Vaandel, Mossel Bay, 1999

The Official Records of the Guards Brigade in South Africa (ORGB), Keliher & Co, London, 1904

Todd, P. & Fordham, D., *Private Tucker's Boer War Diary*, Elm Tree/Hamish Hamilton, London 1980

Trew, P., *The Boer War Generals,* Jonathan Ball, Johannesburg, 1999

Uys, Ian, *Delville Wood*, Uys Publishers Johannesburg, 1983

Uys, Ian, *Heidelbergers of the Boer War*, Uys Publishers Johannesburg, 1981

van Warmelo, Dietlof, *On Commando*, A.D. Donker, Johannesburg, 1977

Viljoen, B., *My Reminiscences of the Anglo-Boer War*, Hood, Douglas & Howard, London, 1903 Watt, Steve, *In Memoriam: Roll of Honour Imperial Forces, Anglo-Boer War 1899–1902*, University of Natal Press, Pietermaritzburg, 2000

Watt, Steve, *In Memoriam: Roll of Honour Imperial Forces, Anglo-Boer War 1899–1902*, University of Natal Press, Pietermaritzburg, 2000

Wulff, L. (ed), *Der Transvaalkrieg in der Karikatur aller Völker*, Eysler, Berlin, 1900

Recommended 'Top Ten' books on the Anglo-Boer War

De Wet, C.R., *Three Years' War*, Archibald Constable & Co., Westminster, 1902. An insightful and highly readable account of the war from the Boer perspective written by one of the most successful Boer generals. This book has since been republished in paperback by Galago, Alberton, South Africa

Griffith, Kenneth, *Thank God We Kept the Flag Flying*, Hutchinson & Co, London, 1974. An enjoyable and masterful account of the siege of Ladysmith. Although the book has been out of print for a long time, copies do appear regularly in second-hand bookshops.

Hall, Darrell, *The Hall Handbook of the Anglo-Boer War 1899–1902*, University of Natal Press, Scottsville, 1999. Very useful for readers who are seriously interested in the Anglo-Boer War. The book contains a wealth of information about personalities, equipment and the constitution of the armies on both sides of the conflict.

Jones, H.M. & M.G.M., *A Gazetteer of the Second Anglo-Boer War 1899–1902*, The Military Press, Milton Keynes, 1999. A comprehensive list of the locations, with brief descriptions of the actions fought, in and around most of the towns and battle sites mentioned in the histories of the Anglo-Boer War.

Maurice, Maj-Gen Sir Frederick & Grant, Capt M.H., *History of the War in South Africa, 1899–1902*, Hurst & Blackett, London, 1906–10. This is arguably the finest reference book about the Anglo-Boer War, containing detailed accounts of all the major and minor engagements of the war, together with detailed maps. It has recently been republished by the Naval & Military Press.

Pakenham, Thomas, *The Boer War*, Jonathan Ball, Johannesburg, 1997. A detailed history that reads like a novel; one of those books that you can't put down. It is readily available, being consistently reprinted.

Reitz, Deneys, *Commando: A Boer Journal of the Boer War*, Faber & Faber, London, 1929. An entertaining and fast-moving account by a member of the Johannesburg Commando who went on to command a Scottish regiment during the First World War. The first of the Reitz trilogy of *Commando, No Outspan*, and *Adrift on the Open Veld*. The latter, covering his exile after the Anglo-Boer War and his experiences during the First World War, was published in 2009 by Stormberg and is readily available.

Schikkerling, Roland W., *Commando Courageous*, Hugh Keartland, Johannesburg, 1964. The diary of an English-speaking commando who returned to his legal practice in Johannesburg after the war. The author describes his experiences, personal bravery and suffering on commando in a humble and humorous style. This is my personal favorite among the thousands of books on the Anglo-Boer War, but finding a copy is like finding hen's teeth.

Todd, P. & Fordham, D., *Private Tucker's Boer War Diary*, Elm Tree Books/Hamish Hamilton. London, 1980. This is an excellent day-by-day account of a private soldier who served in the Rifle Brigade throughout the war. The book boasts an outstanding collection of contemporary photographs and interesting snippets.

Watt, Steve, *In Memoriam: Roll of Honour Imperial Forces, Anglo-Boer War 1899–1902*, University of Natal Press, Pietermaritzburg, 2000. An outstanding record of the more than 25,000 Imperial servicemen who died during the Anglo-Boer War. Details such as their last resting place, how and when they died, as well as interesting remarks ensure that this is an essential book for any serious researcher's library.

Note: Search for any Anglo-Boer War book on the website https://www.worldcat.org/ and you will be given the details of the nearest library that has the book.

Notes

1. Bosman, 1964, p. 29
2. DSAB Vol. 2, 1972, p. 738
3. Romer, 1908, pp. 11-12
4. Yorke, 2000, p. 78
5. Guest, 1902, p. 91
6. Smith-Dorrien, 1925, pp. 276-7
7. Pohl, 1944, p. 81-3
8. Coetzer, 1996, p. 107
9. Bella Crow
10. Guest, 1902, p. 48
11. Scholtz, 1940, p. 21
12. Uys, 1981, p. 9
13. Griffith, 1974, p. 318
14. Schikkerling, 1964, p. 119
15. Uys, 1981, p. 96
16. van Warmelo, 1977, p. 65
17. Hillegas, 1987, p. 265
18. Reitz, pp. 187-8
19. Schikkerling, 1964, pp. 256-7
20. Jurie Swart papers
21. Griffith, 1974, p. 155
22. Schikkerling, 1964, p. 308
23. Fuller, 1937, pp. 134-5
24. Fuller, 1937, p. 243
25. Coetzer, 1996, p. 121
26. Fuller, 1937, pp. 160-1
27. Uys, 1981, pp. 160-5
28. Griffith, 1974, p. 290
29. Izedinova, 1977, p. 139
30. Guest, 1902, p. 55
31. Schikkerling, 1964, p. 169
32. Hillegas, 1987, pp. 86-7
33. Griffith, 1974, p. 262
34. Schikkerling, 1964, p. 1
35. Bryant, 1972, p. 198
36. Fuller, 1937, p. 245
37. Griffith, 1974, p. 324
38. Pakenham, 1997, p. 347
39. Fuller, 1937, p. 113
40. Kestell, 1976, p. 214
41. Schikkerling, 1964, p. 85
42. Fuller, 1937, p. 134
43. Tucker, 1980, pp. 122-5
44. Tucker, 1980, p. 129
45. Izedinova, 1977, p. 181
46. Schikkerling, 1964, p. 60
47. Baker, 1998, p. 37
48. Crum, 1903, p. 49
49. Uys, 1981, p. 80
50. Harfield, 1981, pp. 4-6
51. Ransford, 1969, pp. 72, 76, 78
52. Coetzer, 1996, p. 139
53. Coetzer, 1996, p. 59
54. Griffith, 1974, p. 292
55. Griffith, 1974, p. 311
56. Cd Paper, 1902, p. 126
57. Uys, 1981, p. 117
58. Cd Paper, 1902, p. 127
59. Cd Paper, 1902, p. 125
60. Uys, 1981, p. 127
61. Cd Paper, 1902, p. 127
62. Schikkerling, 1964, p. 259
63. Crowe, 1903, p. 199
64. Griffith, 1974, p. 291
65. Macdonald 1999, p. 232
66. Muller, 1936, p. 154
67. Eliot, 1963, pp. 139-40
68. Schikkerling, 1964, p. 192
69. Griffith, 1974, p. 60
70. Bateman, 1977, p. 85
71. Griffith, 1974, p. 117
72. Uys, 1981, p. 18
73. Coetzer, 1996, p. 127
74. Uys, 1981, p. 197
75. Uys, 1981, pp. 12, 19, 41, 54
76. Bateman, 1977, p. 66
77. Schikkerling, 1964, p. 156
78. Mcffaden, 1999, p. 27
79. Griffith, 1974, p. 80
80. Hall, 1999, 62, 65-6, 86, 98, 121-3
81. Pakenham, 1997, p. 179
82. Eliot, 1963, p. 232
83. Uys, 1981, p. 111
84. Uys, 1981, p. 106
85. Schikkerling, 1964, p. 214
86. Griffith, 1974, p. 183
87. Uys, 1981, p. 69
88. Reitz, 1929, p. 120

[89] Pohl, 1945, p. 79
[90] Lowry, 1902, p. 143
[91] Schikkerling, 1964, p. 368
[92] Uys, 1981, p. 38
[93] Uys, 1981, pp. 38, 50
[94] Reitz, 1929, pp. 210-1
[95] Reitz, 1929, pp. 218-9
[96] Reitz, 1929, p. 220
[97] Pakenham, 1997, p. 479
[98] Kestell, 1976, p. 194
[99] Viljoen, 1903, p. 121
[100] Hillegas, 1987, p. 103
[101] Hillegas, 1987, p. 227
[102] de Wet, 1902, p. 79
[103] Pretorius, 1996, pp. 65-6
[104] Tucker, 1980, p. 96
[105] Jones, 1999, p. 128
[106] Trew, 1999, p. 152
[107] Tucker, 1980, p. 96 (my italics)
[108] Hillegas, 1987, pp. 234-5
[109] Trew, 1999, p. 152
[110] Viljoen, 1903, p. 122
[111] Viljoen, 1903, p. 121
[112] Viljoen, 1903, p. 123
[113] de Wet, 1902, p. 79
[114] Hillegas, 1987, p. 184
[115] Schikkerling, 1964, p. 362
[116] Pakenham, 1997, p. 539
[117] Schikkerling, 1964, p. 367
[118] Griffith, 1974, p. 328
[119] Macdonald, 1999, p. 23
[120] Griffith, 1974, p. 288
[121] Yorke, 2000, p. 79
[122] Griffith, 1974, p. 13
[123] Griffith, 1974, p. 6
[124] Griffith, 1974, p. 263
[125] Bateman, 1977, p. 78
[126] Hillegas, 1987, p. 64
[127] Viljoen, 1903, pp. 178-9
[128] Jones, 1999, p. 60
[129] Fuller, 1937, pp. 113-4
[130] Griffith, 1974, p. 358
[131] Pakenham, 1997, p. 531
[132] Griffith, 1974, p. 2
[133] Bella Crow
[134] Macdonald, 1999, p. 68
[135] Griffith, 1974, p. 66
[136] Schikkerling, 1964, p. 337
[137] Griffith, 1974, p. 244
[138] Fuller, 1937, pp. 116-7
[139] Fuller, 1937, p. 144
[140] Griffith, 1974, p. 65
[141] Griffith, 1974, p. 318
[142] Reitz, 1929, p. 77
[143] Maurice, 1906–10, Vol. 4, p. 26
[144] Goldstuck, 2006, p. 11
[145] Goldstuck, 2006, pp. 13-4
[146] Macdonald, 1999, p. 141
[147] Hillegas, 1987, p. 301
[148] Pohl, 1944, pp. 35-6
[149] Schikkerling, 1964, p. 232
[150] Schikkerling, 1964, p. 380
[151] Coetzer, 1996, p. 204-5
[152] Pretorius, 1996, p. 143
[153] Phol, 1944, p. 24
[154] Coetzer, 1996, p. 135
[155] Schikkerling, 1964, p. 359
[156] Reitz, 1929, p. 301-4
[157] Hillegas, 1987, p. 83
[158] Uys, 1981, p. 78
[159] Orford, 1971, pp. 1, 64
[160] Schikkerling, 1964, p. 205
[161] Orford, 1971, pp. 1, 62
[162] Snyman, 1999, pp. 79-80
[163] Griffith, 1974, p. 82
[164] Griffith, 1974, p. 209
[165] Schikkerling, 1964, pp. 56-7
[166] Creswicke, Vol. 5, 1902, pp. 1-15
[167] Hillegas, 1987, pp. 153-4
[168] Schikkerling, 1964, p. 157
[169] Griffith, 1974, p. 242
[170] Fuller, 1937, pp. 137-8
[171] Jones, 1999, p. 96
[172] Macdonald, 199, p. 233
[173] Schikkerling, 1964, p. 73
[174] Schikkerling, 1964, p. 73
[175] Schikkerling, 1964, pp. 49-51
[176] Pakenham, 1997, p. 572
[177] Hall, 1999, p. 237
[178] Pakenham, 1997, p. 381

[179] Grabandt, 1985, pp. 51, 69
[180] Ransford, 1967, pp. 101-2
[181] Griffith, 1964, pp. 216-7
[182] Pakenham, 1997, p. 425
[183] Hamilton, 1966, p. 456
[184] Coetzer, 1996, pp. 104-5
[185] Griffith, 1974, p. 202
[186] Coetzer, 1996, p. 58
[187] Uys, 1981, p. 74
[188] Hillegas, 1987, pp. 193-4
[189] Uys, 1981, p. 74
[190] Uys, 1981, p. 232
[191] Fuller, 1981, p. 128
[192] Hillegas, 1987, pp. 270-1
[193] Schikkerling, 1964, p. 338
[194] Coetzer, 1996, p. 92
[195] Jones, 1999, p. 17
[196] Coetzer, 1996, p. 95
[197] Macdonald, 1999, p. 285
[198] Uys, 1981, p. 169
[199] Orford, 1971, pp. 62, 64
[200] Reitz, 1929, p. 169
[201] Schikkerling, 1964, p. 304
[202] Chilvers, 1932, pp. 135-7
[203] Rosenthal, 1959, pp. 11-21
[204] Schikkerling, 1964, p. 369
[205] Fuller, 1937, p. 70
[206] Schikkerling, 1964, p. 371
[207] Viljoen, 1903, p. 179
[208] Lee, 1985, pp. 1-2
[209] Uys, 1981, p. 25; Ransford, 1967, p. 115
[210] Macdonald, 1999, p. 155
[211] Griffith, 1974, p. 362
[212] Schikkerling, 1964, p. 73
[213] Rosenthal, 1975, pp. 1, 104
[214] Pohl, 1944, p. 111
[215] Uys, 1981, p. 227
[216] Griffith, 1974, p. 375
[217] Creswicke, Vol. 7, 1902, p. 160
[218] Macdonald, 1999, p. 147
[219] Romer, 1908, p. 119
[220] Fuller, 1937, p. 163
[221] Hillegas, 1987, p. 195
[222] Lowry, 1902, p. 195
[223] ORGB, 1904, p. 181
[224] Crum, 1903, p. 122
[225] Uys, 1981, p. 115
[226] Schikkerling, 1964, p. 159
[227] Schikkerling, 1964, pp. 311-2
[228] Schikkerling, 1964, p. 348
[229] Griffith, 1974, p. 313
[230] Lowry, 1902, p. 191
[231] Macdonald, 1999, p. 71
[232] Fuller, 1937, pp. 89-90
[233] Crum, 1903, p. 54
[234] Griffith, 1974, p. 235-6
[235] Macdonald, 1999, p. 85
[236] Macdonald, 1999, p. 85
[237] Uys, 1981, p. 94
[238] Fuller, 1937, p. 285
[239] Schikkerling, 1964, pp. 245, 252, 278
[240] Schikkerling, 1964, pp. 310-1
[241] Coetzer, 1996, p. 134
[242] Cassell, 1903, p. 352
[243] Hillegas, 1987, p. 73
[244] Macdonald 1999, p. 108
[245] RAMC, 1969, p. 198-202
[246] Lee, 1985, p. 113
[247] Schikkerling, 1964, p. 22
[248] Fuller, 1937, p. 232
[249] Hillegas, 1987, p. 297
[250] Uys, 1981, p. 167
[251] Fuller, 1937, pp 68-9
[252] Schikkerling, 1964, p. 16
[253] Tucker, 1980, pp. 112-3
[254] Lee, 1985, p. 100
[255] Schikkerling, 1964, pp. 266-7
[256] Schikkerling, 1964, p. 267
[257] Griffith, 1974, p. 256
[258] Schikkerling, 1964, p. 213
[259] Pakenham, 1997, p. 438
[260] Griffith, 1974, p. 157
[261] Tucker, 1980, pp. 133-4
[262] Schikkerling, 1964, p. 55
[263] Fuller, 1937, p. 115
[264] Griffith, 1974, pp. 220-2
[265] Rosenthal, 1975, pp. 1, 121
[266] Rosenthal, 1975, pp. 1, 121-2
[267] Jones, 1999, p. 132
[268] Rosenthal, 1975, pp. 119-20

[269] Schikkerling, 1964, p. 301
[270] Griffith, 1974, p. 319
[271] Schikkerling, 1964, p. 245
[272] Fuller, 1937, p. 149
[273] Kestell, 1976, p. 247
[274] Lee, 1985, pp. 52-63
[275] Bryant, 1972, p. 191
[276] Coetzer, 1996, p. 109
[277] Hall, 1999, p. 106
[278] Macdonald, 1999, p. 20
[279] Griffith, 1974, p. 293
[280] Griffith, 1974, p. 30
[281] Pakenham, 1997, p. 574
[282] Tucker, 1980, p. 48
[283] Tucker, 1980, p. 144
[284] Jones, 1999, p. 277
[285] Guest, 1902, p. 45
[286] Schikkerling, 1964, p. 282
[287] Schikkerling, 1964, p. 155
[288] Schoeman, 1950, p. 215
[289] Scholtz, 1940, p. 32
[290] Guest, 1902, p. 14
[291] Bryant, 1972, p. 199
[292] Viljoen, 1903, p. 187
[293] Uys, 1981, p. 84
[294] Uys, 1981, p. 105
[295] Uys, 1981, p. 172
[296] Pakenham, 1997, p. 298
[297] Griffith, 1974, p. 220
[298] Trew, 1999, p. 154
[299] Reitz, 1929, p.43-4
[300] Griffith, 1974, p. 88
[301] Griffith, 1974, p. 365
[302] Coetzer, 1996, p. 252
[303] Griffith, 1974, pp. 62-3
[304] Coetzer, 1996, p. 158
[305] Pakenham, 1997, p. 306
[306] Hillegas, 1987, pp. 68-9
[307] Halpérin, 1952, p. 114
[308] Halpérin, 1952, p. 124
[309] Griffith, 1974, p. 153
[310] Griffith, 1974, pp. 192-3
[311] Hillegas, 1987, p. 304
[312] Schikkerling, 1964, p. 391
[313] Bryant, 1972, p. 195
[314] Pakenham, 1997, p. 539
[315] de Klerk, 1987. pp. 10-1
[316] Fuller, 1937, p. 69
[317] Schikkerling, 1964, p. 205
[318] Schikkerling, 1964, p. 310
[319] Griffith, 1974, p. 255
[320] Griffith, 1974, p. 255
[321] Muller, 1936, p. 42
[322] Orford, 1971, pp. 61-2
[323] Rosenthal, 1975, p. 99
[324] Crum, 1903, p. 55
[325] Griffith, 1974, p. 202
[326] Griffith, 1974, p. 342
[327] Tucker, 1980, p. 67
[328] Hillegas, 1987, p. 301
[329] Schikkerling, 1964, p. 68
[330] Uys, 1981, p. 114
[331] Schikkerling, 1964, pp. 80-1
[332] Tucker, 1980, pp. 74-5
[333] Fuller, 1937, pp. 132-3
[334] Schikkerling, 1964, p. 174
[335] Schikkerling, 1964, p. 175
[336] Ransford, 1969, p. 133
[337] Uys, 1981, p. 70
[338] Reitz, 1929, p. 236
[339] Uys, 1981, p. 188
[340] Schikkerling, 1964, p. 327
[341] Fuller, 1937, p. 129
[342] Macdonald, 1999, p. 66
[343] Kestell, 1976, p. 216
[344] Hillegas, 1987, p. 297
[345] Rosenthal, 1959, pp. 49-55
[346] Kaplan, 1991, pp. 80-1
[347] Chilvers, 1930, p. 125
[348] Chilvers, 1930, pp. 124-5
[349] Chilvers, 1930, p. 125
[350] Macdonald, 1999, p. 40
[351] Schikkerling, 1964, p. 200
[352] Macdonald, 1999, p. 126
[353] Tucker, 1980, p. 36
[354] Schikkerling, 1964, pp. 189, 194, 199
[355] Reitz, 1929, p. 70
[356] Fuller, 1937, p. 97
[357] Schikkerling, 1964, p. 381
[358] Griffith, 1974, p. 309

[359] Griffith, 1974, p. 340
[360] Uys, 1981, p. 129; Jones, 1999, pp. 153-4
[361] Schikkerling, 1964, p. 15
[362] Ransford, 1969, pp. 134-135
[363] Schikkerling, 1964, p. 205
[364] Macdonald, 1999, p. 180
[365] Reitz, 1929, p. 51
[366] Uys, 1981, p. 194
[367] Uys, 1981, p. 215
[368] Schikkerling, 1964, p. 62
[369] Hillegas, 1987, pp. 297-8
[370] Reitz, 1929, p. 62
[371] Reitz, 1929, p. 67
[372] Coetzer, 1996, p. 225-6
[373] Kestell, 1976, p. 147
[374] Schikkerling, 1964, p. 236
[375] Bryant, 1972, p. 202
[376] Coetzer 1996, p. 24
[377] Coetzer, 1996, p. 114-5
[378] Coetzer, 1996, p. 27
[379] Reitz, 1929, p. 143
[380] Schikkerling, 1964, pp. 207, 340
[381] Kestell, 1976, p. 135
[382] Ransford, 1967, p. 113
[383] Ransford, 1967, p. 114
[384] Pakenham, 1997, p. 574
[385] Ransford, 1967, p. 139
[386] Hall, 1999, p. 101
[387] Schikkerling, 1964, pp. 388-9
[388] Coetzer, 1976, p. 71
[389] Bateman, 1977, p. 109
[390] Coetzer, 1996, p. 95
[391] Hall, 1999, p. 105-6
[392] Uys, 1983, p. 240-2
[393] Uys, 1983, p. x
[394] Griffith, 1974, p. 78
[395] Griffith, 1974, p. 95
[396] Guest, 1902, p. 10
[397] Pakenham, 1997, p. 574
[398] Hall, 1999, p. 103
[399] Smith-Dorrien, 1925, p. 401
[400] Schikkerling,, 1964, p. 200
[401] Schikkerling, 1964, p. 146
[402] Schikkerling, 1964, p. 66
[403] Griffith, 1974, p. 269
[404] Griffith, 1974, p. 273
[405] Schikkerling, 1964, p. 360
[406] Fuller, 1937, p. 252
[407] Griffith, 1974, p. 271
[408] Schikkerling, 1964, p. 302
[409] Bateman, 1977, p. 79
[410] Chilvers, 1930, pp. 123-4
[411] Halpérin, 1952, p. 123
[412] Izedinova, 1977, p. 191
[413] Bryant, 1972, p. 204
[414] Ransford, 1969, p. 101
[415] Lee, 1986, p. 36
[416] Schikkerling, 1964, p. 250
[417] Schikkerling, 1964, p. 253
[418] Griffith, 1974, p. 328
[419] Schikkerling, 1964, p. 305
[420] Hillegas, 1987, p. 210
[421] Schikkerling, 1964, p. 129
[422] Jones, 1999, p. 153
[423] Uys, 1981, p. 115
[424] Uys, 1981, p. 141
[425] Uys, 1981, p. 220
[426] Schikkerling, 1964, p. 326
[427] Bateman, 1977, p. 23
[428] Bateman, 1977, p. 89
[429] Hillegas, 1987, p. 288
[430] Hillegas, 1987, p. 289
[431] Hillegas, 1987, p. 290
[432] Coetzer, 1996, p. 147
[433] Griffith, 1974, p. 275
[434] Macdonald, 1999, p. 73
[435] Griffith, 1974, p. 296
[436] Tucker, 1980, pp. 109-10
[437] Griffith, 1974, p. 272
[438] Uys, 1981, pp. 172-175, 231-2
[439] Uys, 1981, p.66
[440] Izedinova, 1977, p. 160
[441] Reitz, 1929, p. 211
[442] Griffith, 1974, p. 256
[443] Trew, 1999, p. 182
[444] Jameson, 1897, p. 265
[445] Longford, 1982, p. 96
[446] Chilvers 2, 1929, p. 108
[447] *Africana Notes and News*, 1959. p. 254
[448] Ash, 2012, p. 25

Index

18th Hussars, 97
18th Mounted Infantry, 62
19th Hussars, 148
1st Loyal North Lancashire Regiment, 142
5th Lancers, 18, 74
5th Royal Irish Lancers, 62

Airlie station, 48-49
Airlie, Lady M., 90
Alberts, Gen H.A., 94
Albrecht, Tpr, 114
Aldershot, 24-25
Aliwal North, 28
Allenby, Col E.H.H., 48, 51, 142
Aloe Knoll, Spion Kop, 42, 63, 117, 149
Amsterdam, 159
Anderson, Lt R., 51
Appelby, Pte, 129
Atkins, J.B., 25
Ava, Lord, 92

Baden-Powell, Col R.S.S., 46, 60, 109, 124, 139
Bagshot, 140
Bailleul, France, 139
Bakenlaagte, Battle of, 92-93
Balaclava, 82
Balfour, 41, 83, 127
Bank station, 113
Barberspan, 122
Barberton, 88, 112, 167, 170
Barker, Lt E.H., 51, 53
Barnato, Barney, 14, 35
Barry, Capt W.J., 161, 164
Barry, Pte J., V.C., 152
Barton's Folly, Fort, 167
Basing, Lord, 30
Bastion Hill, 121
Beattie, W.A., 140
Beatty-Powell, W.C., 161, 163-164
Bechuanaland *also* Botswana, 16, 42, 88, 160
Beck, Tpr J., 31-32, 107
Beerlaagte, 46
Belfast, 20, 31, 52, 66, 68-69, 105, 127, 129, 146, 149-150, 152-153
Bell's Kop, 134-135
Belmont, Battle of, 19, 113, 130, 137
Benson, Col G.E., 93

Bergendal, Battle of (Dalmanutha), 19-21, 33, 35, 48, 54, 61, 66-67, 69, 71, 84, 97, 99-100, 108, 113, 115, 120, 127, 158
Bewicke-Copley, Maj R.C.A.B., 147
Bethal, 72, 134
Beyers, Gen C.F., 56, 74, 138
Beytel, A., 101
Biccard, M., 54
Black Watch, 62, 105
Black Week, 19-20
Blake, Col J.E., 84
Blake-Knox, Surgeon, 72, 102, 116
Bloedzuikerspan, 140
Bloemfontein, 13, 17, 19-20, 41, 43, 48, 74, 77, 80, 89-90, 93, 95, 104, 128, 159, 166, 170
Blood River Poort, 62
Blood, Col, 101
Boer Scouting Corps, 22
Booysens, Johannesburg, 87
Borghys, Lt, 154
Boschkoppies, 78
Boskop, 13
Bosman, Herman Charles, 22
Botha, Cmdt-Gen Louis, 20, 33, 42, 52, 57-58, 61-62, 84, 86-88, 93, 105, 115-116, 118, 131-132, 139-140, 150
Botha, H.J., 115
Botha, Tpr, 105, 107
Bothaville, 30, 96
Botswana *see* Bechuanaland
Bouwer, Tpr P., 32
Bowen, Major, 79
Braklaagte, 32
Brandfort, 48, 90, 94
Brandkop, 48
Breedt's Nek, 51
Breytenbach, Cmdt, 113
Bristowe, Justice, 131
British Expeditionary Force, 142
Broadwood, Gen R.G., 20, 57, 74, 77
Bronkhorstspruit, 14
Bryant, J., 72, 75
Buchanan-Riddell, Lt-Col R.G., 147
Buller, Gen Sir R.H., 19-20, 26, 34, 46, 52-53, 60, 70, 74, 82, 86, 94, 104, 107, 109, 116, 118-119, 122, 136, 147
Bullock, Col G.M., 101, 103, 118
Bulwana Hill, 83, 110
Burger, Gen S., 88

Burgersdorp, 102-103
Burgersdorp cemetery, 15, 47, 141
Burgershoop cemetery, 47
Bush Veldt Carbineers, 58
Bushman's Kop, 74
Butler, Captain J., 92, 94
Buys, Cmdt S.B., 101, 126
Buys, L., 86

Caesar's Camp, 45, 101, 128-129, 134
Calcutta, 92
Caldwell, Maj C.E., 60
Canadian Scouts, 105
Cape Town, 13, 40, 41, 56, 90, 118, 153, 155, 160
Carpenter, Sgt-Maj, 154-155
Cerignola, Battle of, 148
Cetshwayo, King, 14
Chadwick, I., 124
Chamberlain, Joseph, 16-17, 118, 125
Chieveley, 30-31, 55, 76, 139
Childe, Maj C.B., 121
Chrissiesmeer, 50, 53, 73
Churchill, Sir Winston, 21, 30-31, 34, 55, 59, 82, 130, 132, 139, 141, 158
City Imperial Volunteers, 63, 79
Clements, Gen R.A.P., 56
Codrington, Capt, 79
Coffin, Maj P., 110
Coke, Gen J.T., 147
Colenso, 53-54, 61, 74, 76, 82, 84, 86, 107, 118-119, 133, 137, 139
Colenso, Battle of, 19, 49, 52-53, 104, 135, 140
Colesberg, 37, 56, 70-71, 112
Colley, Gen Sir G.P., 14, 79
Colvile, Gen H.E., 140
Commission of Inquiry, 83, 137
Congreve, Capt W.N., V.C., 110, 139
Cook, Col, 147
Cork Militia, 30
cosmos, 79
Cotton, Maj S.L., 66
Coutts, H.D., 124
Coventry, Maj the Hon. C., 160, 163
Craig, Fort, 166, 169
Cronjé, Gen P.A., 19-20, 81-85, 96, 130, 160, 162
Crowle, P.H.S., 23, 76, 80
Crum, Maj, 97
Cullinan, Sir Thomas, 132, 150
Cullingworth sisters, 40, 130

Dam Plaats, 127
Dardanelles, France, 82
Davies, H., 161, 163
de Jager, Danie (sculptor), 17, 80, 85
de Jager, Pieter 61
de Jager, S., 106
de la Rey, Asst-Comdt-Gen J.H., 19, 21, 37, 57, 61, 73-74, 86, 119, 122, 148
de Villiers, Justice J., 88, 114, 117, 131
de Wet, Cmdt-Gen C. R., 20-21, 24-25, 55, 57-58, 74, 76-77, 80, 88, 94, 104, 110, 116, 120, 135, 154, 159
Defence Committee, 82
Delagoa Bay, 40, 55
Delville Wood, 140-141
Dennis, Lt, 114
Devonshire Regiment, 63, 81, 108, 111, 118, 148
Diamond Hill, Battle of (Donkerhoek), 19-20, 90, 104
Dibley, Capt, 22
Dick-Cunyngham, Col W., V.C., 101
Digby-Jones, Lt R.J.T., 114, 117
Doornbult, 147
Doornkop, Battle of (Johannesburg), 20, 62, 79, 157
Doornkraal, 101
Dordrecht, 119
Douglas, Lt-Col William, 50, 140
Doveton, Maj, 42
Dow, Lt J., 73
Dow, Pte J., 73
Dray, Capt, 76, 80
Driefontein, Battle of, 20
Dufrayer, A., 124
Dullstroom, 26, 31, 45, 92, 101, 103, 105, 127, 146, 153
Dundee, 18, 46, 48, 57, 64, 65, 86, 116
Dundonald, Lord, 34, 121, 134
Dunne, bugler, 49
Durban, 19, 41, 57, 98, 127, 146, 162
Dwarsvlei, Battle of, 21, 139, 141

Edmunds, Pte, 96
Edward, King, 118, 139, 141, 150
Egerton, Lt, 44
Eikenhof, 22
Elandshoek, 127
Elandslaagte, Battle of, 61-62, 156
Ellis, Sgt, 57, 113

187

Eloff, Lt S.J., 160, 163
Eloff, Veldkornet, 105
Els, W, 92
Emmett, Veldkornet S.J., 84, 118
Engelbrecht, Martha, 142, 144-145
Erasmus, Col P.E., 110, 118
Erasmus, Gen D.J.E. 'Maroela', 18, 57, 162

Ferreira, Col I., 118
Fleischer, J., 144, 146
Fochville, 22-23
Fordsburg Commando, 70, 90
Fosbery, Capt P.E., 152-153
Fosbery's Post *also* Monument Hill, Belfast, 100, 152-153
Foster Gang, 74
Fourie, Cmdt, 39, 70
Fourteen Streams, 158
Franklin, Petty Officer, 128
Fraser, Tpr, 162
French, Gen J.P.D., 18, 24, 56, 63, 70-71, 79, 82, 97, 140, 142
Fuchs, A.C., 48
Fuller, Lt, 30, 34, 36, 62, 64-65, 78, 84, 101, 104, 126, 128, 133

Garlick, Pte J., 50
Gatacre, Gen W.F., 19, 110
Geluk, 158
Ghandi, Mahatma, 158
Glencoe station, Council of War, 57
Gluyas, Nurse L., 155, 157
Glynn Mine, Sabie, 70
Gordon Highlanders, 62-63, 79, 114, 130
Gordon, Capt W.E., 21
Gough, Col H. de la P., 54
Gough, Maj, 62
Gough's Mounted Infantry, 62
Grant, Lt-Col, 106
Graspan, Battle of, 19, 137
Great Gonerby, 51
Great Trek, 13
Green Point Camp, 90
Greylingstad, 27, 36-38, 41, 98-99, 103, 111, 126, 129, 152
Griqualand West, 14
Groenewald, Cmdt, 45, 59
Groot Zuikerboskop, 127
Grootvlei (South Rand Mine), 101

Guards Brigade, 97, 99
Guild of Loyal Women, 155
Gun Hill, 76, 92

Haig, Maj D., 140
Haldane, Capt Aylmer, 55, 130
Hamilton, Gen I.S.M., 20, 63, 78-79, 82, 108, 114, 142
Hancock, Lt, 58-59
Hankey, Capt, 114
Hannay, Col O.C., 114, 116-117
Harber, H., 128
Harlech, Fort, 137
Harrison, George, 15
Hart, Gen A.F., 54, 110
Hartley, Wallace, 116
Harts River, 122
Hassell, Capt J.A., 28
Hattingh, D., 73
Hay, Col, 79
Hectorspruit, 19, 91, 124, 146, 166
Heidelberg, 26-27, 29, 31-32, 38-40, 46, 49, 86, 105, 107, 113, 127, 132, 135, 154, 158,
Heidelberg Commando, 32, 44, 48, 54, 56, 78, 84, 94, 101, 127
Heilbron, 96, 128-129
Hekpoort, 167
Helvetia, 26, 65-67, 92
Hertzog, Gen J.B.M., 108, 122
Hill, Col, 147
Hillegas, H., 73, 76
Hlangwane Hill, 52, 86
HMS *Powerful*, 43
HMS *Sybille*, 108
HMS *Terrible*, 43, 138
Hockaday, Cpl, 114
Hogg, W.S., 13
Hollander Volunteer Contingent, 26
Howick Concentration Camp, 54
Hughes, Capt M.L., 104, 107
Hunt, D., 112
Hunter, Gen Sir A., 83
Hussar Hill, 34, 136

Ifafi, 103
Imperial Yeomanry, 102, 137
Inglefield, Maj, 56
Inkson, Lt, 104
Inniskilling Dragoons, 50, 96

International Legion, 48
Irene, 48, 151
Isabellafontein, 90
Isandlwana, Battle of, 142
Izedinova, Sophia, 32

Jacobs, P., 44
Jacobsdal, 24, 61, 168
Jagersfontein, 64, 67
Jameson Raid, 16, 18, 20, 40-41, 64, 79, 139, 160-165
Jameson, Dr Leander Starr, 16, 18, 20, 40-41, 64, 79, 139, 160-165
Johannesburg, 12, 14-17, 19-20, 25, 28, 35, 41, 44, 62-63, 74, 79, 87-88, 92, 96, 98, 127, 131, 146, 151, 154, 160-162, 168
Johannesburg Police, 33, 35, 84, 113, 115, 119
Jordaan siding, 62, 64
Jordaan, J., 92
Joubert, Cmdt-Gen P.J., 18-19, 26, 57-58, 116, 138, 151, 159
Jourdain, Lt-Col H.F.M., 121
Juta, J.C., 88

Kabul, India, 139
Kalkkrans, 135
Kamffer, Veldkornet, 46, 83
Kandahar, India, 139
Kestell, Rev, 109
khaki weed, 79
Kimberley, 15, 18-20, 35, 111, 141
King, J.N., 28
King, Lt, 24
King's Liverpool Regiment, 66
King's Royal Rifles, 79, 97, 106
Kipling, Rudyard, 45, 54, 162
Kitchener, Field Marshal Lord, 21, 55, 59, 94, 110, 114, 120
Kitchener's Horse, 154, 157
Klapperkop, Fort, 49
Klein Kalliesfontein, 51
Klerksdorp, 86
Klip River, 83, 113, 156
Knox, Col E.C., 46
Knox, Maj-Gen W. G., 109
Kock, Gen J.H.M., 18, 52
Koedoesrand, Battle of, 61
Koen, Cmdt, 109
Koorn Spruit, 20, 74

Kooyker, L., 162
Kraaipan, 18
Krause, Justice F.E.T., 88
Kriel, 93
Kroonstad, 20, 36, 57-58, 101, 154
Kroonstad, Council of War, 20, 57
Kruger National Park, 34, 146, 159
Kruger, F., 127
Kruger, President S.J.P., 14-18, 35, 40, 57-58, 73, 88, 91, 131, 160, 165
Kruger, Susanna, 47
Kruger's Post, 148
Krugersdorp, 15-16, 21-22, 44, 47, 88, 91, 96, 99, 105, 120-121, 123, 136-137, 139, 141, 154, 157, 160-166, 168-169

Lace Mines, 96
Ladysmith, 18-20, 23-25, 32, 42-46, 48, 52, 57, 60, 62-63, 65, 68, 70-71, 74, 78-79, 81, 83-84, 86, 93-94, 100-102, 108, 111, 116-119, 122, 126, 128-129, 132-135, 140, 152, 156, 166
Lake Banagher, 50
Lake Chrissie *see* Chrissiesmeer, 24, 50, 54
Lambert's Bay, 108
Langlaagte station, 74
Las Palmas, South America, 108
Lawlor, Lt J.L., 66, 67
Leeuwpoort Halt, 34
Leicestershire Regiment, 97
Letchford, Pte, 59-60
Leyds, Dr, 108
Liebenberg, I., 28, 51
Liverpool Regiment, 66, 158
Loch, Lord, 140
Logan, J., 55
Lombard's Kop, 46, 48, 110
London Convention, 15
Long, Col C.J., 52
Lourenço Marques, 41, 56, 109, 129
Lowry, Rev, 97
Lubbe, Cmdt, 43
Lynch, G., 106
Lyttelton, Gen N.G., 116, 147

Maartens, D., 32
Macdonald's Kopje, Majuba, 138
MacGregor, Maj R.L., 48-50
Machadodorp, 67, 69, 88, 91, 99
Mackworth, Maj, 79

Mafeking, 18, 20, 24, 47, 60, 105, 107, 111, 118, 121, 124-125, 157, 160
Magaliesburg, 64
Magersfontein, Battle of, 19, 26-27, 32, 35, 96, 104, 130, 137, 148, 156
Majuba, Battle of, 14, 20, 58, 79, 81-83, 85, 138-139
Malherbe, Veldkornet I., 116
Malmani (Ottoshoop), 160
Malta Mounted Infantry, 110
Manchester Regiment, 45
Maraisburg, Roodepoort, 82, 85, 155, 157
Massamnekop, 42
Matjiesfontein, 156
McKay, Cpl. J.F., V.C., 62
Mears, W., 44, 46
Mentz, M., 146
Methuen, Lord, 19, 27, 55, 122
Meyer, Gen L.J., 18, 48, 57, 140
Meyer, O., 84
Meyrick, Capt St John, 82, 155
Middleburg Commando, 45
Middlesex Regiment, 147
Miers, Capt R.C.H., 158-159
Miller-Wallnut, Maj, 114
Milner, Lord Alfred, 118, 150
Mistake, Fort, 167
Modder River, Battle of, 19, 61, 63, 72, 84, 125, 128, 133, 137
Modderfontein Post, 113
Molteno, 19
Mons, France, 142
Monte Cristo, 86
Monument Hill, Belfast *also* Fosberry's Post, 100, 152-153
Mooi River, 149
Mooifontein, 134
Moord Kraal, 34
Moordenaar's Poort, 56, 159
Morant, Lt 'Breaker', 58-59
Mostertshoek, 20
Mount Alice, 43
Mounted Infantry Brigade, 114
Muller, Gen C.H., 45, 121, 152-153
Munnik, J., 87-88

Naaupoort, 107
National Scouts, 31-32, 101, 105, 113, 128, 154
Naudé, Capt J.J., 26, 112

Neethling, sisters Johanna & Henrietta, 22
Nell, Tpr F., 31-32, 107
Nelson, Lord, 125, 147
Nelspruit, 49-50, 108
Nicholson's Nek, Battle of, 26, 48, 57, 74, 137
Niemeyer, L., 28
Nooitgedacht (Eastern Transvaal), 40, 48-49, 92-93, 113, 115
Nooitgedacht, Battle of (Magaliesberg), 56138
North Lancs *see* 1st Loyal North Lancashire Regiment
Nyeri, Kenya, 156

O'Reilly, Dr, 40
observation balloon, 25, 148, 151
Ogies, 72, 75
Ogilvy, Col D., 11th Earl of Airlie, 90
One Tree Hill (Maconochie Hill), 110
Oosthuizen, Gen S.F., 21, 109, 139, 141
Orange River Convention (Bloemfontein Convention), 13
Orange River station, 54
Ottosdal, 77, 123
Ottoshoop, 160
Owen, C.M., 13, 79

Paardeberg, Battle of, 20, 56, 81, 83, 85, 100, 114, 116, 117, 166
Paardefontein, 28
Paardekraal Monument, 105, 121, 120, 123
Paris, France, 34, 60, 139
Park, Col C.W., 45, 108, 148
Patterson, telegraphist, 40, 130-132
Penn-Symons, Gen Sir W., 65
Pickering, Driver P., 38-39
Pietermaritzburg concentration camp, 44,
Pieter's Hill, 19, 156
Pietersburg, 28, 112, 120
Pilansberg, 42
Pilgrim's Rest, 84, 88, 90, 101, 121, 128
Pitsani, 16, 160
Philippolis, 51
Phol, F., 182
Pohlman, Lt W.F., 84
Pont Drift, 152, 156
Poplar Grove, 20
Porter, Col, 37, 107
Potchefstroom, 14, 74, 138, 161
Pretoria, 14, 17, 19-21, 35, 40-41, 48-50, 55-56,

58-59, 87-90, 100, 110-112, 115, 120, 122, 129-132, 139, 150-151, 160-163, 166
Pretoria Commando, 92
Pretoria Convention, 15
Pretorius, Andries, 13, 54, 64
Prinsloo, Cmdt H., 42, 127, 129, 151

Queenstown, 19

Raikes, Lt, 79
Railway Volunteers, 24
Rainsford-Hannay, Lt F., 61
Randfontein, 161-164
Raphael, Lt F., 105
Rawlinson, Col H.S., 140
Red Fort, 134
Reddersburg, 20
Redelinghuis, 'Roksak', 101, 103, 109
Reform Committee, 16
Reitz, 57
Reitz, F.W., 88
Reitz, Deneys, 29, 54, 56-57, 127, 133, 135
Renew, Audrey, 47
Reynolds, Capt, 96
Rhodes, Cecil John, 16
Rice, Maj S.R., 167
Rietfontein, Battle of, 103, 137, 140
Rifle Brigade, 105-106, 110-111, 119-120, 126, 148, 150, 156
Roberts, Field Marshal Lord, 19-21, 49, 61, 78, 81-83, 124, 130, 139-140
Roberts, Lt F.H.S., 20, 61, 122
Roodeval, Battle of, 21
Royal Dublin Fusiliers, 94, 166
Royal Engineers, 25, 41, 105, 114, 117, 119, 166-167
Royal Field Artillery, 27-28, 35, 52, 61, 63, 77, 96, 119
Royal Irish Fusiliers, 22
Royal Navy, 40, 43, 109
Royal Scots, 48, 50
Royal Signals Museum, 40
Russian–Dutch ambulance, 32, 150

Saartjie's Nek, 112
Sand River, 20
Sand River Convention, 13
Sanna's Post, 20, 23, 74, 77, 80, 90, 94, 95, 120, 125
Scheepers, Cmdt G.J., 58

Scheepers, Tpr, 32
Schikkerling, R.W., 26, 30, 40, 58, 73, 87, 94, 102, 104, 108, 127-128, 132, 152, 154
Schoeman, Cmdt D.J., 136, 150-151, 153
Schoeman, Gen H.J., 70, 112, 115
Schutte, Cmdt, 83
Schwartz, Cmdt P., 148
Scott, Capt P., 138
Scottish Rifles, 36, 37, 111, 129, 147
Ses Myl Spruit, Battle of, 20, 48
Shaw, Pte G., 142-143, 145-146
Shepstone, Sir Theophilus, 14
Silkaatsnek, 21
Skanskop, Fort, 41, 49
Slabbert, L., 158
Slabbert, Veldkornet, 44
Slingersfontein, 37
Smith-Dorrien, Gen H.L., 21, 24, 92, 127, 129, 142
Smithfield, 28
Smuts, Asst-Cmdt-Gen J.C., 56, 64, 67, 73, 113, 132
Sollum Hayata, North Africa, 42
Somerset Regiment, 158-159
South African Constabulary, 96, 158-159
South African Infantry Brigade, 140
Spion Kop, Battle of, 33, 46, 65, 114, 127, 134, 147, 151, 158
Springbok, 73
Springs, 151
Spruyt, C., 56
St Petersburg, Russia, 150
Standerton, 39, 41, 96, 134
State Model School, 40, 130-132
Steenkampsberg, 59, 136
Stellenbosch, 54
Stephens, Capt R., 110
Steward, Capt W., 66
Steyn, President M.T., 17, 57-58, 73, 128, 135
Steynskraal, 135
Stormberg, Battle of, 137
Strathcona Horse, 155
Suikerbosrand, 29
Sundays River, 116
Swanston, Lt A. W., 50, 53
Swart, Jurie, 29, 57

Tafel Kop, 96
Talana Hill, 18, 46, 65

Talana, Battle of, 18, 46, 65, 137
Thaba Nchu, 77
Thackeray, Col E., 140
Theron, Cmdt Danie, 22-23, 44
Thom, Driver, 68-69
Thompson, R.R., 124
Thorneycroft, Col A.W., 114, 117, 147, 151
Thorneycroft's Mounted Infantry, 38
Three Tree Hill, Battle of, 159
Todd, Lt, 57, 79
Trichardt, Capt S.P.E., 32
Trichardt, Cmdt P.F., 45
Tucker, Pte F., 36, 122, 158
Tudor-Trevor, Maj, 73
Tugela Heights, Battle of, 20, 133
Tugela River, 23, 43, 54, 109, 119
Turffontein concentration camp, 44
Tweebosch, Battle of, 86, 122
Twin Peaks, Spion Kop, 93, 117, 147, 149
typhoid vaccine, 107
Tzaneen, 132
Vaal River, 13, 19, 25, 55, 73, 105, 120, 123
Vaalkrans, Battle of, 19, 20, 65, 100, 140
Valsch River, 31, 96
van As, Veldkornet, 154, 158-159
van den Heever, brothers Jack & Gert, 26, 54
van der Merwe, Jan 'Tweefontein', 24
van Diggelen, Cmdt, 162
van Emmenes, Tpr Roelf, 32
van Gogh, Cornelius 'Cor' Vincent, 48
van Rensburg, N., *Seer*, 74-75, 77, 122-123, 127, 133
van Warmelo, D., 28
Venn, Pte, 100
Ventersburg, 13
Ventersdorp, 138, 142-146
Venterskroon, 55
Vereeniging, 19, 150, 154
Vereeniging, Treaty of, 21, 94, 118, 122
Verraaiers Nek *also* Traitor's Nek, 148-149
Victoria League, 155
Viljoen, Gen Ben, 100-102, 104, 113, 134, 146, 156
Viljoen, Gen Wynand, 139
Voight, E., 155
von Braun, Col, 152

von Zeppelin, Baron H., 26-27
Vosloo, G., 148-149
Vosloo, J., 148
Vredefort, 126
Vryburg, 18, 122

Wagner, H.H., 156
Wagon Hill, 42, 60, 63, 79, 81, 92-93, 108, 111, 114, 128, 134-135
Wagon Point, 60, 63, 114, 117
Walker, George, 15
Walkerville, 146
War Office, 60, 78, 82, 134
Warren, Gen Sir C., 42, 110, 136-137, 147
Waterval Boven, 40, 66, 97, 108, 111
Waterval Onder, 49, 65-67, 91, 97, 99, 129, 135
Watkins-Pitchford, Carbineer H., 100
Wauchope, Gen A.G., 19, 107, 156
Weilbach, Cmdt J.D., 48
Wepener, 20
West, Tpr M., 38-39
White, Col H.F., 162
White, Gen Sir George S., 18, 32, 60, 62, 65, 94, 108,
Wiid, P.S., 162
Wilhelm II, Kaiser, 16
Williams, Capt, 78
Willoughby, Maj Sir J., 161-163
Wilson, Gnr A., 62, 159
Wilson, Walter, 29
Witbank, 72
Wolmarans, Maj J.F., 118
Wolvehoek, 32
Wonderfontein, 150
Woodgate, Gen E.R.P., 147, 149
Woodward, Sgt, 29, 31
Wylie, Fort, 52

Yeomanry Hill, 56
Younger, Capt D.R., 21, 141
Yule, Gen, 46, 57, 64, 116

Zeekoehoek, 51
Zeerust, 156, 160
Zulu War, 14, 118, 142